GRANITE *Mariner*

Granite Mariner is published under Catharsis, a sectionalized division under Di Angelo Publications, Inc.

Catharsis is an imprint of Di Angelo Publications.
Copyright 2023.
All rights reserved.
Printed in the United States of America.

Di Angelo Publications
4209 Santa Monica Blvd, #200
Los Angeles, California

Library of Congress
Granite Mariner
ISBN: 978-1-955690-54-6
Hardback

Words: John Long
Cover Design: Savina Deianova
Cover Artwork: Renan Ozturk
Interior Design: Kimberly James
Editors: Jeff Jackson, Willy Rowberry, Cody Wootton

Downloadable via www.dapbooks.shop and other e-book retailers.

For educational, business, and bulk orders, contact distribution@diangelopublications.com.

1. Biography & Autobiography --- Personal Memoirs
2. Sports & Recreation --- Rock Climbing
3. Sports & Recreation --- Extreme Sports

GRANITE
Mariner

JOHN LONG

FOREWORD BY JEFF JACKSON
INTRODUCTION BY RENAN OZTURK

Original artwork by Renan Ozturk
World-renowned climber, artist, filmmaker

CONTENTS

ADVENTURE: STORIES

ACKNOWLEDGEMENTS

AUTHOR BIO

FOREWORD

Jeff Jackson

I've always been a fan of climbing literature. By the time I was fourteen, a year into my obsession, I'd blazed through the canon. Whymper, Harrer, Herzog, Benuzzi, Bonatti, Messner, and Roberts. These were the guys who shaped my nascent understanding of the sport with their taciturn, humble expedition blow-by-blows. And then, one afternoon in 1978, I cracked a *Climbing* magazine and discovered John Long.

Not only was "Largo's" subject matter—bouldering—a long ways from the mountaineering slogs immortalized by the heavies of the genre, but his prose sung, felt spontaneous and polyrhythmic like jazz, and went down like melted butter. Here was writing freed from the conventions of the past, more akin to the New Journalism of Tom Wolfe and Gay Talese—writing that incorporated fiction techniques like close description, dialog, and internal monolog. The point of view was personal and avuncular. Long wrote like an old friend, one who was willing to divulge secrets. The story was funny, sometimes hyperbolic and peppered with apt yet surprising metaphors. It owed something to Mark Twain and tall tales, with a nod to the comic burlesque voicings of poet James Tate, and the supernal asides of Wallace Stevens. In short, it was in a class by itself.

It's been forty-five years since I read that essay, "Pumping Sandstone," and I've continued to read John Long with admiration and pleasure. To say his work is iconic (it is) misses the point. John Long's body of work is a treasure and rests easy on the shelf beside all the authors who've stoked our fires from generation to generation. Crack the cover and jump into a world of adventure.

INTRODUCTION

Renan Ozturk

I visited Yosemite Valley later than most. It was in the middle of my dirtbag era, which was after I graduated from Colorado College in 2003. I gave away all my belongings and hit the road, living in the back of my friend's pickup truck, wintering in Indian Creek or Joshua Tree, summers in Squamish, spring and fall in Yosemite, dumpster diving and climbing all year round.

Yosemite is a magical place. It doesn't matter who you are, the first time you come through the tunnel and see El Cap and Half Dome, they're magnetic. Everybody can understand the draw of the landscape, but when you're in the Valley, you also feel the presence of all those generations of climbers—the characters you read about and talked about. When I was there, a lot of those people were still climbing. Even the great ones from the golden age were still alive. So yeah, Yosemite had a huge impact

I first heard of John Long through Dean Fidelman *(Stone Nudes),* an iconic California photographer. Of course, I'd heard of the Stonemasters, a loose group of SoCal climbers who pushed standards in Yosemite from about 1973 to 1980. Despite a relatively short tenure, the Stonemasters had an outsized effect on climbing culture. As Long writes in "A Short History of the Stonemasters":

> *The way it played out, the original movement diffused into the masses after a few short seasons. The spark was the counterculture animating the young from many countries; but the cliffside distilled our scattered energies into a battle*

cry as close to something sacred as we'd ever experienced. The entire Stonemaster adventure was less of a movement and more like the forcefield you sometimes feel around title fights, live jazz, and felons out on bail. Stuff that can hurl us into other orbits—some cosmic, others terminal—though the force itself, while stout, was never built to last.

The Stonemasters, especially people like John and others who were part of that '70s generation, are still giving back to the climbing community. John's writing is an ongoing account of this lifestyle, and that's important for the younger generations because they may not get the same introduction I had.

Climbing has grown vastly more popular in the last decade, but the vagabonds and the dirtbags are still few and far between. The people who fully dedicate their lives to adventure climbing in the way I did in the 2000s and the Stonemasters did in the 1970s are still a rare breed. The ones that do give up everything to live the climbing lifestyle have likely read deeply into the culture through John's books. That's part of what drives them. And that's what John seems to understand and capture.

The human element is everything for storytelling, and John dives deep into the good, the bad, and the ugly of those characters so that people can empathize and relate to them on a level that transcends sport and distills the essence of the culture. And it's more important now than ever to document the culture in these different forms of writing and film and cinematography. There's not a lot of young dirtbags still doing it and interacting intergenerationally, so books like this are critical to help bridge that gap and continue to feed the soul of the sport.

ADVENTURE
CLIMBING

A SHORT HISTORY OF
THE STONEMASTERS

One Dark and Stormy September Night

A sea of orange trees spread north from the downtown commercial district, thinning as gray foothills climbed into the schist canyons and woody arroyos of the San Gabriel Mountains. Welcome to 1970 in Upland, California, my hometown. A quaint little bedroom community lush for its citrus groves and mountain panoramas. Cozy, familiar, but a prickly fit for my wildness.

I'd often peer out through the busted windows of my homeroom in Upland High, daydreaming about all the mountains I would someday climb, mysterious summits obscured by clouds and ten times the size of 10,064-foot Mt. Baldy (which I'd rampaged around for years), gleaming in the distance. But I couldn't go alone. I needed partners and a way to get to those mountains. So I organized a high school rock climbing club for the sole purpose of enlisting a partner with a car.

The club got shut down after a field trip to Joshua Tree National Monument, when a chaperon caught several students with a short dog of Pappy Van Winkle and a foreign exchange student from Haifa was found wandering the desert in her panties. No matter, since by then I'd partnered with Eric "Ricky" Accomazzo and schooled him on the little I knew about ropework. And we'd be climbing plenty since Ricky had a car—a powder-blue Ford Pinto we drove into the junkyard over the following years, during which Ricky distinguished himself as king of the shit-your-pants runout.

Ricky—an all-everything water polo player, with a manner just as smooth as Mezzaluna—was to climbing what Sinatra was to song. From Yosemite granite to Chamonix ice, Ricky climbed the hardest new routes with a casual artistry that led our Yosemite brother Dale Bard to once ask, "What's that guy made of?"

"He's Italian," I said, which didn't explain Ricky hiking a glassy Royal Arches slab that Dale and I had just backed off and declared un-leadable. Back in high school, Ricky and I were just two kids thrilled to get our feet off the ground. Then we were three.

"You're not going to believe this one, Johnny," Ricky said one day after school.

That morning, on a restless hunch, Ricky drove up into the foothills and started snooping around a mangy canyon for a misplaced Shiprock or Half Dome. Instead, he stumbled across a long-haired maniac running laps on a thirty-foot mud cliff.

"Another climber?" I said. "In Upland?"

"Name's Richard," said Ricky. "Richard Harrison. Says he dropped outta high school because it was cutting into his climbing time."

What were the odds? Nobody quit high school to go climbing back then. Not in the U.S. anyway.

Richard, Ricky, and I were soon scratching over the boulders at Mount Rubidoux, a practice climbing area near Riverside, California. We pooled our money and bought a nylon climbing rope and a skeleton rack, and over the 1970 school year and through the summer, if we weren't climbing, we were reading, thinking, or talking about climbing.

We'd memorized quotes and immortal passages, including the mawkish book jacket copy from *Nanga Parbat Pilgrimage*, *Starlight and Storm*, even *The Ascent of Rum Doodle*. We'd recite the grave stuff *sotto voce* and then yell the gallant summit pronouncements at the top of our lungs, with faux French and German accents we learned from listening to Inspector Clouseau and watching *Hogan's Heroes*. Most of this went down in Richard's cinderblock basement bungalow, later known simply as "The Basement."

Richard lived up in the foothills, above the citrus groves just shy of the mountains. His nearest neighbor was half a mile away. A dirt drive found his split-level lodging (kitchen and bedroom above, basement below), set back from a twisty two-lane road flanking a rocky streambed that occasionally overflowed during winter rains. You needed a compass to ever find the place, and on my first visit, Richard's cranky old German Shepherd bit my leg. Richard's mom, two siblings, grandparents, and twenty-odd critters lived in Old MacDonald's other farm, several hundred yards downhill from The Basement.

An artist friend of Richard's had painted an exposed joist with a stylized cordillera of mountains, starting with K2 by the left wall and ending with the Matterhorn by the door on the right. In the presence of these giants, we dreamed away many evenings, recounting dazzling alpine epics, listening to Jimi Hendrix and Pink Floyd on Richard's squeaky old tape deck, and bonging rag weed he grew in the arid gulch behind The Basement. No one ever bothered us. When you're eighteen, that kind of privacy and the cloistered vibe of The Basement made us feel like sovereigns of a magic castle. And all the while, Richard held court with a corncob pipe.

Richard grew up around artists (his father was a renowned woodworker), favoring lifestyles so daring that the rest of us wondered how anyone could pull them off and stay out of jail. Each Stonemaster (as we later styled ourselves) brought to the group ingredients that were chucked into our collective gestalt. Richard brought the main course: doing just as you pleased. If that squared with others—fine. If not, "Tastes differ," he'd often say, never bothered by public opinion.

Richard went on to climb more routes in more places than most of us combined, always so much on the down-low he might have remained anonymous if not for his full-page photo in Meyers' seminal *Yosemite Climber*, cranking an early ascent of Nabisco Wall with a young John Yablonski belaying. It's curious to consider how that picture and the thousand-and-one adventures that followed all sprang from one dark and stormy September night in 1972.

An Unexpected Guest

The night started out like so many others: strains of Curtis Mayfield's "Superfly" mingling with clouds of weed smoke and incense so thick I could scarcely see the summit of Broad Peak on the joist, six feet away. Wind lashed The Basement as thunder rumbled down from the San Gabriel's.

For months we'd languished—reading, talking, dreaming. Gazing toward a future we wanted with all our might, where our lives would run momentous. Now the waiting felt like a bed of nails, so I once again started in on Buhl's forced bivouac on Nanga Parbat. The heat was gone. I shifted to Messner's solo of Les Droites. The words were cold and lifeless.

We sat there, in the poverty of posers, with no catalyst for our scattered energies. Who were we with no spark? No true north? So ran our first encounter with unclaimed moments, where big bangs sometimes emerge. You never see them coming.

No one remembers who coined it, only that "Stonemaster" materialized in our conversation. Just mentioning the name conjured The Stonemaster himself, and his lightning struck us right between the eyes. We jumped up and started yelling over each other. Rash, reckless plans were voiced at lightspeed, and I half-expected pentagrams to appear on the rafters and horse heads to start bobbing round The Basement. Nobody cared.

Never mind Herzog and Messner, and forget the Himalayas. This was about us—and stupendous rocks, since we were rock climbers, after all. There was El Capitan and Middle Cathedral and hundreds of gallant, historical climbs at nearby Tahquitz and Suicide rocks, and we'd climb them all in a minute. All of this spewed forth the moment we realized that the only thing holding us back was the pissant size of our dreams. It felt like getting birthed out the barrel of a cannon.

The shift from reciting other people's triumphs to chasing your own always provokes the beast of uncertainty. Fear of the unknown. Fear of dying. Fear of fear. Fear and cockroaches are much the same. You cannot kill them all and there's always more. After months upon months, books upon books, our dream at last dashed against the unknown like a fly against a windowpane. Then The Stonemaster threw open the window.

As we kept marching around The Basement and blabbering about the fantastic exploits sure to follow, I held up, knowing The Stonemaster was ushering us onto the rock-scarred faces where the Buhls and Terrays once roamed—and where scores of them had died. Some horrendously. The notion did to death the fatuous heroics that fueled our fantasies, the adventure equivalent of genre paintings. This was real as bone marrow, and I had nothing to scale it off, no metaphor, since our quest didn't feel like anything we'd ever experienced. Either way, we were already two rope lengths up, and had been for a while. No bailing now. The only thing we had was each other and a pole star we could feel but not yet see or imagine.

Around midnight, I got on my bike for the six-mile pedal back to my tiny dorm room at the University of La Verne, where I was slogging through my freshman year. From Richard's house, a lung-busting climb found the steep, twisting, jet-black road rifling down from Mt. Baldy. I could coast for a couple of miles, at what felt like Mach 1, rarely encountering cars while tracking the single white lane line that, in the dead of night, sans headlamp, was my only hope of not flying off the road. But that night, a stiff headwind held me nearly in place, and I floated down the road in a trance, touched by the fragrance of orange blossoms. My life, which was all and only mine, had just begun.

Over the following months, The Stonemaster tornadoed around us, tapping his toes and scratching his balls. Grousing when we dithered at a danger. Tormenting us with the same question: *Who are you, really?*

It sounds prosaic now, but not to teenaged misfits with no charts and little experience. We could only answer through an odyssey, which required a proper crew.

Fortune planted the question in the ears of Mike Graham, Robs Muir, and a handful of other young climbers scattered over Southern California, and all of us were soon on board. From the moment we first cast off, The Stonemaster shot us into action with a velocity that broke one of our backs, busted another nearly in half, killed several outright, and had the other half dozen of us pawing at sloping holds.

Early Journeys

Suicide Rock, in Idyllwild, California, served as our training ground and cultural workshop. East of Suicide, a mile across Strawberry Valley, rose massive Tahquitz Rock, crucible of American climbing mores and incubator of the Yosemite pioneers. Tahquitz always felt hallowed and elderly—like a famous old uncle you were proud of but never visited much because he was, well, old. Suicide felt brand-spanking-new because most of the routes had gone up in the previous half-dozen years—courtesy of Pat Callis, Charlie Raymond, and Bud Couch—and there were plenty more new ones for the taking.

The rock tended toward sweeping (up to about 300 feet), high-angled slabs, faces, and arêtes, with extravagant runouts on polished granite. In an era long before sticky rubber shoes, when traditional "ground-up" methods still held, casting off on a Suicide test-piece had the feel and jeopardy of big game hunting with a spear. And one of the best of the early hunters was Mike Graham, known in later years as Gramicci.

Mike had the long, lean frame of an Olympic swimmer and the insouciant dash of a surfer, which he was, having grown up in Newport Beach. With the gift of a natural and the drive of a beatnik, not once, in all the years I knew and climbed with Mike, did he ever round into top shape. He never needed to. He did everything on native skill and guts.

If you were to ask Jim Bridwell to name the greatest, go-for-broke lead he'd ever seen, it was Gramicci cranking an eighty-foot, unprotected layback during the yet-unrepeated first ascent of *Gold Ribbon,* on Ribbon Falls, Yosemite.

Mike worked at Ski Mart, a big outdoor recreation retailer, and kept us all in the finest gear (later, Robs Muir, Ricky Accomazzo, and I would work at Ski Mart as well). Mike also fashioned the first Stonemaster logo, with the sizzling lightning bolt, forever chalked beneath *Midnight Lightning,* one of the world's most famous boulder problems. It was through Mike that we met Gib Lewis and Bill Antel.

Gib had a bottle-brush blond afro and a learning curve that never flattened out. An adventure sports generalist who later mastered windsurfing and laid down the grimmest ski descents on record, Gib started out strong and just kept getting better and better.

Bill apparently stepped from the shadows straight onto world-class face climbs. I never knew where Bill came from and didn't care because the Stonemasters were like the French Foreign Legion in that regard—your past was forgotten the moment you signed on.

What's more (and decades before the public took note), rock climbing's provenance, mostly written by young white guys, was expansively amended by Carolyn "Lynn" Hill (future World Sport Climbing Champion), Mari Gingery (whose mother was Japanese), and Mariah Cranor (who later ran Black Diamond Equipment), card-carrying Stonemasters, there from Day One. These three women climbed just as hard, sometimes harder, than us fellows, ensuring that by the mid-1970s, the democratization of climbing outpaced all other sports by a wide margin.

So we had a name, a lightning bolt, and marching orders to peaks unknown, but as a group, we'd done little more than repeat Suicide's standard hardman routes and shoot off our mouths. We needed some dramatic victory to assert our arrival and establish the clout of The Stonemaster. But nobody was quite sure what, or how.

Valhalla

Robs Muir and Jim Hoagland were both UC Riverside students and standouts at Mt. Rubidoux and Suicide. It took the pair several tries, but they managed the first continuous ascent of *Valhalla,* one of America's few 5.11s and a route that had a reputation the size of its creator, Bud Couch, a six-foot-four college professor who lived in Idyllwild and lorded over Suicide with flinty disdain.

Bud was the last, and possibly the best, of the traditional line of Idyllwild masters that ran back forty years to John Mendenhall, the father of California rock climbing. Bud had his circle of partners, whose names and photos were peppered throughout the guidebooks. We were awestruck by these guys and secretly wanted their blessing. Instead, they jeered as we tumbled all over their rock.

I was too proud and insecure to roll with such ridicule, but far worse was getting dressed down by the leaders of various outing clubs that rounded out the Idyllwild climbing scene during those dog days. For ages, these clubs had floundered up the same gullies in humorless cavalcades; the very gullies we'd down-climb (unroped, of course) to return to our packs. A couple of times when we ran into a battalion of these people and the leader launched into another diatribe, barking and spitting in our faces, things nearly got ugly.

The whole shebang felt absurd. There you had a cult of illustrious has-beens mostly loafing in the shade, drinking malt liquor and tossing off snide comments, while a regular platoon, led by phobic drill sergeants, queued for their umpteenth slog up some dark and dreary ditch. One of Suicide's most beautiful formations was called the Weeping Wall, and it was crying for good reason. For millions of years, this fantastic rock slab had drawn rain and wind upon itself to fashion resources that were largely going unused.

"Time to step it up," Richard concluded one night in The Basement, "or we ain't going nowhere."

Shortly after Robs' and Jim's victory, we all shot for *Valhalla*, and we all got there. (*Valhalla* immediately became the prerequisite for becoming a Stonemaster, and Mike kept a journal that logged the first dozen or so ascents.) In another few months, we'd repeated every old test piece worth doing, yet the Stonemasters scarcely grew larger for our efforts—efforts that inspired no one but pissed off everybody, leaving them anxious and guarded. But while the duffers trudged up their gullies, and the old guard slowly faded to black, anyone new had a different dance to follow, and eventually, many did. The Stonemasters had arrived, the party was on, and everyone was invited.

Safety in Numbers

The season we all got liftoff saw the Stonemasters pull down dozens of new climbs and first free ascents at Suicide and Tahquitz, and out at Joshua Tree. *New Generations, Iron Cross, Drain Pipe, Ten Carrot Gold, Green Arch, Ultimatum, Le Toit, The Flakes, Jumping Jack Crack, Ski Tracks*, and countless others—all must-do routes for modern crushers—were climbed in rapid succession. Most routes were dispatched mob-style because no one could bear missing out on the glory. Plus, it was always more laughs with a conga line five or ten strong, and far more dangerous because the Suicide climbs were often protected by bolts, and only bolts, and a leader was obliged to run the rope halfway to Kingdom Come before breaking out the drill.

Here was the climbing equivalent of glass blowing: delicate and tricky. You were certain to get burned if the thing got away from you, and it could in a flash. The shoe of choice was either red PAs (Pierre Alan) or brown RDs (René Desmaison). Both edged okay but had the friction coefficient of a shovel. The slightest misstep and you were off for the big one, and nobody took the big one as often or as dramatically as Tobin Sorenson, who knew ninety-nine names for dangerous, but had lost the one for reason.

Once in a Lifetime Experience

Most climbers know of Tobin Sorenson as the madman who, in blue jeans and a "Jesus Saves" sweatshirt, soloed the North Face of the Matterhorn; or who, with the late, great British alpinist Alex McIntyre, made the first alpine-style ascent of the *Harlin Direct* on the Eigerwand; or who joined Ricky Accomazzo on the germinal first ascent of the Dru Couloir Direct, in Chamonix—at that time, the hardest ice climb in the Alps, and one of the first times a team bivouacked while suspended from ice screws. If you had to pick the world's best overall climber from the 1970s, from alpine peaks to Yosemite's big walls, few would argue if you gave the nod to Tobin.

More than a friend and a partner, Tobin was a once in a lifetime experience. He answered The Stonemaster's momentous question, *Who are you, really?* in ways we could never fully grasp.

In Tobin's fierce nature, there was a touch of the feminine, as there is in every prince and pirate. But when he tied into a rope, he was all wildcat. During our early mob ascents, we never goaded Tobin, especially when he grabbed the lead. Rather, we gnashed our teeth and held our breath, because Tobin, though a great natural athlete, hadn't technically caught up to the rest of us, but he charged as though his knickers (back then, he always wore knickers) were on fire. God must have adored him. It is the only explanation why Tobin survived the gigantic ragdoll falls he logged each and every weekend.

His skill quickly approached his ambition and, praise the Lord, Tobin's harrowing falls eventually declined. But so long as he lived, his goals outpaced his capacity—or anyone's capacity. We were too young to appreciate where it all must lead, but from the day he first chalked up, Tobin Lee Sorenson was a dead man climbing. I believe the savage force that drove him and his saint's sense of purpose derived, in large part, from his reverence of climbing history.

Worship came naturally to Tobin, the oldest son of a Presbyterian minister. Though he'd never place another climber alongside the Almighty, Tobin would nevertheless risk your life and his own to secure his place at the table with the Salathes and Pratts and Bridwells—all supreme artists in Tobin's mind.

Emily Dickinson said that art is a house that wants to be haunted. But Emily refers to how a house, inclined by history, naturally attracts the ghosts of the great ones who lived and tangled with the perennial curses. Tobin seemed determined to inhabit the house with his own ghost. Why else would he follow hard cracks out at Joshua with a noose lashed round his neck, or race his sportscar on the wrong side of the road? And how could such madness help forge a distinguished climber? All we knew for certain was that Tobin had some dark need to square off with his Maker every time out.

None of us dared follow Tobin's example, but he helped convert us from delinquents to warriors on a mission—a shift accentuated by the newest Stonemaster, John Bachar, who through talent, courage, and obsessive dedication, transformed himself into one of the greatest figures in twentieth-century adventure sports. Though John always played his own tune—both on the rock and on the alto sax he used to torture us with—early on, he did so within the context of the group, and we all had the edgy rapture of watching John go where no climber had gone before. If ever a Stonemaster carried the name on his sleeve (and he scribbled it on his boots as well), it was John Bachar, Grand Templar of the entire movement.

Double Trouble

Throughout 1973, the group's energy arced up and found expression through several pivotal ascents. First came the *Vampire,* an old Royal Robbins aid route that took the boldest line up the baldest section of Tahquitz. Eight hundred feet long, with a flapjack-thin, expanding flake soaring up the glazed, Southwest Face, the *Vampire* was the closest thing we Southern Californians had to a big wall. When Ricky Accomazzo freed the A4 traverse on the third pitch, via an audacious, sideways leap to the expando flake (an improbable, though easier, traverse was later found slightly lower), any notion we had about what a leader could and should do flew straight out the rain fly. With three 5.11 pitches in a row, the *Vampire* was, along with Yosemite's *Nabisco Wall*, and Eldorado's *Naked Edge,* one of America's first multi-pitch, super free climbs.

The *Vampire* naturally led to Idyllwild's most improbable free climbing prospect: *Paisano Overhang,* a twenty-five-foot, downturned roof crack that went free at 5.12c (the rating was not established for another decade, when Randy Leavitt and Tony Yaniro invented the climbing technique known as "Leavittation" to bag the second free ascent). The combination of grisly wide crack moves and A3 protection gave us a futuristic yardstick to measure any other crack on the face of the earth.

If we could climb something as difficult and poorly protected (a fall would have likely been a backbreaker) as *Paisano,* what could stop us? And so, on the slipstream of these climbs, we made our summer pilgrimage to rock climbing's grandest stage: Yosemite Valley. To that point, we'd made only brief sorties into the Valley, slowly developing our comfort level by picking off a couple of small walls and a celebrated crack or two. But in 1973, the moment the semester let out, we descended on Camp 4 en masse, determined to carve an existence out of Yosemite's soaring expanse.

The Big Valley

Within a few weeks of arriving in the Valley, the Stonemaster campaign gained critical mass; out of necessity, we broke ranks with our small cadre of SoCal partners and teamed up with other kindred jokers. Robs had already climbed the West Face of El Cap and we had some catching up to do.

Richard and Kevin Worrall kickstarted the season with an early ascent of the *Direct Route* on Half Dome. Ricky, Gib, and future alpine hero Jay Smith climbed *The Nose* and I quickly followed suit, tying in with British ace Ron Fawcett. Directly on our heels climbed Richard and soulful English mountaineer Nick Estcourt (who, a few years later, perished in an avalanche, 6,500 meters up K2, during an early attempt on the West Ridge).

During those first months, the Stonemasters lived on the walls. But more pivotal than our first Grade VIs was the bond we forged with Jim Bridwell, the most practiced rock climber in the world and a carry-over from the Yosemite pioneers, most of whom fled The Ditch in the late 1960s.

If The Stonemaster himself had a right-hand man, it was Jim Bridwell, aka, "The Bird." To recount another Bridwell story is to spin a broken record, but his influence cannot be overstated. Uncertainty, the Kryptonite of humanity, was Jim Bridwell's daily bread. To climb with Jim, which we all did, was to embrace the boldest, newest, most outrageous adventure you could, each and every time out.

What followed were a thousand exploits that took Jim and me from El Cap in a day to Venezuela's Angel Falls to the jungles of Borneo. Through Jim, we met Mark Chapman, Kevin Worral, Ron Kauk, Werner Braun, Billy Westbay, Ed Barry, Jim Orey, Rik Rieder, Dale Bard, and many others. During our first few seasons, we were all interchangeable partners.

But this was a many-sided posse. Nature had put a quietness in some, a ferocity in others, but all of us could best see daylight from high places. It was hard to get up high, where the margin for error is thin as a knife's blade and life is merely tolerated. More people had walked on the moon than had been on some of that granite. And all of us, when the sun beat down and the rock turned into rubble, wished we'd never bothered. But we were dancing with life, discovering who we could be, which stokes a fire like none other. And so, surrounded with people who made our hearts smile, we worked ourselves into hot sports, and as Alice was promised, found Wonderland.

When the group's gusto grew too much for us Southern Californians to contain, our original group burst at the seams and The Stonemaster mojo splashed over one and all. By 1974, there were easily twenty-five Stonemasters (an ascent of *Valhalla* was no longer a criterion), and by 1975, most everyone in Camp Four was a charter member of the most unofficial club on the planet.

Years later, French climber Laurent Dubois, writing in *Le Monde*, said the Stonemasters "set a cultural standard aped by monkeys around the world." The way it played out, the original movement diffused into the masses after a few short seasons. The spark was the counterculture animating the young from many countries, but the cliffside distilled our scattered energies into a battle cry as close to something sacred as us heathens could hack. The entire Stonemaster adventure was less of a movement and more like the forcefield you sometimes feel around title fights, live jazz, and felons out on bail. Stuff that can hurl us into other orbits—some cosmic, others lamentable—though the force itself, while stout, was never built to last.

Our Yosemite saga was a subplot in which The Stonemaster himself played a leading role only in the beginning, when this existential experiment harmonized the needs of an entire generation of restless outcasts. It quickly assumed a life of its own, and The Stonemaster's work was done. Knowing that the most valuable technique was the exit, none of us ever saw him go.

From the beginning, The Stonemaster provided a portal into the mysterious, a quest made ridiculous by climbing El Capitan thirty or forty times, something many climbers had now accomplished. After a dozen or so big walls, you could return to find challenge and, no doubt, danger, but you'd no longer encounter an unknown world. When we first jumped onto the Big Lonesome, our relationships, our clothes, even our language morphed to reflect the inner expedition. But over the years, the crazy clothes, lingo, and attitudes became ends in themselves, no longer predicated by jumping beyond our experience. We'd crisscrossed this particular ocean countless times, and in the process, a Stonemaster had come to mean little more than a formidable granite mariner—a rarity when we'd first attacked Suicide and Joshua Tree, but not anymore.

Then Tobin died while trying to solo the North Face of Mt. Alberta (a feat later attempted by another Stonemaster, Mark Wilford). So boldly and so often had Tobin marched point for all Stonemasters, when every summit and every ending flowed into something new; but this time he'd led us into no-man's land, where the future dead-ended with no exit and no retreat. We just hung our heads and stared at our shoes. Everything was fleeting. And when someone was gone, there was nothing left of them at all, forever, but it takes the rest of your life to accept it. If you ever do.

Especially early on, the Stonemasters moved freely between dreams and destruction. Because we were all forced to work on the rescue team (the only way to escape Yosemite's seven-day camping limit), we'd handled our share of corpses. Our founding ranks had also been thinned when Bill Antel shattered his back on Rixon's Pinnacle, and when Gib Lewis fell 100 feet to the deck—right in front of Ricky and me—while soloing the mottled ice falls in Lee Vining in the Eastern Sierras. Miraculously, Gib would return, but Tobin never could, which disgorged feelings that left us shattered, disintegrating into something that didn't translate in human terms.

So died the last of our innocence, and innocence was the lifeblood of every Stonemaster. Our pain was nothing compared to the injustice we felt, which left us dismayed and outraged. We surely saw it coming, and Tobin essentially died by his own hand. But I hated God just then. You come into the world believing a brave heart will live forever. When you learn otherwise, you might love once more, but you'll never again be the same person.

I couldn't bring myself to attend Tobin's funeral—something I later deeply regretted—and instead dug out an old Impressions tape and listened to a song that, years earlier, in the tent cabin of a girlfriend in Yosemite, Tobin and I used to play over and over.

People get ready, there's a train comin'
You don't need no baggage, you just get on board
All you need is faith to hear the diesels hummin'
You don't need no ticket, you just thank the Lord

Tobin was the only apostle among us, but this lyric summed up the come-one, come-all philosophy that spread the Stonemasters so far and wide, and saw so many people from so many places just get on board. But in time, the train got too crowded and the nuclear, personal bond that held together our passion and desires slowly unraveled. And I lost the thread of my life. That's when I understood that a Stonemaster, in their pure and original form, could only be a kid with a restless spirit and unrequited dreams. And I was no longer a kid with dreams, but a man with stories and skeletons.

Grateful? Absolutely. I'd surfed, rather by chance, the critical juncture between cult and culture, had seen the world change before my eyes. And I'd tried to communicate, through direct action, what made life and death so significant to us. But I'd had my turn, knowing one's meaningful days are always numbered. Yosemite and I were done with each other. I stared out over an emptiness so vast it put all my previous encounters with the void into the shade.

A wise friend said that once you know the nature of this emptiness, like an Atlantic squall, you can plot a course through it. Or you can play grab-ass on deck as the winds tear the sails to shreds. The only course I knew was to return to Yosemite, and it only took a few days and a few climbs to know I was playing grab-ass once more.

I went to Vanuatu, Borneo, Irian Jaya, and other places I can't remember and could never pronounce. Once again, the great unknown provided salvation and spared me the bitterness, dread, and ennui that, following one's first shattering letdown, drive many into the bottle and into the grave.

At long last, I found myself back in The Basement with Richard. It would be our last and shortest confab in our secret castle—Richard soon moved to Red Rock in Nevada and never came back. Almost by reflex, we started in with the stories, though this time, the stories were our own.

With Nuptse as our witness, soaring off the dusty joist, we recounted how, through sweat and fear, but the whole while laughing, we drew near The Stonemaster—not so much a being as an island in our souls. Through many epics did we find him, striving to become who we most revered, though not owing to our route-finding skills; rather, because The Stonemaster had sought us all along. By no other means could you find Wonderland, where the young and strong alight for a time and jump just as far as they can. Every old Stonemaster knows the place, still feels the wind on their faces, and in other haunts and in other ways, we might jump beyond ourselves. But only the young can live on those craggy shores, and we would land there no more.

MOOD INDIGO

Richard, Jay, and I made good time, despite the angry weather, and climbed most of the way up Washington Column before bivouacking on Overnight Ledge, three rope lengths from the top. Night came tenderly but our hunger felt murderous once the adrenaline wore off.

Jay had brought a zip-locked block of cheese, swimming in yellow varnish after cooking in the haul bag all day. We wolfed it down in no time. Same with the summer sausage and family-size can of Dinty Moore stew. This was our first go at scaling a big wall, and knowing the hunger of the castaway.

We'd planned to start three days before but got washed out by a late summer thunderstorm that flash-flooded camp and the Visitor Center, close by Yosemite Falls. Now we had no water at all, swilling the last of it to gag down that funky cheese. No worries, said Richard. We could sleep the night away and climb off the wall in a few hours next morning. Then tank up on water once we got down.

We slouched back, wasted, three wannabe rock stars, shoulder to shoulder on our little granite bench.

Between roping up at the base and clawing over the summit lay a vertical gulf we could gaze past but never fully plot beforehand. The sorcery came from crossing that gulf with an unproven strategy made up on the spot, which felt risky as hell. Without a reckless curiosity about the unknown, where all things seem possible, we wouldn't have gotten far. A dozen years later, we'd have fifty walls bagged between us, and half of those were crapshoots.

Richard kept fiddling with gear, pitching a few broken bits out into space and us chuckling anxiously as they plummeted through the night before clinking off the wall a thousand feet below. I so feared falling through the air, but tumbling through my mind was my greater fret. Dissolving into the crypt of self. Big walls as body snatchers. I'd quested up there, offering myself to fear, as the void reached up, grasping at my feet, dangling off Overnight Ledge. Slowly, the white noise died off, leaving signal, which is soundless and always right now.

To whom did this silence answer? Not to me. The world of sounds and shades and ten-thousand forms was no longer arrayed around me as the focal point. The order of things had flopped, somehow. Now everywhere was the center. Perhaps this was how the world perceived itself.

I had no idea, starting out that morning, as we idled up the trail, shouldering vicious loads. Inaccessibility was part of the magic. If anyone could stroll up here, most of its power would be lost. We were experienced climbers—not on this scale, it is true—but we were hungry for trouble and knew about ropes and pitons and going up. We all felt confident we were where we belonged.

Around noon, a fiery breeze blew the clouds away and heat waves welled off the rock, blistering to the touch. We'd climbed too high to safely retreat, otherwise we would have. The most heinous quality of heat is its unrelenting strength, which no one can understand until it is endured. We panted, foreheads banging, seeking the tiny patch of shade beneath the haul bag.

Then clouds rolled in like foaming breakers, darkened and snarled, as rain teemed from the sky for what felt like hours, us still stranded in slings. Finally the sky broke apart and the rock, scarfed in mist, dried out. For another hour, we dangled there, staring into the blue distances, wondering if Nature had lost Her mind (spinning the dial on the thermostat like that), shivering ourselves back to action. Rangers said the swing in temperatures was the largest in a day since they began keeping records in the 1890s. Now, hours later, we sat stupefied on the ledge, wondering how this mercurial mountain could apprehend such extremes.

I never know a mountain till I've slept on it. But beat down like that, sleep refused me. The lights and campfires gleamed in the valley. My mind went blank. A quiescence without beginning, crawling with ancestral fears. Scared me shitless. It must have spooked the others as well because we all started talking furiously about nothing, blue stars winking back at us. It felt like being in church, almost, till a hankering for a sip morphed into brain-frying, soul-murdering thirst. It happened—like everything else in this circus-mirror world—one-two-three.

We'd climbed through the heat wave and had downed maybe a quart of water per man, many quarts shy of the required dosage. That triggered, on a time delay, a thirst like a freight train that ran us right over.

We sat there, crying out for a drop. Anything. Staring at the moon, trying to will it across the sky. Time became the enemy. The mountain, monstrous. At first light, like three bursts of fire licking the wall, up we climbed, summiting in a daze, our mouths and eyes glued shut.

We staggered into forest and traversed right over a saddle to the start of North Dome Gully, a mostly treeless series of slabs and sandy ledges marking the start of the descent route. The storms of centuries had deposited a riot of teetering boulders into this ditch, bristling with snaggle bushes. The sky was blue and, already, the gully heaved with heat mirages. Jay warned to stay far left because out right loomed the Death Slabs, steep and naked granite covered with pine needles, where a traveler, dying of thirst and loaded with ropes and ironmongery, only went to die.

We trundled down, breathless and seeing double, through a maze of boxcar boulders and manzanita. Gaping at the Merced River, half a mile below, meandering from Tenaya Canyon and wending through the valley. A silvered strand of life, us shrieking inside at the sight of it. There, but tragically out of reach. We would gladly have sold the other guy into slavery just to have one cool inch of that river.

I couldn't make out Richard's words, just followed his hand, pointing to seep, drizzling from a fracture in the wall of the ditch. Clear water. Living water.

We'd all three stripped down to short shorts and sneakers, our thirst just as roaring and naked as our bodies. I reached a hand into the thread of drizzling brightness so intense that my mind stopped. It was the most unguarded moment of my eighteen years on earth.

Jay clawed at the drizzle, trying to catch it. Then rooted through the haul bag, retrieved our tin Sierra cup, and held it below the trickle. We watched, agonizing second after second, as the cup began to fill. Jay couldn't wait and tossed down a spoonful. I wrenched the cup from his hands and held it under the drip, and we kept doing this in turn till round about noon, our bodies filled back out and we could see straight and make words again.

We pushed on, as if floating in slow motion through a Hieronymus Bosch painting, found by tilting life on edge for 1,200 feet and emptying its pockets. We'd never suspected a world so stark, so vivid as heat and cold and hunger and thirst. The absoluteness of water dripping from a rock. The teetering minarets and flying buttresses. Even the white rags of clouds, shredding as we strove for the silver river.

GREEN ARCH

Tobin Lee Sorenson (1956–1980) was widely considered the world's greatest all-around climber during the 1970s. More than a climber, Tobin was a once-in-a-lifetime experience, a charmed man-child who embodied the Stonemaster ideal so perfectly that decades later, all who knew Tobin still hold him in awe and reverence.

One Saturday morning, during the spring of 1973, five or six of us hunkered down in the little breakfast joint in Idyllwild. Tahquitz Rock was our oyster. We'd pried it open with a piton and, for months, had gorged at will; but the fare was running thin. Since we had ticked off one after another of the remaining new routes, our options had dwindled to only the most grim or improbable.

The week before, Ricky Accomazzo had scoped out the Green Arch, an elegant arc on Tahquitz's southern shoulder. When Ricky mentioned he thought there was an outside chance that this pearl of an aid climb might go free, Tobin looked like the Hound of the Baskervilles had just heard the word "bone."

Since the Green Arch was Ricky's idea, he got the first go at it. After fifty feet of dicey face climbing, he gained the arch, which soared above for another eighty feet before curving right and disappearing in a field of knobs and pockets. If we could only get to those knobs, the remaining 250 feet would go easily and the Green Arch would fall.

The lower corner and the arch above looked bleak. The crack in the back of the arch was too thin to accept even fingertips, and both sides of the corner were blank and marble smooth. But by pasting half his rump on one side of the puny corner and splaying his feet on the opposite side, Ricky stuck to the rock—barely—both his rump and his boots steadily oozing off the steep, greasy granite wall. It was an exhausting duty just to stay put, and moving up was accomplished in a grueling, precarious sequence of quarter-inch moves. Amazingly, Ricky jack-knifed about halfway up the arch before his calves pumped out. He lowered off a bunk piton and I took a shot.

After an hour of the hardest climbing I'd ever done, I reached a rest hold just below the point where the arch swept out right and melted into that field of knobs. Twenty feet to paydirt, but those twenty feet didn't look promising.

There were some sucker knobs just above the arch, but those ran out after about twenty-five feet and would leave a climber with nowhere to go, no chance to claw back onto the route, no chance to get any protection, and no chance to retreat. We'd have to stick to the arch.

Finally, I underclung about ten feet out on the arch, whacked in a suspect knife-blade piton, clipped the rope in—and fell off. I lowered to the ground, slumped back, and didn't get up for ten minutes. I had strawberries on both ass cheeks and my ankles were rubbery and tweaked from splaying them out on the far wall.

Tobin, unchained from the pine, tied into the lead rope and stormed up the corner like a man fleeing Satan on foot. He battled up to the rest hold, drew a few quick breaths, underclung out to that creaky, buckled, driven-straight-up-into-an-expanding-flake knife-blade, and immediately cranked himself over the arch and started heaving up the line of sucker knobs.

"No!" I screamed up. "Those knobs don't go anywhere!" But it was too late.

Understand that Tobin was a born-again Christian, that he'd smuggled Bibles into Bulgaria, risking twenty-five years on a Balkan rockpile, that he'd studied God at a fundamentalist university, and none of this altered the plain fact that he was perfectly mad. Out on the sharp end, he not only ignored all consequences, but actually loathed them, doing all kinds of crazy, incomprehensible things to mock the fear and peril. (The previous year, out at Joshua Tree, Tobin followed a difficult, overhanging crack with a rope noosed around his neck.) Most horrifying was his disastrous capacity to simply charge pell-mell. On straightforward routes, no one was better. But when patience and cunning were required, no one was worse.

Climbing, as it were, with blinders on, Tobin would sometimes claw his way into the most grievous jams. When he'd dead-end, with nowhere to go and looking at a Homeric peeler, the full impact of his folly would hit him like a wrecking ball. He would panic, wail, weep openly, and do the most ludicrous things. And sure enough, about twenty-five feet above the arch, those sucker knobs ran out and Tobin had nowhere to go.

To appreciate Tobin's pickle, understand that he was twenty-five feet above the last piton, which meant he was looking at a fifty-foot fall, since a leader falls twice as far, as he is above the last piece of protection. The belayer can rarely take in much rope during a fall because it happens so fast. Normally, he can only secure the rope—lock it off. But the gravest news was that I knew the piton I'd bashed under the roof would not hold a fifty-foot whipper. On really gigantic falls, the top piece often rips out. In Tobin's case, the next-lower piece was some dozen feet below the top one, at the rest hold; so, in fact, Tobin was looking at close to an eighty-footer—maybe more—with rope stretch.

As Tobin wobbled far overhead, who should lumber up to our little group but his very father, a former minister, a quiet, retiring, imperturbable gentleman who hacked and huffed from his long march up to the cliffside. After hearing so much about climbing from Tobin, he'd finally come to see his son in action. He couldn't have shown up at a worse time.

It was like a page torn from a B movie script: us cringing and digging in, waiting for the bomb to drop; the good pastor, wheezing through his mustache, sweat-soaked and confused, squinting up at the fruit of his loins; and Tobin, knees knocking like castanets, sobbing pitifully and looking to plunge off at any second.

There is always something you can do, even in the grimmest situation, if only you keep your nerve. But Tobin was totally gone, so mastered by terror that he seemed willing to die to be rid of it. He glanced down. His face was a study. Suddenly he screamed, "Watch me! I'm gonna jump."

We didn't immediately understand what he meant.

"Jump off?" Richard begged.

"Yes!" Tobin wailed.

"NO!" we all screamed in unison.

"You can do it, son!" the pastor put in.

Pop was just trying to put a good face on it, God bless him, but his was the worst possible advice because there was no way Tobin could do it. Or anybody could do it. There were no holds. But stirred by his father's urging, Tobin reached out for those knobs so far to his right, now lunging, now hopelessly pawing sweet nothing as he plunged through the air. The top piton shot out and Tobin shot off into a spectacular, tumbling whistler. His arms flailed and his scream could have frozen brandy.

The lower piton held and he finally jolted onto the rope, hanging upside down and moaning softly. We slowly lowered him off and he lay motionless on the ground, and nobody moved or spoke or even breathed. You could have heard a pine needle hit the deck. Tobin was peppered with abrasions and had a lump the size of a turnip under one eye. He lay dead-still for a moment longer, then wobbled to his feet and shuddered like an old cur crawling from a creek.

"I'll get it next time," he grumbled.

"There ain't gonna be no next time," said Richard.

"Give the boy a chance," the pastor threw in, thumping Tobin on the back.

When a father can watch his son pitch eighty feet down a vertical cliff, and straightaway argue that we were shortchanging the boy by not letting him climb back up and have a second chance at an even longer whistler, we knew the man was cut from the same crazy cloth as his son, and that there was no reasoning with him. But the fall had taken the air out of the whole venture, and we were through for the day.

The "next time" came the next summer. In one of the greatest leads of that era, Ricky stemmed the entire Green Arch on his first try. Tobin and I followed. Tobin would go on to become one of the world's true super climbers during the late 1970s. But nothing really changed: he always climbed as if time were too short for him, a Dostoyevskian gambler with the family jewels.

I've seen a bit of the world since those early days at Tahquitz, done my share of crazy things, and have seen humanity with all the bark off, primal and raw. But I've never since experienced the electricity of watching Tobin out there on the quick of the long plank, clawing for the Promised Land.

He finally found it in 1980, attempting a solo winter ascent of Mt. Alberta's North Face. His death was a tragedy, of course. Yet I wondered if God Himself could no longer bear the strain of watching Tobin wobbling and lunging way out there on the sharp end of the rope, and finally just drew him into the fold.

THE ONLY BLASPHEMY

At speeds beyond 90 miles an hour, the California cops jail you, so I keep it down in the 70s. Tobin always drove flat out, till his sports car exploded in flames on the freeway out by Running Springs. Tobin was a supreme artist, alive in a way the rest of us were not. But time was a cannibal for Tobin, who lived and climbed like he had only minutes before existence ate him alive. When Tobin perished attempting to solo the North Face of Mount Alberta in winter, our only surprise was that he hadn't died sooner.

I charge on toward Joshua Tree National Monument, where two weeks before, another friend had "decked" while soloing. I inspected the base of the route, wincing at the grisly bloodstains, the tufts of matted hair. Soloing is unforgiving, but a warrior, with a touch of card sharp, can usually pull it off. You just have to be realistic, and never stove to peer pressure or pride. Do it for private reasons, whatever those might be. Or don't do it.

At 90 miles an hour, Joshua Tree comes quickly, but the stark night drags.

The morning sun peers over the flat horizon, gilding rocks shining on the desert carpet. The biggest stones are 150 feet high. Right after breakfast, I run into John Bachar, widely considered the world's foremost free climber. For several years, Bachar's traveled widely in his red VW van, chasing the sun and the hardest routes on the planet.

Most all climbs are easy for Bachar. He has to make his own difficulties, and usually does so by ditching the rope. He dominates the cliff with his grace and confidence, never gets rattled, never thrashes, and if he ever gets killed climbing, it will be a gross transgression of all taste and you'll curse God for the rest of your life on aesthetic grounds. Bachar has been out at Joshua Tree for several months now and his soloing feats astonish everyone.

It is wintertime, when college checks my climbing to weekends, so my motivation is there but my fitness is not. Right off, Bachar suggests a "Half Dome day." Yosemite's Half Dome is 2,000 feet high, so we'll have to climb that much footage (roughly twenty small climbs), there at J. Tree, to log our Half Dome day.

Bachar laces up his boots and cinches the sling on his chalk bag. "Ready?"

Only then do I realize he means to climb all 2,000 feet solo, without a rope. To save face, I agree, thinking: *Well, if he suggests something too crazy, I'll just draw the line.* I was the first to start soloing out at J. Tree anyway.

We cast off up vertical rock, twisting feet and jamming hands into bulging cracks; smearing the toes of our skintight boots onto tiny bumps and wrinkles; muscling over roofs on bulbous holds; palming off rough rock and marveling at it all.

A little voice occasionally asks how good a flexing, quarter-inch hold can be. If you're solid, you set curled fingers or pointed toes on that quarter-incher and push or pull perfunctorily. And I'm solid.

After several hours, we've disposed of a dozen pitches and feel invincible. We up the ante, to the threshold of expert terrain. We slow, but by early afternoon, we've climbed twenty pitches; our Half Dome day is history. As a finale, Bachar suggests we solo a 5.11—an exacting drill, even for Bachar.

I was already hosed from racing up twenty different climbs in a few hours, having cruised the last half dozen on rhythm and momentum. Regardless, I follow Bachar over to Intersection Rock, the communal hang for local climbers and the site for Bachar's final solo.

Bachar wastes no words and no time. Scores of milling climbers freeze when he starts up a left-slanting crack, climbing with flawless precision, plugging his fingers into shallow pockets in the 105-degree wall, one move flowing into the next, much as pieces of a puzzle match-fit together. I scrutinize his moves, making mental notes on the intricate sequence.

After thirty feet, he pauses, directly beneath the crux bulge. Splaying his left foot onto a slanting edge, he pinches a tiny flute and pulls through to a giant bucket hold. Then he hikes the last 100 feet of vertical rock like it's a staircase. A few seconds later, he peers over the lip and flashes that sly, candid snicker, awaiting my reply.

I'm booted up and covered in chalk, facing a notorious climb, rarely done, even with a rope. Fifty hungry eyes give me the once-over, as if to say, *Well?* That little voice says, "No problem," and I believe it. I draw several deep breaths. I don't consider the consequences, only the moves. I start up.

A body length of easy stuff, then those pockets, which I finger adroitly before pulling with maximum might. This first bit passes quickly. Everything is clicking, severe but steady, and I glide into bone-crushing altitude before I can reckon.

Then, as I splay my foot out onto the slanting edge, the chilling realization comes that, in my haste, I have bungled the sequence. My hands are crossed up and too low on that tiny flute that I'm pinching with waning power.

My foot starts vibrating and I'm instantly desperate, wondering if and when my body will freeze and plummet. I can't possibly down climb a single move. My only escape is straight up.

I glance down beneath my legs and my gut churns at the thought of a freefall onto the boulders, of climbers later cringing at my red stains and tufts of hair. They look up and say, "Yeah, he popped from way up there."

My breathing is frenzied while my arms, gassed from the previous

2,000 feet of climbing, feel like concrete. Pinching that little flute, I suck my feet up so as to extend my arm and jam my hand into the bottoming crack above. But I'm set up too low on that flute and the only part of the crack I can reach is too shallow and accepts but a third of my hand.

I'm stuck, terrified, my whole life focused down to a single move.

Shamefully, I understand the only blasphemy—to willfully jeopardize life—which I have done, and it sickens me.

Then everything slows, as though preservation instincts have kicked my mind into hyper gear. In a heartbeat, I've realized my desire to live, not die. But my regrets cannot alter my situation: arms shot, legs wobbling, head on fire. Then fear burns itself up, leaving me hollow and mortified. To concede, to quit, would be easy.

That little voice calmly says: "At least go out trying." I hear that, then punch my hand deeper into the bottoming crack.

If only I can execute this one unlikely move, I'll get an incut jug and can rest on it, jungle-gym style, before the final push to the top. I'm afraid to eyeball my crimped hand, scarcely jammed in the bottoming crack. It must hold my 205 pounds, on an overhanging wall, with scant footholds, and this seems ludicrous, impossible.

My body has jittered here for close to a minute. Forever.

My jammed hand says, "No way!" but that little voice says, "Might as well try it."

I pull up slowly—my left foot still pasted to that sloping edge—and that big bucket hold is right there. I almost have it. I do. Simultaneously, my right hand rips from the crack and my weight shock-loads onto my enfeebled left arm.

Adrenaline powers me atop the "Thank God" bucket, where I try and suck my chest to the wall and get my weight over my feet. But it's too steep to cop a meaningful rest so I push on, shaking horribly, dancing black dots flecking my vision, glad only that the terrain, though vertical, is casual compared to below. Still, it takes an age to claw up the last 100 feet and onto the summit.

"Looked a little shaky," says Bachar, flashing that shameless snicker. I want to slap it off his face.

That night, I drove into town and got a bottle. The next day, while Bachar went for an El Cap day (3,000 feet, solo, of course), I wandered through dark rock corridors, scouting for turtles, making garlands from wildflowers, staring up at the titanic sky—doing all those things a person does on borrowed time.

Postscript: On July 5, 2009, John Bachar died while free soloing on the Dike Wall near his home in Mammoth Lakes, California. He was fifty-two years old, an iconic rock climber, and a legend in the world of adventure sports.

Thirty-one years before, I wrote this essay, stating that if John ever got killed climbing, I would curse God for the rest of my life on aesthetic, not moral, grounds. Now, I'm not so sure I want to curse God, or anyone, for the rest of my life, though I'm saddened to have to live it knowing John Bachar is not out there somewhere, tangling with Old Man Gravity.

But maybe he still is. He's just higher than I can see from here.

THE LAST PITCH

"Watch me close," I said to Ron, remembering my first time on this pitch, several years before. "This might get funky."

I felt anxious, amazed, primed—everything all at once. El Capitan in a day was a done thing. In traditional-style rock climbing, free-climbing a genuine big wall remained the last and greatest prize. We wanted to be first and here was our chance to close the deal, eleven pitches up the overhanging East Face of Washington Column.

From the start, I'd warned the boys that this last pitch might shut us down, so we were bursting at the seams from the suspense of battling all the way up here and still not knowing.

"Get us off this thing," said Ron.

Ron Kauk was only a kid. Seventeen, I think. I outweighed him by sixty pounds, but Ron had caught me falling many times, so I didn't question his hip belay. John Bachar, third on the rope, reached an arm from a patch of shade, passed me a couple slings, and said, "You're the man."

That helped. All the way up, we'd cheered and prodded one another as aid pitch after aid pitch fell to our free-climbing efforts, pitches that soon became classics: *The Boulder Problem Pitch*, with its fingertip liebacking and scrabbling feet; the *Enduro Corner*, a soaring dihedral that goes from thin hands to big fingers, right to the belay bolts; the thrutching *Harding Slot*, a claustrophobic, bottomless flare that was destined to dash the hopes of so many Europeans; and the flawless *Changing Corners*, a vertical shrine of shifting rock planes with an ocean of air below. For over a thousand feet now, the blond-orange cracks kept connecting in remarkable ways, and we kept busting out every technique we knew. Never before had we experienced a route so continuously difficult. To our knowledge, no climbers ever had.

Fifty feet to go.

My toes curled painfully inside my EBs, but I reached down and cranked the laces anyhow. Sweat dripped off my face onto the rock. We passed around the last of our water as I racked a few small pitons and several Stoppers and Hexcentrics on the sling around my shoulder. I slowly chalked up, glanced over at John, and said, "I'll take some tunes, if you please."

John reached into his day pack and punched the button on our little cassette deck. Jimi Hendrix's "Astro Man," our theme song for the route, blared through the top flap. John flashed that insolent grin and said, "Rock and roll, hombre."

John Bachar. He looked more like a math geek than an athlete, with his elfin build, stringy blond mop, and two shiny silver buckteeth. Back in high school, I'd get midnight calls from John about his new climbs or boulder problems, meaning I immediately had to beg a car or even hitchhike to Stoney Point or Mount Rubidoux so I could bag these routes as well.

Meanwhile, John began his lonely quest to become the world's greatest solo rock climber, a ritual he practiced for an astonishing thirty-five more years before it finally took him out. But just then, smirking on that ledge, he was eighteen years old, and looked about twelve.

I took a last sip of water and shuffled out on the tapering ledge, around a corner and over to moderate lie-backing up the left side of the short pillar, ending at a twenty-five-foot headwall.

All the way up, the rock had been diamond-hard, but here it turned to sand. Two summers before, on my first big wall, flambéed by a heat wave, I'd nailed this last bit via rickety pins bashed into a rotten seam. I'd wondered out loud, to Ron and John, how we might free-climb the section; one glance confirmed we never would. However, just right of the seam and straight up off the pillar, the vertical face bristled with sandy dimples and thin, scabby sidepulls. I'd have to toe off pure grain and yank straight out on these scabs, praying they didn't bust off. The only protection was several tied-off baby angles slugged into that seam.

While organizing our gear, I'd talked big about not bringing a bolt kit and about high adventure, cha cha cha. What an ass. I couldn't hang my hat on those pins. The only nut was in the lieback crack, ten feet below. It was one of those surreal fixes where I was plainly screwed yet somehow had to make do.

I reached up and grabbed the first sidepull. It felt serious just to hoist my feet off the pinnacle, and I stood sulking for several minutes. Here was the chance of a lifetime and I was too gripped to commit. Maybe Ron should have a go? He would race up this, I thought. Ron was the most gifted climber we had ever seen. He'd hiked the *Endurance Corner* like a staircase. Same with the *Harding Slot*. Nothing could stop him.

Ron first turned up in Yosemite when he was fourteen and it was like Sitting Bull returning to Standing Rock: the chief had finally come home. The elements were living things in him, and the rock and even the Valley itself seemed fashioned just for Ron. In some nameless way, fundamental as chain lightning, Ron Kauk was father to us all. Not long after that afternoon on the Column, Ron would spread his wampum across Europe, hurling it at the Karakoram and beyond, closing the circle on the traditional era of climbing. But I couldn't call him now.

Too anxious to sleep, turning this last pitch over in my mind like a pig on a spit, I'd fairly dragged Ron and John out of their sleeping bags, then had burgled the two leads up to this crumbly face. Now I couldn't muster the sack to pull a single move.

I hated this situation. I loved it, too. Not a soul, not even God, stood between me and the decision I faced. Do or fly. The moment my feet left that pillar, my life would change forever.

Gritting my teeth and fingering those useless pitons, I peered up at the flaky holds, shifting foot to foot on my tiny stance. It felt like the route was taunting me, playing my ego off itself so I'd lose patience, crank into something stupid, and plummet terribly as the whole Valley howled.

But fuck it. There were holds, and I only had twenty-five feet to go. Maybe less. I glanced left and growled, "Here goes." Then I blanked my mind and pulled off the pinnacle.

After a body length, it felt unlikely I could reverse any of this, so I accepted that I was basically soloing. Strangely, I relaxed. If this was what the route demanded, I'd go with it. The climbing wasn't nearly so hard as I was making it. Scared as I was of snapping an edge, I cranked a series of screwball twisty moves to avoid reefing too hard on suspect handholds and keep some weight over the granular footholds.

After about ten feet, I stretched high off a flexing carbuncle and pinched the bottom of a big grimy tongue drooping down, clasping both sides in turn, anxiously wiggling a few sketchy wired nuts into the flaring grain. The only pins I had that would fit behind the tongue were bashed into that seam below.

Fifteen feet to go.

Bear-hugging like mad, I gunned for the roof, feet bicycling the choss. Grains rained down. The tongue flexed and groaned. My eyes zeroed in on the short hand crack extending down from the roof, but after a few more bear hugs, I'd only reached a sloping sandbar, which I'd have to straight mantel to stretch a hand into the crack.

This was bullshit. If I blew off here, I'd go for a monster whipper and probably hitt the ledge. I hated this route with all my heart. Piece of shit goddamn garbage wall from hell! What the fuck?

"What's going on over there?" Ron yelled from around the corner.

"Just watch me," I yelled back.

"We can't even see you," said Bachar.

"Just watch the damn rope," I said.

I splayed my feet, soles flush on the crud, one hand pawing the tongue as I raked the sandy berm, trying to get down to solid rock. Cocking into a mantel at last, I pressed it out like molasses, gingerly placing a foot on the crunchy veneer and stepping up with my teeth chattering and no handholds. Finally, I could stretch up to the crack, sink a hand jam, and slot a bomber hex.

I leaned back off the jam and gazed down at the pitiful wires bristling from the tongue and the loose face, patted with chalk marks, plunging to the tied-off pegs. The wicked hard climbing I feared never came, the real challenge being the crap rock.

All told, this was like the best pitch I'd ever done. Perfect, really. And beneath the pinnacle, diving 1,200 undercut feet straight into the talus—a face of wonders. I felt like the Valley's favored son. Reaching out over the roof, I could just clasp a good, flat-top hold. I pulled up and realized my hands were on top of Washington Column.

We called it *Astroman*. Following an early ascent, the British ace Pete Livesey called it "the world's greatest free climb," a title that stuck for the next twenty years. During that time, the last pitch, "the sting in the tail," cleaned up nicely following a thorough brushing and hundreds of ascents. Several long, thin pitons were welded behind the tongue, as well as some copper-heads. But the caveat for the last pitch remains the same as it did in July 1975: *Don't fall.*

GUILTY PLEASURES

On the world's first big multi-pitch sport climb

Lynn Hill and I spent the winter of 1981 in Las Vegas, climbing daily at Red Rocks and plowing through nights at dead-end jobs. After roughly ten seasons of climbing 300 days a year, my learning curve had flattened and I found myself singing the same old song. I wasn't the first "famous" climber whose future looked like outer space, so I kept switching venues rather than instruments. Everything would change that summer during a filming gig at Venezuela's Angel Falls, a jungle gusher sufficient to deliver me into television production and book writing. Never again would I climb full time.

Several years later, Lynn joined the international competitive circuit, became world sport climbing champion for what seemed like forever, free climbed *The Nose* on El Cap, and became an adventure sports icon. But that winter in Vegas found us in flux, searching for direction. Soon we'd find our separate ways, but before leaving Vegas for good, we'd also find the archetype of the nascent American sport-climbing revolution. Or more accurately, the archetype found us.

If ever an area lent itself to sport climbing, it's Red Rocks; but back then, the idea of gym-bolting the now-popular sport areas never crossed our minds. We still followed a traditional approach. Bigger and bolder always meant better, so partly from a sense of duty, but more from force of habit, we focused on the many unclimbed crack systems that slashed a half-dozen giant canyon walls. Only later would we realize that the classical "trad" days had already died.

Since arriving in Vegas a few months before, we'd established a handful of long free climbs, often scaring ourselves stiff. Trying to limit bolts and pitons, or avoid them altogether—which is asking for trouble on the sheer, friable sandstone—we'd sometimes find ourselves belayed to cosmetic nuts and running out the rope on vertical, iffy rock. On the steeper lines, busting out onto the face was generally suicidal. The red sandstone offered ample holds, but usually ran too steep for lead bolting.

On one route, Lynn traversed from a bombay chimney onto the vertical face, busted a hold, and logged an airball screamer for the ages. Only a doubtful friend in the guts of a flare stopped her from smashing into the boulders from sixty feet. We had enough other frightful episodes that the most startling lines—massive, surging faces upwards of 1,000 feet—remained futuristic projects to gaze up at in wonder.

Then we met local climbers Jorge and Joanne Urioste, who, back then, comprised roughly a third of the hardcore Red Rocks climbing fraternity. Jorge knew a great line when he saw one, and he saw plenty. He also understood that the old trad rules could ruin a climber should they try to lead those tempting unclimbed faces. So Jorge began leading would-be face climbs on aid, installing bolts at convenient places—hardly a new tactic, though usually applied to brief holdless sections of short testpieces, and, to my knowledge, never before the MO on what essentially were short wall climbs.

Jorge would dress the pitch, then Joanne would work the moves on a top rope till she could free-climb the whole enchilada in one go. The bolting went slowly and the climbing slower yet. Jorge, an anthropology professor at UNLV, enjoyed limited free time, so his ascents entailed miles of fixed ropes—meaning Jorge would siege each climb till the bolts were placed and Joanne had free-followed every move. Joanne would often need multiple days to free a single pitch, some of which were borderline 5.12. Once the climb was "done," Joanne would return with another free climber and tick the redpoint.

Not surprisingly, the few Red Rocks locals were alarmed by the Uriostes' disregard for traditional style, a style that kept adrenaline levels high but also kept us in the cracks. I've wasted half my life on questionable pursuits, but I've never told others how to climb, or live, or die. Nevertheless, Jorge's tactics privately confounded me.

As I scratched my head in the scree fields, Jorge quickly bagged a slew of outstanding lines (including what later became some of the most well-traveled multi-pitch routes on earth). A few of Jorge's routes looked as if he'd loaded a Gatling gun with quarter-inch bolts and stitched a 1,200-foot vertical face, bottom to top. In fact, Jorge hand-drilled every bolt he ever placed. The few times Lynn and I repeated a Urioste composition, the climbing felt surreal. So accustomed were we to shouldering a bulky rack and placing gear that cast off with nothing but quickdraws, and clipping bolts every eight feet, felt almost criminal. The experience immediately cast me onto the indefinite ground between two worlds: one known and established, the other a strange but alluring universe where fun meant everything and fear counted for nothing.

No question, Jorge had queered the very rules I'd slavishly followed since first roping up. Other climbers with more natural courage or recklessness embodied the old trad ethic with native ease. In uncanny, elusive moments, I could get after it like a Bengal tiger. But when I started redlining, only devotion to the classical verities kept me so hidebound. I fudged the rules, certainly, but trying to maintain an idealized level of boldness had set my experience on fire. So to see Jorge engineering the risk and uncertainly out of the game was both perplexing and enticing. I had a vague inkling I was looking at the future, and the possibilities seemed boundless.

That year, Jorge and Joanne were working on their biggest, steepest, most outlandish climb yet, a varicolored, 1,100-foot convex plaque towering over the tumble of Oak Creek Canyon, half a dozen twisting miles into the Red Rocks' backcountry. They'd pushed the route about 750 feet. On several sections, Joanne hadn't yet attempted to free-follow, though Jorge thought it possible to free most, if not all, of the climbing up to their high point. Possibly because Lynn and I were two of the few active climbers in the area or, more likely, because we lived a few blocks from the Uriostes, Jorge invited us to explore the free-climbing prospects. The expedition felt odd from the start. I wasn't used to someone so thoroughly setting my table, and during the two-hour slog into the cliff, I felt like a burglar casing a job.

The bewildering angles of both Oak Creek Canyon and the surrounding bluffs made everything appear askew, so we couldn't get a coherent fix on the wall until nearly reaching the base. It looked similar, in length and angle, to the business section of the *Prow* on Washington Column. I figured we'd get hosed at a jutting roof, 120 feet above. Maybe sooner.

No climber, anywhere on earth, was trying to establish new free routes, ground up, on anything remotely resembling the wall just above us—a 1,100-foot, vertical-to-bulging face with not a single prominent crack for the duration. On such a steep wall, there clearly were no places to stop and hand-drill protection, and you'd need a lot of it because much of the face appeared smooth as fine china.

Lynn led the first pitch, a steepening ramp/corner gleaming with that glassy, black desert varnish that earmarks the slickest stone on earth. She quickly pawed to the belay and yelled down, "Easy 5.10."

Joanne and I followed. Above the first belay, the wall jacked up to dead V, and I cautiously worked over blocks and eyebrow roofs that looked stout from below but passed at 5.9. Hanging off a jug, I gazed at the ladder of quarter-inch bolts cutting around the roof to the headwall above. Much obliged, Jorge. A big stretch, one heaving layback move, then incuts to a hanging belay. Maybe easy 5.11, but exciting with those quarter-inchers.

The next lead looked like 5.10 yet provided the only moderate pitch on the lower wall, following generous rails and passing a regular cavalcade of those quarter-inchers. Somewhere during that pitch, I knew we were on to something rare.

The cliff was steep as a skyscraper. Because the route began halfway up a high canyon rampart, resting above a long approach slab spilling into shade, I felt as if we were climbing on a wall triple the size. We'd peer up, dangling from sling belays, wondering if we could climb ten more feet, only to find hold after hold, with ready bolts to clip. After a few leads, I was charging with more momentum than I'd felt in several years.

The route had, so far, traced intermittent cracks, which abruptly thinned to a shadow; for unknown reasons, on the section just overhead, Jorge had skimped on the bolts. Though only rock-bottom 5.10, I found myself a good ways out on a quarter-inch "coffin nail," pulling on vertical rock that would require 100 ascents to totally clean up. Then an easy crack led to another sling belay beneath a headwall.

I lashed off, leaned back, and started laughing. I'd never climbed anything remotely like this. After the first pitch, the few nut and cam placements had dried up. If Jorge hadn't pre-rigged the bolts, we wouldn't have made it past the first pitch. For us to just waltz in, clip, and go wasn't climbing as Lynn or I understood it. But damn, we were having a blast.

Far below, arid, brown plains—today a solid grid of prefab homes and soulless office plazas—swept gently into the gaudy Las Vegas Strip, twenty-five miles and a world away. Just above, a thin, bottoming gash snaked up a bulging piebald wall, occasional bolts festooning both sides. This looked hard and sustained. It was Lynn's lead, and I was glad.

Flexible folk are rarely mega-strong and strong folk are rarely flexible, but Lynn has a wealth of both qualities, and I always had to lump it. As she steadily bridged, Gastoned, crimped, and jammed up the pitch, the rope hanging free between bolts, Joanne and I sighed, wondering how we'd manage. Several times, between bolts, Lynn paused to slot a wire. Then the rock bulged slightly, and she started cranking for keeps.

Stemming her left leg out at about chin level, toeing off some burnished nothing. I would never walk again if I tried that move.

"You bring the ascenders?" I asked Joanne.

"Nope," she said, craning to see Lynn 110 feet above. "I think she's got it now. It eases there."

Fortunately, I have a three-foot reach advantage on Lynn Hill, and could stretch past the acrobat moves, thieving by on sidepulls and shallow jams. While it lacked a definitive crux, there were long stretches of 5.10. Overall, the pitch felt about 5.11c, and closely resembled a modern sport-climbing lead, save that it hung 800 feet up a wall and actually had holds.

The fixed ropes ended here, with 400 vertical feet looming above. Much as we wanted to press on and bag the whole climb, without Jorge's first installing another stack of bolts, we had no chance. It crossed my mind to grab our little rack, cast off, and hope for the best, but the next few hundred feet looked bulging, bald, and periodically loose. And even if I had a bolt kit, the steepness shot down any chance of lead bolting without aid slings. Yet, with luck, and a few more days of toil, the whole mother might go free—a concept so wonderful that, down at the base, I suggested Jorge immediately get back to work. A short, stout man with the perseverance of an Andean mountaineer—which he'd been in the Bolivia of his youth—Jorge finished bolting a month or so later. The next weekend found Lynn, Joanne, and me back at the highpoint.

I remember some reachy 5.11 face work on the sixth pitch, and how the rope dangled in space as I belayed the girls up. Pitch seven looked improbable, wandering a bit and working through several projecting white ribs. Lynn got that one and she got a dandy—and scary as well. Most every long Red Rocks route passes through a vein of choss, with a few gong-like flakes.

The wall kicked back maybe fifty feet above. If Lynn could smuggle past this last bulge, we were home free.

Lynn Hill. We called her "Little Lynnie." She was a prodigy and we all knew so from day one. She carried her gift with quiet ease rather than chest pounding or smug humility. Back then, no female had ever climbed remotely as well as the best guys, so when Lynn began dusting us off—which she did with maddening frequency—folks offered up all kinds of specious explanations, refusing to believe a female, and a five-foot, one-inch article at that, could possibly be so honed.

Out at J. Tree, they said Lynn shone, owing to quartz monzonite's superior friction, which catered to her bantam weight. In Yosemite, her success hinged on small hands, which fit wonderfully into the infernal thin cracks. On limestone, she could plug three fingers into pockets where the rest of us managed only two. Even after a heap of World Cup victories, it still took the climbing world an age to accept Lynn as the Chosen One, and perhaps her legacy was never sealed, once and for all, until she free-climbed *The Nose*, on El Capitan, the world's most famous rock climb.

From the early days in Red Rocks, it would take her several years to become "the" Lynn Hill. Nevertheless, she was always a supernova, especially on that funky pitch way up what would become the seminal *Levitation 29.*

"Watch me!" Lynn yelled, giving me a head's up, as she liebacked up a sandbar, her feet pasted at shoulder height. Ten more feet and Lynn pulled onto easier ground. Modern topos call this pitch 5.10+, but it's basically unratable, what with the band of loose white rock and the bizarre, sideways moves. An easy crack led a few hundred feet to the top. We rapped the route, stripping the fixed lines.

I can't remember if it was Joanne's twenty-ninth birthday, or if that came shortly afterwards, but it factored into naming the climb *Levitation 29*. The route has seen thousands of ascents and has cleaned up nicely. In her autobiography, Lynn called the route her favorite of all time. In real-world terms, that was the start of American multi-pitch sport climbing, and it happened on one of the finest samples you'll ever find. Luck of the draw.

Over the radio today, I heard Sarah Vaughn singing a classic Hammerstein lyric, which ran, "When I grow too old to dream, I'll have you to remember." The majestic hike in, the soaring wall, and the radiant novelty of scaling that great stone wave—an impossible feat prior to *Levitation 29*—are going the way of all memories. But the visceral thrill of roving the open face, pulling for glory, starry-eyed and amazed to be alive, lingers still.

HEADING NORTH

Reject the angel. Kick the muse, made ill by limitation. And forget our fear of the scent of violets. The true struggle is with the duende.

—Federico Garcia Lorca

The first person I met when I stumbled into Camp 4, in May of 1971, was Jim Bridwell, sitting on a rock and smoking a Pall Mall. Several small magazines covered rock climbing back then, and Jim was their cover boy. New routes on El Capitan. All those photos of Jim free climbing like mad. Photos I'd studied for days, pouring over the ecology of ascent.

I told Jim if he ever needed a partner, I was available. This was my first time in Yosemite Valley, and I promised Jim I had many things to do.

"Like what?" Jim asked, and I said, "Like the Left Side of Reed's Pinnacle."

Bud Couch, longtime Pharaoh of Tahquitz and Suicide Rocks (my home crags), had recently gotten hosed on Reeds. By checking off the pinnacle, I counted on putting Bud and Suicide behind me. I was seventeen years old. Jim was twenty-six, I think. He showed me where to stash my backpack full of junk; we tossed a rack together and hitchhiked down to Reeds. I could not kick off my Yosemite campaign with a better partner. So far, so good. Yet I wondered: was Jim Bridwell packing the *duende*?

My mother had dropped me off at the Greyhound bus station in Upland, California, at 6:05 a.m. that morning. I spent the next eighteen hours thumbing through *In Search of Duende*, by poet Federico Garcia Lorca, as the near-empty bus chugged up the Grape Vine and across the central valley, past Prospero, Cawelo, Famoso, finally dumping me at Yosemite Lodge round midnight.

Lorca, gay and defiant, had been executed by firing squad during the Spanish Revolution. That sounded epic. And it felt arty, rolling through Calico and Delano, glossing the verse of a Spanish insurgent. But Lorca the person felt made up as Waldo or William Tell and *el duende*, a spontaneous physical and emotional response to life, was probably moonshine as well—and I loved the sound of it.

El duende springs up inside us, said Lorca, when we hear the bold flamenco. *Duende* gives us chills. Makes us smile or cry or punch a sailor man. *Duende* hangs the moon, for the love of *Dios*—then runs off with our sister. This *duende*, whatever it was, if it was, had that something, doubtful and hazardous, to keep my mind off the uncertainty awaiting me the moment I stepped off the bus.

Reed's Pinnacle was a flat-topped, 350-foot-high exfoliation slab, leaning against the main wall and soaring for the northern rim of the valley. The first pitch, which Bridwell let me lead, burrowed behind the left side of the pinnacle, and I thrutched up a cavernous chimney—feet on one side, back on the other—then up to a stance at some slung chockstones. Secure, but I wasn't used to chimney's anywhere near that steep. The ropes dangled free below me. It was dark in there, too, and Lorca had promised that every darkness has its *duende*. The black stone felt cold. From the hidden bowels, a chilly draft wafted out that smelled of middle earth.

I looked up and shuddered. How the chimney, arcing up in a granite wave, shot into shadows, narrowing as it went. Like the dusk, I imagined, at the end of the world.

"Climbed many wide cracks?" asked Jim, joining me atop the chockstone.

"Loads," I said.

"How many?" he asked again, looking straight through me. Those copperish volts on my tongue were fear.

"None . . ."

"Better watch me close, or you'll never make this," said Jim, with his raw, hard rock aesthetic.

Jim started ratcheting up the narrowing maw, working the thigh-wide space between sweeping planes of granite with heel-toe locks, while arm-barring like a champ. He'd slotted a small, wired nut maybe twenty feet off the belay, but rope drag dislodged it and it slid down the rope to me.

"No worries," said Jim when I broke the bad news. "I could call this 5.7 if I wanted to."

Jim, fifty feet overhead, entered the business part of the pitch with not a single piece of protection between him and my belay. It was like looking up an elevator shaft at someone splayed in an open bomb bay door. The real shit. Jesus, did I really belong here?

Lorca described how the *duende* surges up inside of us, from the soles of our feet. It is truly alive. Boils our blood. But sometimes, Lorca warned, it acquires a fatal character, and contrives the means to kill you. I could hear Lorca laughing at his executioners. But that was Bridwell, secure at the next belay ledge, chuckling down that he'd meant to scare me all along. Just because.

I barely followed Jim's lead on a top rope, him coaching me up every move, finally belly-flopping onto his belay ledge with gaudy red holes in my knees and elbows.

The arrival of the *duende,* said Lorca, "is the subtle link that joins the five senses to what is core to the living flesh, the living cloud, the living ocean of love liberated from time."

Some *maestra* in Pamplona might have told me what that meant. It sure sounded like Reed's Pinnacle, and my adventure with Jim, who, the following day, led me over to Sunnyside Bench to attempt a brand-new route, tried many times, and infamous for spitting people out of it, aptly coined "1096," a code name used by law enforcement rangers to indicate a madman was on the loose. Mark Klemens made us a trio.

Mark had climbed with Jim for years and likely was the finest of the Golden Era, off-width masters. His first ascents of *Cream, Steppin' Out, Basket Case,* and many other body cracks remain test pieces today, fifty years after Mark first led them with bong bong pitons and lug-soled Robbins boots. Bad ass.

Mark took first shot at the lead, wriggling behind the flake, glommed onto the vertical wall like a giant hand, tilted right about 20 degrees. A fist crack in the back of the flare, in concert with thuggish chimneying, allowed Mark to jackknife up an inch at a time as the cruel pod labored to belch him out. The many previous failures (including much-published photos of people plunging off the thing), and how improbable it looked as a rock climb, made the adventure feel uncertain—a feeling I avoided like stomach flu, but which Jim and Mark charged after. Mark kept battling hard.

Lorca warned that the *duende* wounds. "And in trying to heal that wound that never heals, lies the strangeness, the inventiveness of a man's work." Like climbing rocks for little reason and no pay. I didn't know nothing. Except I was scared and elated.

Mark fought most of the way up the forty-foot flake before lowering off, exhausted from hanging sideways and upside down to place protection.

Jim tied in and ratcheted up to the high point in a minute. Jim clasped the outside of the flake, and with his spontaneous sense of *vérité,* and the last nut far below, swung out into a go-for-broke lieback, hand-over-handing up to a small, sloping ledge a dozen feet higher. In one ferocious stroke, *1096* was a done thing. Felt like we'd stolen Christmas.

I mean, how could these guys walk up and dick the damn thing like that? They'd just shown me how, Mark sneered, and it was my turn, so what was I waiting for? Mark was unapologetically old school. Meaning he was salt, and salt is harsh.

"Want me to climb it for you, too?" he asked.

"Bite me," I said, shimmied behind that flake, and started worm-driving more sideways than up, the flake leaned right so far. All that bleak cross-pressuring between palms, back and shoulders, butt cheeks and knees, grinding each down to the wood as my left hand punched for iffy fist jams in the bowels of the grainy flare. Fear and desperation, not wanting to embarrass myself to my heroes—only these kept me going, till I reached the end of the flare. Wheezing like Hurricane Katrina. So close, but what to do? I couldn't move.

How many times over the following fifteen years would Jim and I find ourselves—on the face of Angel Falls, in the middle of Borneo jungle, squared off with bikers in a Coachella Valley bar—momentarily frozen. Doubt in every direction. Only in such agonizing spaces do we learn how to conduct business. The problem, as always, is fear.

When you're slacking, wrote Lorca, the *duende* slacks. When you dither, or are scared, the *duende* just stands there, twiddling its thumbs. But when you go for it, as Bridwell had, the *duende* comes on like rolling thunder.

"Grab the edge!" Bridwell yelled down. I did, and immediately hinged into a Frankenstein lieback, feet pasted up by my hands, slapping for all I was worth. A final lunge and I caught the lip of the sloping ledge, pulled myself onto it, and collapsed at Jim's feet. There were only a few 5.11s in the Valley back then, and *1096* had to be one of them.

"It has to be!" I gasped out.

"It's not," Mark yelled up.

"It's close," said Jim.

Over the decades, *1096* became the industry standard for 5.10++ wriggling. Owing to its bizarre geology, there is no standard way to climb it. "It's a chimney," says Mountain Project, a favored climbing directory. "It's a flare, it's a fist crack, it's a lieback . . . It's a classic!"

The *duende,* on the other hand, glowing with the magic of a Persian illuminated manuscript, with the weirdness of a sixties sci-fi book cover, remains impossible to define. Who cares what it is, really, so long as it gets the next rash teenager with a pack full of junk onto the 6:05 Greyhound, heading north.

THE REAL DEAL

The Tao of Paul Gleason, Stonemaster Emeritus

A century-old aerial photo of Upland, California—on display in the Upland City Library—shows a sprawling orange grove, like a borderless green quilt, spilling off the San Antonio Mountains into the alluvial flatlands of Pomona Valley, forty miles east of Los Angeles. SpongeBob might have grown up here; General George S. Patton, Mark McGwire, and Tom Waits actually did. So did Richard Harrison, Ricky Accomazzo, and I.

Back in 1970, we were sixteen, and most local rock climbing—which wasn't much—flowed through the Sierra Club and several Boy Scout explorer troops. The Riverside Search and Rescue (SAR) Team, allied with the sheriff's department, formed a menacing third party. In that bygone age of love beads and leisure suits, if you didn't hitch on with one of the official outfits, you were nothing.

The groups disapproved of outsiders winging it in their sport; you either played by their rules or slipped someone $20 to school you on the side. I paid the $20 to Jack Schnurr, a SAR member (and excellent teacher) who taught me basic rockcraft in one afternoon, and another $20 to Bob Dominic, a former Eagle Scout who guided me for a day at Tahquitz Rock. Since it took ages to raise forty bucks, I declared myself fully "taught" after two sessions. I passed on my training to Ricky and Richard, and we collectively bought a rope and a skeleton rack.

Dominic had first told me about Mount Rubidoux, a popular bouldering area near Riverside. In mid-summer, Rubidoux is a parched and smoggy wasteland choked with brambles and fox heads. But in early winter, clover and wildflowers blanket the mountainside, and the air is cool and clear. Motoring up the single-lane road en route to the towering summit crucifix, you pass scores of boulders, from ten to forty feet high, rearing off the angled hillside. A Monument for Peace sits near the apex, with a stone-and-mortar bridge and minaret bearing a brass plaque commemorating 100 nations, erected 125 years ago by a forgotten local dreamer.

Something pacific, a presence, it seems, lingers about the mountain that, starting in the early 1900s, attracted thousands for Easter sunrise services, a now-ubiquitous ceremony that began there on the summit of Mt. Rubidoux. When the Santa Ana winds blow, you can look north to the snow-covered San Gabriel Mountains, and beyond for a hundred lifetimes.

From the first afternoon at Rubidoux, we were snubbed by anyone with a rope because we were clearly neither Boy Scouts (the cigarettes) nor from the Sierra Club (our boom box blaring the Mahavishu Orchestra). We were feral and annoying. With little gear and less experience, we badly needed help. But every organized group of climbers would strip our top ropes and elbow us into the weeds. In the daffy dynamics of early 1970s climbing, such handling was an initiation ritual, and junior group members instructed us to seize the opportunity, suck up to the leaders, and plead to join. But we no more belonged in one of those groups than Tikis belong on Mars. So we stumbled down our own path, making the game up as we went.

I'd screwed up most everything, especially relationships, because I'd never learned to blend or comply. But up on the steep, I learned to move with new harmonies, taking what the rock gave me. Ricky, Richard, and I had found something to love, and the future, which can plague a teenage mind, began to take the profile of great granite walls on the horizon.

We had no money and limited access to a car, so after school we'd often hitchhike out to Rubidoux and boulder till we couldn't make a fist. We'd been climbing for a few months when Paul Gleason picked up Richard and me hitching home and drove us twenty miles to our doorsteps in his rust-pocked VW Bug.

I don't remember how it all got started, but we began meeting Paul out at Rubidoux at the oddest hours. With his lumberjack frame, shoulder-length red hair, and Van Dyke moustache/goatee ensemble, Paul resembled Buffalo Bill Cody with twenty pounds of gristle packed on. Paul was entirely free of guff and posturing, which had a calming effect on a tightly wound kid like myself. I badly needed somebody to live up to.

I started copying everything Paul did, even down to the way he walked—a sort of Cro-Magnon shamble with firm, collected purpose. Paul wore white Navy pants—longtime costume of the Yosemite Valley hardmen—and in a week, we all had them as well. Paul smoked a corncob pipe ("Missouri Meerschaum"), cycling between Flying Dutchman and ragweed, a sacrament Richard and I adopted straightaway. The challenge was trying to match Paul move for move on the boulders, nearly impossible because he was one of the best climbers of that era.

From the early 1950s to about 1972, Stoney Point, in the San Fernando Valley, and Rubidoux were the bouldering hotspots for aspiring California climbers.

Joshua Tree soon usurped both venues, but one need only visit Rubidoux on a cool winter day to appreciate the area's biting diorite and highball bouldering.

As early as 1968, the preternatural Phil Haney and crimp wunderkind Ben Borson established a stack of Rubidoux problems upward of V8. Lunging, jumping, crimping, and open-handing absolutely nothing, Haney tamed overhanging rock fifteen years before sport climbers made it their native turf. Nevertheless, the sage and gatekeeper of Mount Rubidoux was Paul Gleason.

Around 1970, when most Southern California climbers were slug-

ging angles into Tahquitz granite, Paul made annual junkets to Colorado to bone up on John Gill's infamous Dakota sandstone problems,
returning to SoCal with revolutionary strategies—like the use of gym-
nastic chalk and hatefully tight "varappe" boots. More important, Paul,
one of the first to repeat John Gill's Mental Block and Eliminator dy-
nos at Horse Tooth Reservoir, near Fort Collins, understood that a fit
climber, willing to huck and deadpoint, could yard up most anything.
Without the direct mentoring of its original members by Paul Gleason,
those of us who later became the Stonemasters might never have realized that, in the early 1970s, the field of free climbing stretched before
us with the breadth and sparkle of open ocean.

Once we fell under Paul's laconic tutelage, our learning curve so
steepened we could barely hang on. Like many effective coaches, Paul
inspired by virtue of who he was, not through what he said, which was
never much. His praise and suggestions were laid on with a feather,
which made us listen that much closer.

We'd watch Paul send the Wall of Glass, say, with its dynamic start
and twenty-five-foot 5.11 slab finish. Then, rather than sing his own
song, he'd return to the base and say, "I figure one of you boys should
get that today."

We'd pull ourselves silly and scare ourselves crazy, taking jumbo
skidding whippers into the shrubs trying to make good on Paul's pre-
diction. A "Nicely done," or "You're starting to move real well," was
the most we'd hear. When I finally climbed the Wall of Glass, and stood
where Paul had stood on top, I felt like Spartacus and Paul quickly
ferreted out the corncob and we huffed and hacked and howled. For the
first time in my life, I felt like I'd joined the world.

Paul modeled a different rendering of a human being, one based on
quiet enthusiasm and awe for living. In a word, love. Not the quixot-
ic, emotional article, but some nameless spark that ignited my natural
gratitude for being alive and for expressing that stoke on the boulders,
which Paul readily admitted were minerals, nothing more. But the

movement itself, a continuous creative act, was to fashion a state of being that glowed, pulled from the vastness of non-being one foot and one handhold at a time. Cash money never changed hands. Nobody noticed our failures and little victories. But we were stirring life with a magic wand and it felt like we owned the world.

I'd always been paralyzed by judgments—from family, coaches, and everyone else who couldn't contain me. I'd taken it personally, and a rebel the size of Godzilla had for years marched point in my life. I started rock climbing to show the world who was wrong or die trying. After a few months around Paul, I no longer pushed so hard off everyone.

Paul initially played it easy with us, but as we rounded into shape, the curriculum grew increasingly grueling. Paul had ambition and focus when it came to bagging new boulder problems—he'd chart moves out on graph paper and file the edges of his PAs with an emery board. For Paul, ascending a hard new boulder problem was a soul adventure he'd authenticate by howling at the sky, dancing in place, and, of course, stoking the hallowed corncob. From the moment he bagged a new climb, we knew that Paul would lead us over to that ghastly slab or ceiling till we'd all succeeded. Paul's corncob was not for lonely harvest.

I still remember sitting with Paul on top of the forty-foot Joe Brown Boulder, gazing into the vastness. And Paul would say, "Pretty amazing we can see at all, don't you think?" Such comments threw me, as I generally wolfed down reality in chunks, which gave me heartburn bad. "How does anyone stand on such a small hold?" he might say in the middle of a problem, and I'd tumble off wondering what the hell. Once I started pondering things I'd long taken for granted—walking, thinking, remembering, forgetting—I awoke to a nuanced world.

I'd swing by Highland Outfitters, an outdoor sports shop where Paul worked, and we'd sneak off to boulder. Or I'd pedal my bike to his house in Claremont and we'd motor out to Rubidoux. Paul was no saint and struggled with his share of problems—trouble with his wife, too little money, an equivocal future. He'd drop into a mood. I'd dig, and he would run down some difficulty. I'd say, "That sucks." Paul would crack an ironic smile and promise it was all just part of the deal. Hate it or love it, the choice was ours. I later learned that Paul and his younger brother Phil (also a skilled climber) were both sons of an evangelist minister. Pop must have had an authentic holy streak, because something supernal had rubbed off on both his sons.

As we slowly climbed up to Paul's level, I distinctly remember the afternoon out at Rubidoux when he told me, in his unassuming manner, "John, you're going to be an outstanding climber. You're strong and your technique is starting to get good. You'll go as far as you want to."

I had no way to know how good I was or could become because I didn't know myself and couldn't see ten minutes into the future. But Paul could, and over the next year, he made us understand that while he might have the talent, it was not in the cards for him, or anyone else he knew in SoCal climbing, to really go after it on the big stones. That fell to Richard, Ricky, me, and several other young SoCal climbers who had adopted the cheeky name of The Stonemasters. Paul believed we'd realize the unrequited dreams of many SoCal climbers and had a plan to get us started.

"There's this crack out at Tahquitz," he said. "I nailed it last weekend and was thinking how you boys might free climb the thing if you could muster the effort."

Paul described a soaring, 150-foot offset, first climbed by Royal Robbins, which went from wide hands to fingers. It sounded fantastic. "It's worth a look," Paul concluded.

Two days later, we freed the Bat Crack (5.11), the first chapter in a saga that picked up again that May, in Yosemite Valley, the mecca of world rock climbing.

When I returned to attend college after ninety days in the Valley, Paul wanted to hear all about our summer exploits. I talked his ear off for weeks about hooking up with the heroes of American climbing (all twelve of them) and venturing onto Middle Cathedral, Sentinel, Half Dome, etc. Nobody could have been more excited for us than Paul, but when I swore up and down that he could—and should have—climbed all those routes with all those people, I was unprepared for his answer.

"Why?" he asked. I instantly gave him fifty reasons. "Those are your reasons, John. And they're good reasons," he said, "because it's your path. But it's not mine."

"It could be," I insisted.

"Maybe," he said, and then paused for a long beat. "The way you're made, you had to go there and wrestle the beast," he said. "But I don't, because it doesn't fit me."

He talked quietly about family, his low-key life, the bouldering he still loved, and other things since forgotten. He told me the rewards he got from living his life according to his own inner compass were no greater, and certainly no less, than my own.

What Paul didn't tell me was that he'd quietly returned to the fire-fighting community that he'd broke in with as an eighteen-year-old on a "hot shot" crew. Climbing was Paul's passion, but fire science was his calling and vocation. Over the following three decades, Paul Gleason revolutionized wildland firefighting, becoming a legend (and college professor) in the process, inventing protocols and strategies that were standardized across the world, saving entire communities, and untold lives, in the bargain.

Paul had crazy skill and creativity, but his genius was that of a mentor, which is no mean feat. The relationship between mentor and student is specific and charged. The mentor informs and shapes his students desires which, after a fashion, are often his own. The student has the thunder, but the mentor can see the route ahead. It is not always obvious where the power lies. Over time, each one can convince himself that he has created the other. But Paul never rolled like that. His true influence came into its own when Rubidoux, Yosemite, and all the rest were largely behind me. Instead of living off the past till I just dried up and blew away, I'd see the future glow with the promise of the days when the corncob burned hot and El Cap was king.

Back in 2003, when Paul was slowly expiring from colon cancer, his younger brother, Phil (an early Valley partner of mine), got hold of me and gave me Paul's phone number. Making that call thrust me into labyrinths to which no one can fully escape.

Paul sounded composed, even content with the inevitable; I found myself reaching for his muted voice. All I could do was praise Paul for having faith in us long before we did. Most of all, I thanked him for being himself. Paul gave us permission to find our own way, and, in a sense, we did it all for Paul. I told him so.

"I really appreciate hearing that," he said. "It was a pleasure knowing you. I was always proud of you guys."

I can't say why—who knows how these things work—but despite the deep sting of the moment, I felt strangely optimistic.

"See you on the other side," I said.

"I'll be waiting," he said.

A few weeks later, Paul Gleason, son of a traveling evangelist minister, seminal wildland fire fighting educator, world-class boulderer and mentor to all of us Rubidoux kids, climbed clean out of sight.

That summer I visited Rubidoux after a four-year absence. The crisscrossing footpaths, the pepper trees, the whale-backed formations, every hold on every boulder — all were draped in memories. So was the small dirt grotto below the Borson Wall, where Paul, Ricky, Richard, and I, starving for escapades, would yank ourselves stupid on the bulging, saber-edged face, passing the corncob hand to hand. My return was a kind of eulogy to a past long lost but still lingering, like chalk dust on the holds.

As the sun dove into the west, I trudged to the top of the Joe Brown Boulder and gazed over an expanse I'd grown up with. In the self's own maze, I needed a trusted other to show me who I was. And with Paul, it had less about daring do and more about grasping his gift of acceptance, and making it my own.

Still, we needed a place to do it all. A personal launchpad. Like the top of a storied boulder. From this airy perch, I had ventured off and now had come full circle, keeping an eye out for Paul, lumbering around the corner, tamping his pipe, scanning the rock for the next great boulder problem, and calling us to task.

I flashed on a Jean Courbet painting (one of his Trouville seascapes) I'd recently seen at the Norton Simon Museum. Up close, streaks of unblended paint, trowled on thick with a palate knife, appeared abstract. But back up a few paces and those seemingly random blotches of shade and color resolved into the world. So it went with Paul's lapidary methods, hinging on mere suggestions, all proposed with practiced looseness.

Climbing, like literature that lasts, is not, finally, its medium nor its style; rather, something before, behind, above, and beyond all words and all movements. None of us outlives our own time. What does is the charm of discovery, and what a person becomes when it's the air you breathe and the ground you cover. A sparkle silently passed on from Paul to us, which led both up, and into the valleys of the soul, where someday the rope runs out.

I stood up and gazed out past the snow-capped San Gabriel's, trying to appreciate that I was there at all, seeing, remembering, struggling to live up to Paul's doctrine that "it's all part of the deal."

HAUNTED HOUSE

Big Rock is a small, scrappy climbing area in Southern California. Technical climbing first came to the crag in the late 1940s, when soldiers from nearby March Air Force Base sieged the water-trough running up the middle of the 150-foot-high face. Throughout the 1950s and '60s, Big Rock was one of several training grounds for the RCS (Rock Climbing Section of the Sierra Club) and the Riverside Mountain Rescue Team. Meanwhile, generations of Los Angeles- and San Diego-based climbers arrived by the van load and clambered over every inch of the smooth diorite slab, bringing the business.

When a motivated core group binge climb at a small fry area like Big Rock, routes sometimes get done like *English Hanging Garden* (FA, John Gosling, 1970), which was so damn hard that when we found it in the early 1970s, those who'd once climbed at Big Rock seemed like super heroes stepped from Marvel Comics. We had nothing living to go on because the pioneers had left the building.

Just as we entered high school and began learning the ropes, authorities closed down Big Rock as construction began on a nearby dam and reservoir project, comprising the Perris Lake Recreation Area. So my generation never overlapped with the old guard who established all those exciting climbs, suddenly abandoned. When we started sneaking onto Big Rock, as an army of workers built out the dam and reservoir, the place felt like a lost wing of the Smithsonian. We were anxious to follow the chalk marks of the caste of Big Rock veterans who had dominated Southern California climbing for over a decade. Their numbers included Lee Harrel, Paul and Phil Gleason, Pat Callis, and Charlie Raymond, who developed Suicide Rock (when the latter two were students at CalTech), the preternatural Phil Haney, Keith Leaman, John Gosling, chain-smoking Don O'Kelly, and his son, Donny, plus a few others (many were members of an ambitious Eagle Scout group, we later learned). How had this entire generation of SoCal pioneers just up and vanished? What had gone on here at Big Rock? We had to find out.

We started parking out on the highway, half a mile away from Big Rock, and sneaking in. We were well clear of the workers, derricks, and skip loaders, so by the time a foreman was bothered to chase us off, we had usually scaled a handful of routes and were good to go. When the same cranky boss kept catching us, we started leaving a half pint of Old Forester on the boulder near the base of the slab. Then we were free to climb all day—no questions asked. These were simpler times.

Once the dam was completed, they reopened Big Rock to climbing, and for the last thirty years, countless SoCal climbers have learned the ropes there. But our glory days out at Big Rock were when we first visited the place and seemed to have it all to ourselves, knowing we were using the footholds of the climbers whose names were strewn across guidebook pages of all the local crags. They were gone now and there was nothing but rusty quarter-inch Rawl Drive expansion bolts, widely spaced, to suggest that here at Big Rock, they had smoked their Marlboros, ate baloney sandwiches on white bread, and took huge skidding falls, if the rumors were true. Legend says they took pictures of each other with Keith Leaman's Kodak Brownie, stuffed in a gym sock crammed inside a Folgers Coffee can. But no one ever saw a single photograph. Only their routes remained, proof that they'd mastered small hold and friction climbing and learned how to engineer face climbs. Back in the day.

It felt like boarding a time machine when throw-back articles started appearing on Supertopo.com about Big Rock's salad days.

"Just mention Big Rock and my fingertips burn and my calves tighten," wrote Phil Gleason who, along with his brother, Paul, were central figures in the 1960s Big Rock zeitgeist. "I can still feel the excitement we used feel when driving up and first seeing its 'huge' bald face. I remember the sweet-sage, desert-rock smell after a rainstorm. Our first taste of the addicting intoxicants of adventure, and the warmth and magic of climber camaraderie. Wandering around the place in a happy little band, discovering and working on boulder problems till one, then the rest of the group unlocked the mystery. We were famous to each other, back when thrills were cheap, laughter came easily, and pleasure was as simple as the sun coming over that dome of rock and warming the chilled belayer."

Sometime in the 1990s, brothers Phil and Paul Gleason returned to Big Rock after a thirty-year absence. "*The Nose* was virtually gone," wrote Phil. "The Ring climb was destroyed. The cliff that used to sport the wonderful little climb, No Exit, was in rubble. Sitting on the ledge at the top of The Trough, looking out across the manmade lake, I felt that melancholy one feels when cherished places have changed forever. I cannot replace those things now lost in time, but I take pleasure in knowing some kid is approaching Big Rock with sweaty palms, fearing yet craving their first lead."

Big Rock was but a brief aside of the larger drama we all eventually acted out in Yosemite and beyond. Its charms are mostly lost on outsiders, but were dear to us owing to its regional legacy, which reads like the high school diary of the home team. Our early history always exerted a special hold on us; and to every successive generation, Big Rock will feel like a wall of phantoms, when the past meets the present where the rubber meets the rock. It's an unremarkable place, but it still feels enchanted, as for a moment in time, we had it to ourselves, when the dam was forming up and the entrance fee was a short dog of cheap bourbon.

At an old, abandoned crag, the anxious silence reaches back to the long lost who worked out a passage on the rock. Decades later, at the juncture of back then and not yet, we rope up for a route and climb it right now, riding old routes into the future, following the line of phantoms whose bones might well be dust. We are the same ghosts following the same holds, dangling side by side at the belay, paying out the memories. The collected astonishment, ingrained in the rock, murmurs to those still on their way, fearing yet craving their first lead.

Every route is voodoo. Every crag is a haunted house.

VOODOO CHILE

Several miles distant, draped in high noon haze, the Northeast Face of Mount Wilson hove into view. Richard pulled his old VW van onto the gravely shoulder, as he'd done every day that week. We climbed out, silently smoking cigarettes and staring out at the mile-wide heap of Aztec Sandstone, trying to understand the mountain's power, its chasms, hanging forests, and iron-striped bands of rubble. For years, whenever I'd study a big new route, it would murmur to me, like someone had pressed a seashell to my ear. Now in the hush of the desert, Wilson had the standalone, Sphinx-like feel of time in mineral form. Shapes, identity, being—all seemed to dissolve in its shadow.

"They're calling for rain this weekend," I said.

Richard tugged the corner of his walrus mustache. He had the thickest beard I'd ever seen and not once can I remember him clean shaven. The stash and the stubble, along with his bandana, were personal trademarks. So were new routes, and we were looking at one. A big, lonesome one.

Only in the cross light of late afternoon did the 1,700-foot, diamond-shaped Aeolian Wall stand out from the shambling monolith, rising 3,000 feet off the desert floor and ruling the southwestern skyline. Aside from a route along the left margin of the Aeolian (established six years before by Red Rock, Nevada, pioneers Joe Herbst and Larry Hamilton), Old Man Wilson had gone it alone. Fine by me. Winter was near and we could let the Old Man be.

Richard toed his cigarette out in the sand and shoved the butt in his pocket, as he always did. "Tomorrow, then."

I was burned out bad, but Richard knew I couldn't refuse a big new route.

We wheeled off for Las Vegas and Randal Grandstaff's dirtbag hacienda, sunk in a parched arroyo south of McCarran International Airport. Rent monies to Grandstaff were squandered on white magic charms and slot machines, so some months before both gas and electricity were cut. Why was I still living like this? We went outside to barbecue and organize gear for tomorrow.

After summer in Yosemite and fall in Red Rock, the last of our gear hung sadly on one sling. The bolt kit, crucial tackle for big new routes, was down to a single drill bit and three ¼-inch Rawl "coffin nail" bolts—sketchy in sandstone, but marginally better than nothing. I felt along our one shitty rope, formerly our haul line, grimy wraps of athletic tape covering holes in the sheath.

"We're golden," said Richard.

We'd climbed nonstop for a decade, ticked big routes from Venezuela to the Arctic Circle, and we'd always walked away. But challenging the Old Man with one rope wasn't golden. It was asking for trouble. Richard Harrison never asked for trouble. He sought it out, wrestled it away from the steeps, chewed it off the bone till it became his flesh and blood. Blame it on Joe.

We were barely seventeen when Richard and I met Joe Herbst out at Joshua Tree and he coached us through a couple of grainy chimneys, his forte. He'd recently climbed El Capitan, a feat in the early 1970s. Around the campfire, Joe's eyes went glassy as he described a place called Red Rock, a short ways west of Las Vegas, with nameless canyons and sandstone walls half a mile high, all unclimbed. That Easter, Richard and I rode the Greyhound bus from our hometown in Upland,

California, to Blue Diamond, Nevada, south of the Red Rock Canyon National Conservation Area, where Joe and his wife Betsy managed a Boy Scout camp and lived in a trailer.

Joe was busy with the scouts, so for our first big multi-pitch adventure he suggested we bag the second ascent of *Jubilant Song*, a route he had established that summer. "We're on it," said Richard.

We laid out our gear on the floor of the trailer, Joe thumbing our mismatched carabiners, replacing this chock with one of his own in the going-to-battle ritual known to climbers from every land. That night I paced, checked the packs, recoiled the rope, even laced on my boots a few times to make sure. How could Richard snore like that?

Joe dumped us on the highway with a hand-drawn topo map describing wild burro trails, barrancas, and sandy slabs we luckily followed to the base of Windy Peak. We hit a big roof on pitch four and I traversed out right, slotting a tiny wired Stopper, the first I'd placed, wondering out loud if a wafer of aluminum cabled with a guitar string could possibly hold a fall.

"They couldn't sell the thing if it didn't work," Richard yelled over. Made sense. I pushed on.

We turned the roof and gained the upper corner. Snow started falling. Three pitches later, we swam over the top in a whiteout. Joe said the descent was "fast," but provided no details, so we tromped along a ridgeline in the vague direction of the road. Twice we got cliffed, dead-ending at fatal drops, and had to reverse directions. We couldn't see ten feet ahead. What was the desert thinking? The sunrise had cooked us hiking in, and now our cotton pants and sweatshirts were plastered with slush and soaked though.

We nestled into a grotto, smoking bowls of Flying Dutchman tobacco in corncob pipes, a practice we borrowed from our mentor, Paul Gleason. Richard's hands shook when he waved a match over the cob. We laughed, though it took a while to know why. Here was the trouble that had sought us all along. Our teeth clacked but we held position, dangling in midair as the alchemy of the big rocks crushed our pasts and made us over in their own image. You don't come all the way back from that.

We stumbled into a gulch and charged blindly for the sound of truck horns, miles off. A blast of light shone through the clouds and finally we saw the road. We both had convulsive shivers when we hailed a passing car and got dumped at the dirt road snaking off toward Herbst's trailer, slogging the two miles through shin-high drifts to get there. The trailer was locked. Herbst had gone looking for us. We weren't Buhl on Nanga Parbat, or Herzog on Annapurna, or any of the great ones featured in the books we lived on and could recite nearly line for line. But we were goners if we stayed outside.

I broke a window and filled the tub, and we stuck our frozen feet in the hot water, furiously smoking our corn cobs through the screaming barfies until the sensation in our legs returned and we laughed again. That's when I knew we could never suffer some middle-register existence. We'd keep our eyes fixed on the horizon till the day the sun went down.

Richard blew out a cloud and said, "So what's next?"

"Dunno," I said. "Maybe throw a rack together and wait till Joe gets back."

But rain and snow fell from the sky for days, and we barely left the trailer for the rest of our trip.

≜

Early the next morning, we push-started the van and motored for Mt. Wilson. A prospector's trail led to the mouth of the canyon. Ten minutes along a dry streambed and we veered left toward the lower wall, a chossy, 1,500-foot washboard bristling with trees and thorn bushes. Toward the top, we roped up for a scruffy 5.9 corner that landed us on a sandstone terrace with a pine tree that cast a shadow like a thundercloud. A steep slab swept off the ledge toward the start of the upper wall. We needed to gain a horseshoe-shaped bowl above the slab, where a ramp wound up and left.

Richard shouldered the skeleton rack of gear. Our eyes met.

"Here goes nothing."

He ran the rope eighty feet over rickety holds before sinking the first bolt. A short ways higher, he found a crack and banged home a small piton, sunk another bolt, anchored to both, and brought me up. The U-shaped bowl was still a hundred feet away.

"Only got the one bolt, just so you know," he said, sounding like Clint Eastwood in *Hang 'Em High*, a film we'd watched so many times that early on, we walked and talked and even spit like Clint. Richard worked a cheroot for a while, but could never keep it lit.

"Watch me close . . . if you wanna learn something," I said, borrowing a line from our Godfather, Jim Bridwell.

Richard chuckled. "Educate me."

The wall above steepened, the holds thinned, and I didn't get far before imagining myself cartwheeling onto Richard's head. I placed our last bolt. The rock above was smooth as a bottle and the bottom of the bowl hadn't gotten much closer.

"I can lower to the belay and we can rap off a single line," I said. We'd have to leave the rope and down solo that 5.9 corner below, a stunt I wasn't high on but figured we could do if we had to. "But once I cast off from here . . ."

Not to mention that once I committed to the remaining slab, retreat was physically impossible with one rope, that the only way off was up.

≙

It had gone that way since our first tour of duty in Yosemite. We weren't sure how to get started, so we'd called Joe Herbst for marching orders.

GRANITE *Mariner*

"Washington Column was made for you guys," he had said. Meaning we should skip the crumbs at the Cookie, Arch Rock, and the other short crags where Valley rookies traditionally break in, and jump on the big walls straight off. This sounded reckless, but I wanted to be like Joe. Richard already was.

We invited our high school pal, Jay Smith (later a legendary alpinist), to join us for our first Yosemite big wall: the East Face of Washington Column. I still can picture Richard casually nailing the Enduro Corner, smoking, of course, and Jay worming through the infamous Harding Slot. When he cut the haul bag loose, Richard and I watched amazed as it zoomed thirty feet into space. Richard took the ride himself because he could.

At the next belay, I asked him what gave with all the horror stories we'd read about hauling a bag (ours, an Army duffel, was feather light), not realizing our mistake in packing so little water. We had no water at all when we groveled onto Overnight Ledge, three pitches from the top.

Richard apologized for not bringing more water, but it wasn't his fault. During the first ascent of the *East Face*, in 1959, Warren Harding and Chuck Pratt nearly perished from heat and thirst. Five years later, caught in a heatwave during the first ascent of the South Face of Mount Watkins, the pair once again ran out of water, and clawed to the top more dead than alive. Neither man was a fool. A short memory is prerequisite for all wall climbers.

When the three of us finally stumbled down from the East Face, we dove into Mirror Lake, fully clothed. Richard, who couldn't remember nothing, racked up for the Prow, also on the Column, that afternoon. A day later, joined by our hometown friend and partner, Rick Accomazzo, we climbed the Prow, rested a day, and fired the South Face, with one rope, a day pack, and a gallon of water on board. Over the following decade, we ran out of water many times, until I finally forgot how to forget.

≜

The U-shaped bowl might as well have been on Neptune. The slab below was steep and blank. We were out of bolts. Richard asked what I was waiting for.

From the moment we set foot on Old Man Wilson, we'd mostly free soloed, but now tied in and thirty feet off Richard's hanging stance, I moved with extreme diligence because I doubted my one ¼-inch coffin-nail bolt, not to mention the belay anchor, could withstand a big fall. Our only certainty was that I was going.

I juked around, trying various lines and downclimbing back to the bolt before finding an unlikely traverse along a flexing black scab, followed by easier but runout dogpaddling to the bottom of the bowl. Richard followed in nothing flat. Per ham and eggs, they say the chicken is committed but the pig is all-in. We were all in.

Richard cast off, lie-backing a fold inside the bowl. The higher we climbed, the less I liked the looks of the knee-wide roof crack jutting into space at the end of the fold. We only had one big nut. Someone was going to die.

"Looks like Paisano Overhang," Richard chuckled, peering out at the roof. That was also Richard's wise idea, free climbing Paisano Overhang, a twenty-five-foot, down-jutting roof crack at Suicide Rock, our home crag. He was sure it would go. So was Rick. Since I had the oversized fists, it fell to me to prove the boys right. Depending on who you ask, Paisano Overhang was the first no-doubt-about-it 5.12 in the country, and Richard made the most of it.

It started with his allegation—to a climber who witnessed the climb from a distance—that I'd taped my hands to fit the crack. This jackass story spread like Covid 19. Every time we were called on to describe the ascent, Richard hopped it up a little more, until finally I'd managed the roof by lacing on boxing gloves, gifted to me by Muhammad Ali.

I keep peering at the roof crack, half a rope length overhead, regretting I'd ever seen Mount Wilson. Who was this heap named after, anyhow? Maybe Woodrow Wilson, the president who committed us to World War I. Or was that William "Tubby" Taft?

"Only gonna get bigger, you keep eyeballing it like that," said Richard, handing me the measly rack.

I started bridging along the fold toward the overhang, luckily finding a flake that skirted around left to a small ledge. The crack above melded into pleats and dihedrals so situated that we couldn't see where the route might go. Our guesstimate put the summit about 800 feet away. Twisting ramps and shallow corners, unseen from below, kept connecting, though the higher we climbed, so rose the odds that somewhere soon the crack would blank out or run into a holdless roof, leaving us stranded.

Richard snubbed out his Camel and dove into an off-width crack, vanishing around a corner as vultures started circling in my head.

Whenever I arrived in midair like this, forecasting doom, I immediately started jonesing for escape. Nothing scared me more than total, irreversible commitment. Richard was never conflicted like that because he was a vulture himself. I tried to be. On inspired days, I soared with the best of them. But at times like these, when there was only one way and possibly none, I'd lock up, drawing raw jolting breaths, blood pounding in my temples and the air roaring in the back of my throat like some wild animal snared in a bear trap. For years, I'd been addicted to this feeling, and the rush of charging in a rampage. Fear is better than heroin, but I didn't want to die. Walking that edge is the pact we made with trouble, all those years before, in a shady little space we called "The Basement."

⚌

The Basement, as described in the Stonemaster story, was a walk-in bunker beneath a 1950s-era split-level house stuck in the boulder-strewn foothills of the San Gabriel Mountains. A dirt road found it. The place had so much weed smoke billowing out the open door that small planes swooping overhead, en route to the local airport in Upland, were known to drift wildly off course and land in Cucamonga, even Buckeye, Arizona—as the story goes.

Long before The Basement birthed the Stonemasters, and served as our nest and launching pad, it was Richard and me, two nobodies from nowhere who couldn't belong if we tried. We liked people fine, but so much of life seemed distasteful and beside the point. And who cooked up all these rules? By some miracle, we'd been made alive, with a gusher of potential experience too fleeting and expectant to waste time working and dogging down loot. What did a job ever buy you but distance from the things that made life interesting: encountering elemental forces and drinking from the source; wrestling dragons and sparring with gravity? But what we wanted, body and soul, was magnitude.

Initial efforts were mundane. Mostly fighting up sandy gullies and scaly faces out at Joshua Tree. They were all ours, but even we didn't care. That is, until we free climbed Vampire, Le Toit, and The Flakes: iconic, 800-foot aid climbs at Tahquitz Rock (established by our hero, Royal Robbins). We were vultures ever after, none hungrier than Richard Harrison. For going on forty years, he never landed.

The breeze died and silence slithered into canyons and over the face of Old Man Wilson, shrouded in shadow. Lashed up high, we felt as much a part of the place and the stone as a petroglyph. But one of my hands kept reaching for the ground.

The rope kited off as Richard mounted out of sight. The intensity of belaying is made so by the long silences, when you learn what it means to be alone. I didn't like it. The next new route had always stretched before me like a starlit bridge over the dimness of my life. For weeks,

I'd watched it waver; now it crashed. The rope came tight.

We climbed for hours, eventually joining Joe's original route along the left margin of the Aeolian Wall, which we quickly followed to the top. The thrill sprang less from the route we climbed than the one I kept imagining, the one we couldn't get off with one rope, the one nobody knew we were on and never would till our bleached bones were discovered years later, if at all. The climb in my head was always the best one.

A little scrambling found a cairn on the summit. We stood there smoking cigarettes, absorbing the panorama. We were snowflakes in the sun, but the desert *lasts*. If Richard took anything from the mountaineering books we devoured early on, it was a special appreciation for summits, and an eye for the classic line.

Ambitious peak-baggers had worked out a route on the Byzantine backside of Mt. Wilson, but even if we could have found and descended it, we'd have landed miles from the van. So we scrambled across the right shoulder, looking for a shorter way off, Richard hobbling like a man with a peg leg, pulling the limb behind him. Years before, he'd caught a staph infection that settled in his hip socket. By the time they discovered what it was, cartilage and bone had dissolved. He left the hospital in a body cast and walked with a pronounced limp for the rest of his life. That he ever managed these Red Rocks death marches, or climbed 5.13 on one good leg, is a wonder.

We dove into the most promising-looking gulley and started descending toward the flats and the urban sprawl, where folks were hunkered in digs—bigger the better—arrayed with handsome stuff and significant people seeking meaning through theater, five-course meals, gadgets, witty conversation, prayer, sex, and intoxicants. We weren't so different in our search for prodigious experiences. But few of us kept a permanent address. We had dangerous dreams and rambling feet, and when they said *go*, we had to follow. We ate whatever food there was, generally skipping the belongings and formalities and going straight for the sex, intoxicants, and a piece of rock with size. Mainly we were broke—and I was sick of being broke. But I still prayed if I had to, and this time I meant it because little else could get us down a 2,500-foot rotten gulley with one rope and little gear.

We started the first of many half-rope-length rappels off saplings and horns. When we couldn't get an anchor, we downclimbed until we found one. The wall steepened and the trees thinned out, forcing us to leave a nut here and a piton there, until we were tying off little more than house plants, holding our breath as we rapped the doubled line.

We finally ran out of nuts and held a board meeting on a shattered ledge. The last 500 feet of junk wall plunged beneath us. Water and candy bars were long gone, and so was most of our gear. A couple of shrubs festooned from the lower wall, but no other signs of natural anchors.

We sat on the ledge and shared our last smoke, gazing off at the wonderland of jutting buttes, bluish draws, and brusque peaks, outlined one against the other like a deck of stony cards. Swaying and rising at the shadowline of light and darkness. Of something and nothing at all. What painters call infinitude.

A month later, Richard and his wife, Tina (childhood sweethearts since our early days in Yosemite), would move to Las Vegas, and Richard extended his legacy all across this vast cordillera, mentoring a band of fledgling vultures, collectively known as the Adventure Punks. For twenty years running, they mined Red Rock for some the world's great adventure routes: the 2,000-foot Lone Star, in Black Velvet Canyon; the 2,500-foot Resolution Arête, also on Mt. Wilson; Blitzkrieg, a towering, super remote wall that no one was even sure how to get to before Richard and Sal Mamusia first climbed it in an audacious, one-day blast. And, of course, the supernal Cloud Tower, the "*Astroman* of the Desert," and near the top of every trad climber's tick list. But that all dangled in the future. Now we had to get down this last stretch of vertical gully. We rigged the rappel off a threaded chockstone that skittered and rained gravel when weighted.

"Someday we'll go too far," I said.

"Someday we'll have no choice," said Richard. "But right now, we're golden."

Richard backpedaled off the edge and into the void, shadows racing up to meet him. It took three more decades—during which I was lucky to see Richard and Tina once a year—before the shadows finally caught him.

≜

In late summer, 2014, I got word that Tina had cancer and there was nothing they could do. For most of their adult lives, they'd lived there in Las Vegas, on the edge of town, where year after year Richard wheeled off for Red Rock, or on far-flung road trips, and made history by stealth. The specialist tills a given crop, restricting his scope to the area under cultivation. Richard quietly worked the whole garden: from bouldering to big walls, from sea cliffs to desert towers. And few knew a thing about his gardening.

Sometimes I'd get a postcard. More likely I'd hear rumors about him and John Bachar free climbing the D7 on the Diamond, say, or bagging Shiprock and the Totem Pole. Whatever I'd dreamed of doing, Richard was "on it," all over the Americas, sometimes with his daughter, Lisa, the apple of his eye.

In the years after I stopped climbing full time, homesick and missing fellow vultures, I'd occasionally spoken to Richard and he always said the same thing: "It's all good. Family's good. You know, just looking for the next new line."

Sometime around his fiftieth birthday, he went from leading 5.13 adventure routes to lying in a coma with a bleeding ulcer. We almost lost him. A few years later, Bell's palsy paralyzed his face, but he still bounced back. Other maladies he never mentioned drained off a little more life force. When I saw him out at Joshua Tree, at Todd Gordon's international climber's ghetto, I was shocked by how his body had betrayed him.

Then Tina got glioblastoma multiforma, an aggressive brain tumor. When I heard she was fading, I hopped on the first plane to Vegas. Tina was still lucid and walking fine. But Richard was a bag of bones, his skin hanging like parchment off his frame, his eyes fixed on a measureless panorama. Something fierce was erasing him from the inside, but he never said what and I never asked.

We moved into the small living room. Richard, a voracious reader, proudly showed me a few first editions of Mark Twain, our favorite author, and a dog-eared copy of the original Joshua Tree guidebook, the one in print when we first ventured to J. Tree in high school. We sat on the couch and thumbed in, running our fingers over grainy pictures of the old Desert Rats waging war on the first routes we ever climbed. We'd both been in the mountains too many times to remember, but at bottom we were desert people, and these were leaves of gold.

We paused at the photo of guidebook editor John Wolfe, c. 1968, jammed in the Waterchute, our first 5.10 route. Despite John's awkward position, all knees and elbows in the flare, we knew at a glance that he belonged right there, as water fits into the sea.

We fret, slave, ponder, write, draw, brag, beg, marry, love, meditate, cheat, grovel, drink, lie, and serve, chasing this perfect belonging. Sitting on that couch, gathered by shadows, we knew we were lucky because we'd found it. We found it out at J. Tree on the Waterchute, on a hilltop of tumbleweeds and boulders at Mount Rubidoux, on El Cap in an ice storm, and on a long-forgotten climb on Mount Wilson. All those places where all of a sudden, the world was made new. All those places where we belonged. Nothing made this clearer than being in the presence of dear friends dying before my eyes.

We leafed through other books from which we had drawn our heroes, giants we honored through rebellion, as the brat defies his parents, stoked by the hope of doing things they wouldn't or couldn't do. Of course, we were loyal containers of their traditions, none more than Richard, his every new route preserving essential family rituals. Tackle all climbs ground-up. Limit bolts so far as he could, and strive for the on-sight flash. With skin in the game, he liked to say, you're always playing with real money. In this regard, Richard Neil Harrison, trad climber to the bone, was a billionaire. Yet even the greatest traditions are less like endless cycles and more like choruses to a classic song—a song that, like every song, has an ending.

Tina stayed behind with their beloved dogs, Nikki, Sam, and Puppy, as Richard walked me to the door. There was death in that house and it scared me and broke my heart. I'd come to climbing chasing *glamourie*, a Scots word denoting a magical world—while ruin loomed on the horizon, a fact I always resented. Meanwhile Richard tilled the whole garden. Always had. My face must have said what I couldn't.

"Don't worry," he said. "We're golden."

Things quickly went south for Tina. And she was gone. Four days later, Richard collapsed in his front yard. Through his death, the desert that lasts came into its inheritance, reclaiming one of its own.

≙

The second-to-last rappel was partially free hanging and ended on a small ramp. Our entire rack lay in the gulch we'd descended, save for one last knife-blade. We scratched around and managed to slug the blade home in a thin crack where the ramp met the main wall. The rising ring told us it was bomber.

If I could get down this last rappel and not die like Tobin and John and Tim and what seemed like half of the guys we'd grown up with, I could walk away and get a place with stuff and conversation with deep thoughts and important feelings and a fridge full of nice food, things I later got and never know what to do with—except for the food.

I rigged the blade with my chalk-bag sling, chucked the doubled rope into space, and peered over. The ends seemed to reach the ground, and fortunately they did, with a few feet to spare. We stumbled out to the dry streambed as darkness fell. And darkness in those canyons is true darkness.

It took us many attempts to push-start the van. We wheeled off the Scenic Drive loop road onto the SR 159, in turn West Charleston Boulevard, heading for Vegas, and Old Man Wilson was lost from view.

NIAD (NOSE IN A DAY)
The First One-Day Ascent of El Capitan

Warren Harding, George Whitmore, and Wayne Merry are lashed to a hanging stance, 3,000 feet up El Capitan. It's November. The days are cold and short, and afternoon shadows streak up the wall beneath them. They gaze overhead, and despair: Will they ever get off? Will it ever be over?

On this, their final push, the trio has been on the wall eleven days, twice as long as any American has ever spent on a rock climb. Below looms a pitched battle, every lead sieged. They've met tasks no rock climber has ever encountered, let alone mastered—wild pendulums, nailing expanding flakes, and the back-breaking toil of hauling hundreds of pounds of supplies up the cliffside. And now, only a fifty-foot headwall bars them from the summit of the mightiest rock wall in the contiguous United States. But that headwall, that last fifty feet, is dead blank and overhanging. They'll have to retreat 350 feet to Camp 6 and a good ledge, and tackle the headwall in the morning.

Warren Harding has other ideas. Never mind the swollen hands and frayed ropes; ignore the rats that gnawed through haul bags, the rain and sleet and chilling retreats, or the running feud with the rangers; and forget the private terrors and sleepless nights because finally, hanging in a web of tattered slings, Harding can nearly spit to the top. Light? He don't need no stinking light!

So, Harding starts bolting. And in an epic no climber should ever forget, he hammers through the night, finally punches home the twenty-eighth and last bolt, and stumbles to the top just as dawn spills into the valley. The first ascent of *The Nose*, arguably the greatest pure rock climb in the world, is done. It is November 12, 1958.

≙

When I started climbing in 1969, if you ever met someone who had climbed El Capitan, you went up and touched their robes. It wasn't until the summer of 1971 that I made it to Yosemite.

To the teenager whose dreams are staked wholly in rock climbing, as mine were, that first trip to the base of El Capitan is a life event. You park on the loop road fringing a lush meadow. The tour bus chugs past and over the loudspeaker you hear, "And, at 3,143 feet high, and over a mile and a half wide, El Capitan is the largest piece of exposed granite in the world." (This oft-repeated claim is false. The Trango Towers, lining the Ruth and Baltoro Glaciers, are larger.)

You stumble into the forest and wend through the pines that finally open up, and there—before you, above you, around you—a sea of granite soars straight off the talus, stunning for its colors and sheer bulk, and terrible for the emptiness that sets in your gut as your eyes pan up its titanic corners and towers.

Faint voices trickle down and you squint up, up, finally spotting two specks. And you shudder. So you do your little climb at the base, then hike down, stealing glances over your shoulder. Then you walk out into the meadow and just stare up at nature's magnum opus.

≙

If someone had told me, as I stood in the meadow after that first trip up to El Capitan, that I would someday climb it in one day, I would have laughed in his face. But that was before I had met Jim Bridwell, before I'd climbed *The Nose* with British ace Ron Fawcett, and before climbers considered themselves adventure athletes. (That mindset entered with a bang in the early 1970s.)

And that was also before a certain article appeared in a climbing magazine, featuring Reinhold Messner and Peter Habeler after their ten-hour blitz of the 4,600-foot North Face of the Eiger. The shot, a freeze frame of old-school, Tyrolean panache, showcased the duo in matching guides' sweaters and saber-creased knickers. Behind them, the ice-plastered Eigerwand stabbed the sky.

"The greatest speed climb ever," claimed the article. "Never to be surpassed . . ."

Kicked back in Yosemite's Mountain Room Bar, Jim Bridwell looked annoyed, his index finger drumming the photo. He shoved the magazine aside. We'd set the record straight, Bridwell announced. And on a class cliff, not some "heap." (Bridwell would later climb the Eiger himself.) That business about "we" caught my attention. And so it happened that, over a couple of draft beers, the plan came together to try and climb *The Nose* in one day.

It broke down like this: I was the designated free climber and would lead the first leg to the top of Boot Flake, seventeen pitches up—comparatively straightforward crack pitches we presumed would go quickly. Billy Westbay, a Colorado climber superb at both aid and free climbing, would lead the more intricate middle section from the Boot to Camp 5, the twenty-fifth pitch. Then Bridwell would take it on home with the last seven.

In my mind, the plan quickly took on fantastic importance, the kind only a nineteen-year-old could attach to it; and so began a long winter of running stairs, trying to climb fifty pitches in one day at Joshua Tree, backing off (but not foregoing) all vice, and largely ignoring my studies.

When Jim, Billy, and I stalked toward the base of El Capitan on Memorial Day, 1975, I felt like I was going to hoist the flag over Iwo Jima.

≜

We started at 5:00 a.m., in the dark. The first four mixed pitches went under headlamps, and smoothly. That put us onto Sickle Ledge and *The Nose* proper, where the Southeast and the Southwest Faces converge to form the great sweeping prow the route is named after. Beyond a fourth-class bit off Sickle Ledge, I started fumbling with some dicey stemming. I had no pro, my headlamp was flickering on and off, and dawn light was slow in coming. I finally pawed up to a bolt and yelled down that I'd have to wait a few moments before trying the pendulum so I could see what the hell I was doing.

Jim yelled up to get going, so I blindly swung right and somehow found the hand crack. In a minute, I hung in slings as Jim and Billy raced up behind—Jim jumaring the lead rope, Billy on the trail rope, both funky nine-millimeter lines. (One of the ropes, a tired old yellow one, had several holes in the sheath and a long oil stain on one end; but there was no use asking about it now.) The climber jumaring the free rope would wind-sprint up to the leader with a third rope and start belaying him before the climber cleaning the previous pitch had arrived. That was the concept, anyway, and was meant to save time. But since I hadn't placed any protection, they both arrived at once, and quickly.

And off I went. A strenuous flare led to a long bolt ladder and the first of the spectacular pendulums—a wild running swing right to the Stoveleg Crack (so named because on the first ascent, Harding nailed it using four crude pitons forged from the legs of an old stove scavenged from the Berkeley city dump).

You lower down about sixty feet, then start swinging back and forth. Now at speed, you go for it, feet kicking hard, digging right, hurdle a corner, feel the momentum ebbing so you dive—yes, dive! If you've chanced it right, you plop a hand into a perfect jam just as your legs start to swing back. You kip your torso, kick a boot in, and you're on line. The laser-cut fracture shoots up the prow for 350 feet of primarily perfect hand-jamming, each pitch ending in stark hanging belays.

I had hoped for a number of fixed pitons, but found few. We'd only brought a couple of big nuts, none of which I took on the first 5.10 pitch, thinking the fixed pins I saw above were good, soon to discover that the eyes had been blasted off by greedy hammers. (This was long before camming devices, remember.) I didn't get a single nut in that pitch.

I kept climbing recklessly fast and Jim and Billy kept gassing up the lines so quickly that they gained the belays sucking wind. Then one would hand me the rack and I'd start charging once more.

I took our few big chocks on the next lead, but only got one in. Two hundred feet higher, I chugged up an oily off-size slot and mantled onto Dolt Tower—and was face to face with two Colorado climbers just slithering from their bags. It was 7:00 a.m.

Dolt Tower (named after Bill "Dolt" Feuerer, one of Harding's partners during initial efforts on the route) is flat and spacious, and is the first place to kick back and take stock of things. Perhaps 20 percent of all parties bail straight off from here because, while the cliff below plunges straight to the deck, the summit still seems miles away. Like the horizon, you can go toward it for days and never draw closer. If you ever get up there, don't be fooled by the illusion. If you've gotten this far, only your mind can defeat you. And to be sure, climbing El Capitan is first and last an odyssey through your mind.

I tensioned right, into a steep lie-backing corner, and ran two pitches together. Aside from the pendulum points and the bolt ladder above Dolt Hole, I'd managed only a couple of nuts in the last eight pitches—a sketchy performance that would almost get me. But not just yet.

An easy bend and we were on El Cap Towers, a perfectly flat granite patio. Now, above the comparatively low-angle Stovelegs, the upper wall rifles up into razor-cut dihedrals. Out right looms the fearsome sweep of the Southeast Face, which during dawn light, draws fabulous hues into its keeping. There lie the world's most notorious nail-ups. Since Royal Robbins, Check Pratt, Yvon Chouinard, and Tom Frost first scaled it in 1963, with the North America Wall, what dramas this great sprawl of granite must have seen. All the tense leaders, their terrors and doubts and battered hands, hooking and bashing their way up its over-hanging immensity. And all the mooneyes glaring at belay bolts hanging half out of its gritty diorite bands, where a dropped peg free falls for ages, striking nothing but the ground. A precious few specialists thrive on this kind of work, but I've never been one of them.

Across the valley looms the great tinctured bulk of Middle Cathedral, a monster without the menace; and far out east, perched in the sky, clouds boil over Half Dome's cleft North Face, twilight's ancient custodian.

≜

We took a short break about halfway up the wall. It wasn't much after 7:00 a.m., so we slacked off a bit, knowing we had only to keep going to make the top by early afternoon. Our tactics were basic since we'd each done the route only once before. Had we known some years later that elapsed time would become a priority, we might have pressed on at the same rabid pace. But just then, simply climbing El Cap in one day was the goal.

We peeled off our sweaters, cinched them into a knot, and pitched them off. This left us in circus-colored bellbottoms and psychedelic shirts and vests—an intentional parody of the orthodox threads Habeler and Messner wore in that cover photo. Down below, the meadow started filling with our friends, with an occasional car horn encouraging us to even greater speed.

We'd made no secret about our plan, and over the previous few days, dozens of climbers came to wish us luck. Did we need any gear? Did we need a ride to the base? Did we want someone to meet us on top? Mike White, a Valley regular, summed it up when he told me to "do us proud." We had all of Camp 4 to account to if we failed.

Just above El Cap Towers, an unprotected chimney gained the top of Texas Flake, a thick exfoliating block shaped like the Lone Star state. Just off it, a fifty-foot bolt ladder finds Boot Flake—detached and resounding to the thump—previously an exciting exercise in expando nailing, but recently free climbed at stiff 5.10. I clipped up the bolts, reached the crack on the right side of the Boot, and immediately cranked into a layback, anxious to power it off and be done with leading. Foolishly, I chose to run out the entire Boot.

I was likely about thirty feet above the bolts, and eighty or so feet above Texas Flake, when a cramp paralyzed my right forearm. My fingers curled into a fist and I couldn't straighten my arm. The fall looked huge and would land me straight onto Texas Flake. (Forty-five years later, Quinn Brett, one of America's finest adventure climbers, took this very fall, tragically leaving her paralyzed from the waist down). I dangled off an ever-creeping left jam and desperately tried to shake out. No good. Panting, I jerkily downclimbed a few moves, slotted in a borderline nut, and hung on it long enough to jiggle the cramp out. Then frigged up to the top of the Boot, clipped off the cabled four-bolt anchor, and kissed the rock. My part was done. It wasn't quite 8:00 a.m.

Jim had the lead switch all worked out. I clipped the rack onto the haul line and slid it down to Billy, then put him on belay—on the haul line. He drew a deep breath and shot off across the King Swing, an enormous pendulum left. He latched the first fixed pin, lowered, then swung left again and fired up into a steep groove.

The course now passes through a 300-foot gray diorite band involving the only nebulous climbing on the route. In a magnificent bit of anything goes, Billy would yank up on a bashie, crank off some laybacking, edge up onto a fixed pin, go unprotected over loose face climbing, pendulum this way and tension that way.

Since this was only his second time on the route, the going was largely unfamiliar, but he shot up it like he knew it all by heart, showing a skillset shared by few. In an hour and a half, we were on Camp 4, several small shelves below the Great Roof. Billy dashed on, clipping up a string of antique ring angles.

≙

Billy had worked the winter on Wyoming and Montana oil rigs. January days had dropped to 20 below, when a twelve-pound pickaxe ricochets off the frozen earth. The rig's bore-shaft continuously puked "gumbo"—driller's mud—which basted him and instantly froze on his clothes like quick-set cement. The pay wasn't bad, but only thoughts of blitzing *The Nose* had seen Billy through those twelve-hour shifts.

When Frost, Pratt, Robbins, and Fitschen made the first continuous ascent of *The Nose* in 1960, they all agreed the Great Roof was "easily the most spectacular pitch in Yosemite." Not for challenge, but for the splendor of the colossal arc of creamy granite, which ends at an edge-of-the-world sling belay. Billy got us there before noon.

A pitch up the Pancake Flake, thin as a flapjack in spots, a vertical jamming pitch, and we were on Camp 5—another terrace in the sky. It was barely past noon, and we only had to keep plugging away at an easy pace. Or Jim did, since he now had the lead. And Jim needed a breather.

Billy and I had spent the previous months doing long routes and honing up. Jim, meanwhile, was down in San Diego, teaching ropecraft and rescue techniques to a group of Navy SEALS, doing little to no actual climbing, spending his evenings at local taverns drinking lager and playing pocket pool—courtesy of the US Government. Then jumping straight onto *The Nose* with Billy and me. At that time, there probably wasn't another climber alive who could have gotten away with this.

≙

Jim Bridwell . . . Like Billy and me, he came from nowhere in particular. Just under six feet, weighed 170, maybe less. Had been a top high jumper and hurdler in high school. Got a track scholarship to San

Jose State. He'd passed the tough military exams to become a fighter pilot, but declined in the face of the Vietnam debacle. From that moment
on, his only ambition was to become the best climber he could be. He'd
revolutionized the sport, yet he was entirely modest.

By Camp 6, the last big ledge two pitches higher, I regretted not
having worn a harness as my swami belt—three wraps of two-inch
webbing—felt to chafe right down to my spleen. We'd all worn our
free-climbing boots, which were too damn tight. The water ran out.
Jim smacked his thumb with the hammer. When the trail line snagged
a pitch higher, instead of rappelling down to free it, I simply yanked
as hard as I could, eventually pulling off a granite torpedo the size of
a small boy. "You idiot!" Jim yelled, as the granite torpedo detonated
on the slabs far below. I silently hoped I hadn't killed somebody. We
carried on . . .

We were over 2,500 feet up the wall now, into the prime terrain.
Here the exposure is so enormous, and your perspective so distorted,
that the horizontal world becomes incomprehensible. You're a rocke-
teer, dangling in a kind of space/time warp. And if there is any place
where you will understand why people climb mountains, it is here in
these breezy dihedrals, high in the sky.

Pitch after pitch fell beneath us, and by the time we gained the final bolt ladder, we just wanted off. Other routes are steeper, more exposed than *The Nose*. But no route has a more dramatic climax. The
headwall is short—fifty feet—and after that, everything ends abruptly
after a few friction steps. But since Harding's day, some madman has
re-engineered the last belay so that it hangs at the very brink of the
headwall, a mind-boggling nest where all thirty-four pitches spill down
beneath your boots. It's a masterstroke, that hanging belay, for it gives
climbers a moment of pause at one of the most spectacular spots in all
of American climbing. Cars creep along the loop road three-quarters
of a mile below, broad forests appear as brushed green carpets, and for
one immortal moment, you feel a giant in a world of ants. Then you

stumble up a slab for a few body lengths, onto flat ground at last, and suddenly it's over.

△

On the summit, there was no celebration, no elation at all. Topping out on El Capitan after the first one-day ascent should have been one of those few momentous occasions in our lives. But, typically, we were caught in the transitional spin and none of it registered.

During those first few instants on top, curious reactions are the rule. Whether you've taken four hours or four days, you are a different person than the one who started some 3,000 feet below. I've heard of climbers hugging boulders, punching partners, and weeping openly—some from relief, some sad that it's over. I have seen other climbers babbling incoherently, and I once saw a middle-aged Austrian team simply shake hands, give all their gear to another team who had also topped out the Salathé Wall, to their left, and stroll off for the Falls trail, their climbing careers at once made and finished right there. For us, I only remember coiling ropes and booking for the East Ledges descent route, everyone cussing at having not brought a pair of sneakers. We got down to the loop road just as darkness fell.

As we stumbled around a bend, El Capitan burst into view, shimmering under a full moon. If you want to know something of the world's age, look at El Capitan in the moonlight. My feet suddenly felt fine, and for a long beat, we three just stood fast and gaped up at it. And the majesty of the cliff, and what it meant to us to have climbed it in one day, finally struck home.

GRAVITY

I was hauling the pig (haul bag) to the top of the Half Dollar, 800 feet up the Salathé Wall, when a roaring sound hit me like a punch. My head jerked right, and way over on the skyline, I saw a human body pinwheeling from the bridge of *The Nose* all the way down to the toe of the South Buttress, some 3,000 feet later. Then, silence.

The body came and went in no time, but I didn't move for what felt like an age, frozen at the anchor by the violence of a human meteor punching a hole through the sky.

The haul bag was still half a rope length below. The pulley, racks, and neatly stacked cords, draped about the anchor, and me standing there, eight pitches up El Capitan—it all felt outrageous and insane. I glanced down at my partner, Ed Barry, ratcheting up on ascenders and cleaning the pitch.

"Did you see that?!"

"No, but I sure the fuck heard it." The violence of that sound is with me still.

I finished hauling the bag. When Ed pulled onto the ledge, we sucked back against the wall and started chain-smoking.

This was my first full summer in Yosemite Valley after graduating high school a month earlier. Our mentor, Jim Bridwell, the biggest cheese in Yosemite climbing, said we had to get up on El Cap while we still were green and could find an epic. Epics were a climber's bona fides, and we needed one to prove our commitment.

Now I hated Bridwell. And climbing. Next morning, we rapped off and I hitchhiked back to Southern California. It was June 8, 1973.

I kicked around my folks' place for a few days, doing yard work and sleeping like a wild animal, on and off or not at all. The *LA Times* reported that Michael Blake, 19, of Santa Monica, California, had fallen from the "last rope" of *The Nose* route on El Capitan. For reasons under investigation by park rangers, the line had severed and Blake had died. I must have run into Blake out at J. Tree, or up at Tahquitz. Back then, few Southern California teenagers were scaling El Cap. But I couldn't put a face to his name.

I was eighteen and my life didn't flow; it spun and churned. But once I locked sights on Yosemite, the currents raced in one direction. Now every hour, and sometimes more, the blur of Michael Blake surged through my mind like a riptide. It took the rest of that summer and many winter weekends out at Joshua Tree before the ferocious downfall of Michael Blake slowly ebbed to silence.

I returned to Camp 4 the following May, the moment school let out. Straight off, I ran into Beverly Johnson. The previous autumn she'd made the first all-female ascent of El Cap, with Sibylle Hechtel, and I wanted to hear all about it. But Michael Blake's accident jumped in from the shadows, and Bev turned gray.

"I just got to the belay at the end of the Great Roof," (1,800 feet up *The Nose)* she said, "when I heard what sounded like a rocket lifting off." She looked up and nearly got cleaned off the face, by Michael Blake mortaring past.

Bev wasn't climbing much just then, she said. A couple of summers later, she soloed the Dihedral Wall, also on El Cap, and I wondered if that's what it took to purge Michael Blake from her life. (Bev was nails like that, until she later died in a helicopter crash.) I kept going to Yosemite, climbing walls for another decade until I finally got enough during a heatwave on Mount Watkins, gasping up a first ascent with Bridwell, Kim Schmitz, and Ron Kauk.

⚎

Fast-forward four decades and change. I'd written so much about climbing in Yosemite that even I couldn't face another John Long story about back-in-the-day. Then Dean Fidelman wrangled a deal to publish a large-format artbook on Yosemite climbing in the 1950s, and he asked me to write the text. That meant research, as it was twenty years before my time. It took a year of haggling and revising before we finally finished *Yosemite in the Fifties: The Iron Age.*

Shortly after the book launch at Patagonia's shop in Santa Monica, I got a call from Jerry Volger, a stranger to me but a local Venice, California, man. A nephew had gifted him a copy of our new book. There was magic in the '50s, said Jerry. He knew because he'd been there, and when he cracked open our book, it all came rushing back. He wanted to meet in person, though he never said why. I had too much going on to swap climbing stories with a hometown duffer, but for nameless reasons I felt compelled to go.

I met Jerry for breakfast a few days later, at a deli down in Marina del Rey. He had a collared shirt, a face thrown wide open, and the eyes of a kid full of beans. Adventure people often have those eyes. The curious thing is how most of us die with a secret part of us never growing old.

"I'm ancient," said Jerry, now pushing eighty, "but there was a time . . ." And we both flew back to the Valley. Much as I had, Jerry came to climbing through athletics. "I was a great surfer," he said. "I did all the sports."

Jerry had partnered with many of the Californians whom I'd idolized and frequently saw during my high school days out at Joshua Tree and Tahquitz. But by 1973, and well into his thirties, Jerry still hadn't managed an ascent of El Capitan, the pot of gold for all California climbers.

"Then I met a young man bouldering out at Stoney Point," said Jerry. "An up-and-comer named Michael Blake."

My hands gripped the table and I stared at Jerry, unsure which surprised me more: my recoil at hearing Blake's name, or that through some coldblooded fluke, I was eating breakfast with Blake's last partner. I had largely forgotten Blake for going on thirty years, though at random moments—and emphatically just then—a kind of lunatic film clip of his fall would flash through my mind, shoved back into shadows as soon as the clip rolled out.

"I was there," I said. "Over on the Salathé. I saw Blake falling down *The Nose*."

Now Jerry stared at me. His wrinkled hands reached for his coffee cup.

"When I decided to call," he said, "I looked up your name in the white pages and there were over fifty John Longs. But I was ready to ring them all to try and find you, to thank you for doing the book. The first number I tried was you."

I must have scowled. From the darkest cranny in my mind, where I'd stuffed all the other junk, the ghost of Michael Blake sprang out like a Jack-in-the-box, and was standing on the table with a shattered look, like a kid left out in the cold.

"What happened up there?" I finally asked Jerry. "I know the rope broke but I never heard how."

I wasn't worried about asking awful questions and rattling an old man, and wasn't amused that curious forces had shoved us together. Blake was back. We had to deal.

"I was hanging from the bolts at the last belay," said Jerry—then he stopped.

I'd visited that belay numerous times, at the top of the final headwall, hanging over an unplumbed void, the trees and river, and tiny cars creeping along the loop road, feeling miles away and more like a mirage than anything real. Just above this last anchor, the wall rolls back abruptly after a few friction steps, and you're standing on the northern rim.

"Mike was coming up the last bolts," said Jerry, "which, if you remember, run a little sideways. I'd just hauled up the bag and tied it off when he yells up for me to look down. Mike was clipping up the bolts with aid slings, pushing one jumar up the rope as a backup. He wanted to stop at this great spot and take a photo."

Jerry sounded unsure about what followed, so the details are soft. Apparently, Blake stopped just below Jerry's belay, standing on a tattered sling threaded through an original Warren Harding bolt, and started framing the pic as Jerry, looking straight down, leaned back from the anchor to shutter a hero shot.

The only written report I found was from *Off the Wall: Death in Yosemite*, co-written by then-park-ranger "Butch" Farabee Jr. The summit bolt ladder was sixteen years old, the write-up reminded, and when Blake put his full weight on one of the final bolts, "it gave way, yanking out of the wall."

The moment the bolt pulled, Blake must have wrenched onto his one jumar (a dodgy technique that betrayed his inexperience) and it popped off the rope. Because Blake hadn't tied in short (which limits the distance you can plummet), Volger watched him free fall roughly 150 feet to the end of the line (tied directly to his harness), which snapped taut as a bowstring "and severed against some unknown salient on the face," wrote Farabee. "Literally within feet of finishing a Grade VI route, Blake fell 3,000 feet off El Capitan all the way to the base of the Dawn Wall."

And Jerry Volger watched him go the entire way. I only caught the ending.

"What happened next?" I asked.

"Not . . . sure," said Jerry. He looked old and vacant. "Next thing I remember was meeting some hikers on the Falls Trail, five or six miles away."

We sat silently, sipping our coffee. Rilke said that a ghost's greatest fear is aloneness, and I wondered if Blake, hovering around the table, was still holding Jerry hostage. The thought didn't feel strange because the whole encounter ran like a hallucination. I shifted focus to those final moments on the bolt ladder, hoping a few facts might find us solid ground.

Shortly after the accident, rangers and several climbers from the rescue site had humped up to the summit, roped down, and inspected the last belay. The haul bag, I was told, still hung off the bolts, as did most of Jerry's gear, including a ragged end of lead rope dangling in the void.

"You must have untied and soloed to the top," I said.

After he'd just watched Blake go the distance, those last friction moves must have felt lethal in lug-soled Robbins boots.

"It's all a blank," said Jerry, staring at nothing. Part of him had never gotten off that bolt ladder—the part he couldn't remember, which had blanked his recall for those lost hours stumbling down the Falls Trail, and had fogged both our minds even then.

"After the accident, I struggled," he said. "Finally, a friend told me I'd had a shock and had to rest." Jerry never climbed again.

We kept talking, but I've no idea for how long. The same gravity that had pulled two strangers together had hurled a teenaged climber to the ground, merciless fallout from a force so weak that scientists can barely measure it. Yet it took all of our words and silences to finally take the measure of our experience and the ghost of Michael Blake, no longer alone through our remembering. Slowly, without us noticing, as Blake dropped into the ether, Jerry and I were just a couple of people talking to each other.

When the bill came, I asked the waitress to take a picture of us with my cell phone. Later, at home, when I studied the photo, nothing in either of our faces suggested it took forty-four years for all three of us to finally stop falling.

SPEED [TRAP]

"HOW FAR'D SHE FALL?"

"Far enough to blow the helmet off her head," said Tom. "Rescue team short-roped her off the wall, and they airlifted her out. Don't see how you survive that fall, but she did—barely."

August, 2017. We'd just arrived in Yosemite Valley for a video shoot, finding Tom Evans in a corner of the cafeteria, editing photos from the rescue, which he took from El Capitan Meadow using his "big gun" tele-photo lens. Whoever is climbing El Capitan, Tom shoots them for his elcapreport.com ("Unique in all the World!"), highly prized by Valley cognoscenti, and which Tom updates every evening in his van.

Tom paused on a shot of the chopper in midair, the black and tan bulk of El Cap rising in the background. At the end of a rope far below the chopper, rescue ranger Brandon Lathum and climber Quinn Brett—who was strapped into the litter—dangled in space like spiders on a string.

"Speed climbing *The Nose*?" I asked.

"What else?" said Tom. He looked ill.

Word trickled in over the following days. Quinn broke four ribs, punctured a lung, and bruised her liver in the fall. She also suffered a burst fracture of her twelfth thoracic vertebra, "typically a severe spinal injury," according to her doctors. If they knew how severe, no one was saying.

Friends started a YouCaring campaign, donations streamed in from a dozen countries, but still no word on Quinn's prognosis. Two months and three operations later, while rehabbing at Doctors Medical Center in

Modesto, California, Quinn started blogging:

Will I ever walk hand in hand with Max again? WALK hand in hand. BE with Max?

Live a life without diapers and worrying about shitting in the middle of the night because I have no control?

WHAT THE FUCK!

This from the woman who popped handstands on gusty Patagonian summits, who ran "Rim to Rim to Rim" (45 miles, 22,000 feet elevation gain/loss) in the Grand Canyon, and stormed up dozens of Yosemite big walls, several in record time. She was a spark on the tinder of American adventuring until, during a speed climbing run on *The Nose* route of El Capitan, she fell 120 feet and body slammed off another flake below. Now, she was paralyzed from the belly button down.

Sometimes I am depressed, wonder if I should be here. I can't believe that this is where I am at. I am scared. I am sorry. I am overwhelmed.

Reading these words at home in Venice Beach, California, I pushed back from my desk as a long-forgotten scene bubbled into memory. I studied the cell phone photos in Quinn's blog—the heinous road rash, the Frankenstein gash from spinal fusion surgery, and now the horror-stricken timbre of her voice, like she woke up screaming—and thought to myself, "Damn. That could have been me."

≙

Memorial Day, 1975. Seven years before Quinn was born. Jim Bridwell, Billy Westbay (both lost from us now), and I cast off to attempt the first one-day ascent of *The Nose*, the world's most sought-after rock climb.

"Pull this off and we'll never live it down," Jim laughed as we geared up in the dark at the base of the wall. Twice that year, teams had attempted the NIAD (Nose in a Day), bonking in the upper corners, half a mile over the trees. The NIAD was a prize and we meant to get it. I tied into the rope and charged, hell-bent. I had recently turned twenty-one.

Shortly past dawn, I pendulumed right into the Stoveleg Crack, a laser-cut slash bisecting the sweeping granite nose where the Southwest and Southeast Faces converge. The ground dropped away as pitches that normally took an hour were dispatched in minutes, a speed achieved through constant motion and placing little to no protection. Jim promised plenty of fixed nuts and pitons in the crack but I only found a few. The climbing was steep and thuggish, but secure, so it didn't matter. Going fast was all that mattered.

By 7:00 a.m., now a third of the way up the wall, I stormed up a ladder of bolts drilled into the rock, gunning for Boot Flake, a fifty-foot granite scab describing a boot if you eye it dead-on from El Cap Meadow. I'd climbed *The Nose* once before and remembered the crack along the Boot's right side as secure but off-balance. I chalked up and started tomahawking my hands into the wavy fracture. The first twenty feet felt solid so I pressed on, not bothering to place protection in the crack and waste time, jamming for the shelf and bolt anchors atop the Boot. Nearly there, my left arm cramped and my hand curled into a claw. I'd meant to fully hydrate the night before but sipped on beers instead. I shook my frozen arm, my right hand creeping from a greasy hand jam.

My eyes darted down fifty feet to my last protection. When I pitched off—not if, but when—I'd ragdoll down and smash into Texas Flake, the jagged-edged atoll where Jim and Billy were moored, 100 feet below. I wasn't thinking about getting busted in half or even dying, but the shame of dreaming so big and performing so small. A pretender who should have known better.

I glanced at my jammed hand, melting from the crack. I had one big hexcentric on my rack and, when the cramp briefly released, I fumbled the nut into the crack, clipped in the rope, and slumped onto it. Cold sweat streamed down my neck as the mango-sized nut pivoted in the crack. I shook my arm out, reset the nut, and groped up the last bit to the shelf and the anchors. It was 7:20 a.m.

Billy grabbed the lead, swung left, and streaked across the "Gray Band" of diorite that girds El Capitan. Before I could catch my breath, the vortex of our speed ascent sucked me off the anchors and across the wall, blowing away my near miss on Boot Flake—behind me now, but I'd screwed up hugely and squeaked by on luck, nothing else.

Forty-three years later and I'm cringing in the Oval Room at the Fairmont Copley Plaza Hotel in Boston, Massachusetts, hearing about the fall I should have taken by the climber who took it—at the exact same place on Boot Flake.

"Tell me about the climb," asks Ashley Saupe, hosting The Sharp End podcast. I'm at the annual American Alpine Club gala and the band's all here, heroes and has-beens, spanning generations, everyone strands in a web stretching from the Oval Room to Yosemite Valley to the Himalayas and beyond.

Quinn gazes at Audrey with liquid brown eyes and says, "Last time I'd been in Yosemite with Hayden Kennedy, he'd taken a big fall off Pancake Flake halfway up *The Nose* during a speed push. And he came down and had a giant hematoma on his hamstring, and he and I sat by the river, and he soaked his leg and talked about how that felt. Like, he took a sixty-footer and was freaked out and he said, 'Quinn, I don't know why we're doing this speed climbing thing.'"

Hayden was doing what athletes always do at the thin end of the wedge: seek to break new ground. A competent team at a casual pace can climb El Cap trade routes with trepidation, but little fear for their lives. Hundreds do so every season. And dedicated climbers usually look to throw down a quick time, to confirm their skill and fitness, if only to themselves. Nobody wants to be the climbing equal of jazz great, Paul Desmond, who played his sax so slowly you could still hear his lines a decade after he passed.

Chasing record times, however, means no pausing to strategize, to place adequate protection, or drop anchor and regroup, however briefly. You simply charge, hell-bent, using your experience and instincts as collateral. Gravity never sleeps, so the potential danger is towering. It's also optional, and a throbbing rope burn can make even crushers like Hayden Kennedy wonder, *Why?* The question is part of the web, though hidden at first. As the adventures run together and seasons pass, partners, friends, and acquaintances drop into the void so abruptly that it rips holes in the web. The question lives in those holes.

The day before Quinn and Josie McKee headed up on *The Nose*, they learned that Hayden, 27, and his girlfriend, Inge Perkins, 23, had gone backcountry skiing below Imp Peak, Montana. A hard slab avalanche plowed down a gully and buried them alive. Hayden clawed his way out, and dug for hours, but Inge was gone. That night, lost in the dark, Hayden killed himself.

"When Josie and I pulled into El Cap Meadow, the morning of our climb," says Quinn, as the podcast rolls, "I was texting my boyfriend about Hayden, struggling with his death. Josie and I were like—we'd planned on climbing *The Nose* so let's just go. So, out of habit, we put on our climbing gear and, out of habit, we walked to the base because that's what we did. Climb. Fast. Next thing you know we were going."

After the first one-day ascent in 1975, the NIAD remained an infrequent feat performed mostly by Valley locals. Nobody ever remembers the second team to do anything, so little glory accrued from repeating the NIAD. However, the experience was so huge and exhilarating that a burn up *The Nose* became "obligatory for hard men" throughout the '70s and '80s, albeit on a limited scale.

This all changed in 1990, when former pole-vaulting star, "Hollywood" Hans Florine, made speed climbing his life work, scaling El Cap nigh two-hundred times, setting speed records on most every route he bagged. His attention never strayed far from *The Nose*, where he shifted gears from one-day ascents, to elapsed time, turning the NIAD into a race ("the Indy 500 of speed climbing"). This, critically, gave leading climbers a prestigious world record to set and to break—forever. Now the NIAD, like the 100-meter dash, could never fall out of fashion.

Hans' closing statement came in 2014, while partnered with Alex Honnold (who later won an Oscar for *Solo*, the highest grossing documentary in history, about his no-rope ascent of El Capitan in 2018). The pair lowered *The Nose* speed record to a blazing two hours and forty-six minutes (2:46). His 2015 release, *On The Nose: A Lifelong Obsession with Yosemite's Most Iconic Climb*, was a bestseller in the outdoor industry. His record with Honnold felt beyond reach.

Women joined the hunt in the 1990s, though many felt female promise was scarcely tapped until 2011, when Libby Sauter and Chantel Astorga took down *The Nose* in 10:40 (the record had stood at 12:15 for a decade or so). Brett and Jes Meiris responded, clocking in at 10:26. Later that summer, Mayan Smith-Gobat and Chantel Astorga lowered the time to 7:26. In 2013, Smith-Gobat, partnered with Sauter, starched the route in 5:39, in 5:02 the following spring and, later that fall, set the speed record at 4:43 (surely one of the greatest and least-recognized feats in female sport).

Of the many who've climbed El Cap in a day, few had the time and inclination for the grueling prep work (years of skill-building and practice burns up a given route) required to take a run at a speed record. But for those who did, the action was fierce and dodgy. To most everyone else, speed climbing, like most all ascent, was simply another roller coaster. Fast and thrilling but at the end of the day, back on the ground and all out of breath, you ended up right where you'd started.

≜

The morning after Quinn's accident, I drove to El Cap Meadow and found Tom behind his camera, hunkered in a little gravel clearing by a stunted pine, close by the Merced River. For all who have scaled El Capitan, the Meadow exerts a gravity that pulls you there, where climbers loiter (often around Tom, where the banter is rare and relentless) in random groups, or wander off alone and stare at the monolith. The wall is still a long way off, but at 3,000 feet high and several miles wide along the base, it feels like you can reach and touch it.

You sit there and bask in its raw basal force, recalling life up high, and the spells of dark brood when you'd wonder why you were working harder than you ever worked in your life, beating down the fear when below, there were tanned tourists to chase and beer to drink and sandy riverbanks to lounge on and do nothing—and everything. The answer plunged below you on the rock: You were climbing El Capitan.

Most of the ragged ensemble I found in the meadow had been on hand for Quinn's rescue, and the atmosphere felt grim. Brad Gobright wandered over. Twenty-nine and cool as an iceberg, Brad had climbed for twenty-one years, hiking world-class climbs across the Western States, often without a rope. A native Southern Californian, like myself, Brad also grew up clawing over the quartz monzonite domes out at Joshua Tree National Park, a high-desert destination area north of Palm Springs. The previous fall, he'd climbed *The Nose* half a dozen times with partner Jim Reynolds, and eleven more times that season, honing their game for an all-out run at the speed record. I asked Brad what he thought happened to Quinn on Boot Flake. His eyes never left El Cap. "No idea."

The man was locked in. Scanning the rock like a predator. Absorbed in a half-remembered forcefield I could feel and almost taste. Labels and limits, I recalled, stood no chance in that forcefield, which makes the game so seductive, and sparks the craving to throw all your marbles at *The Nose*. We all underestimated the heat, once we had.

Brad's partner, Jim Reynolds, had said in an interview, "The closer we're getting to the record, we're pushing the boundary between dangerous and reckless just a little bit more. So we're starting to wonder: can we just take a little bit more risk and get it finished, so we don't have to come back and take all that risk again?"

Eleven days later, Brad and Jim Reynolds pulled the trigger. Gobright led from the ground to the top of Boot Flake, 1,300 feet up the wall, placing but three cams over that distance. They smoked the route in 2:19:44, breaking Honnold and Florine's record by four minutes.

In Josh Lowell's and Peter Mortimer's feature-length documentary, T*he Nose Speed Record*, Honnold later said: "When Brad and Jim did the record, at the top they had an entire sixty-meter rope between them but nothing clipped, no gear between them, and Brad was literally just holding onto the bolts with his fingers. And I'm like—what are you guys doing?!" The inference being that Alex and Hans levitated up *The Nose* on savvy and legerdemain, while Gobright and Reynolds burgled the record through recklessness. Brad, among the world's most accomplished big wall free climbers, played along because he knew better.

"Alex tells me, 'Dude! You guys are really sketchy,'" said Gobright. "I'm like, 'Yeah. It's sketchy. But that's why I got the record . . . and you don't.'"

The following fall, Gobright perished in a rappelling accident while climbing in Mexico, and Reynolds flummoxed the adventure world by climbing up and down 4,000-foot Mount Fitz Roy, in Patagonia, with no rope.

≙

"What about your fall off Boot Flake?" asks Ashley. We're half an hour into the podcast and half the crowd looks ready to run. Quinn straightens and describes reaching the crack, and how the rope gets stuck below but there's a great loop of slack out in her lead rope, so she starts jamming out the Boot with no belay, "because that's the way you climb the pitch. Josie yells up that we're at two hours, which is, like—sick.

We're on a really cruiser pace."

As Quinn nears the top of the Boot, Hayden Kennedy flashes through her mind. She gropes for a camming device, slung to her harness, which she might slot in the crack in an emergency. Like now. Except she's dropped the cam. Or maybe placed it already. She isn't sure which. Only that everything is racing south—just as it'd gone for me, and for dozens of others present who've battled critical moments and inexplicably escaped, while Quinn did not. A dreadful few among us are sole survivors, and sit still as statues as Quinn recounts the moment: feet paddling, hanging for her life on Boot Flake, fumbling gear and thinking, "'I shouldn't do that,' or, 'I shouldn't have done that.' One second of a feeling like in an elevator," says Quinn. "Then—falling. Granite whooshing before my eyes. Thankfully, I don't remember the rest."

Quinn briefly reviews the rescue operation (a more technical extraction is hard to imagine), and Ashley asks how her recovery is going.

"It's been a pile of shit," says Quinn, "and it's been amazing, with the people who've come to help me."

Audrey mentions the YouCaring fundraiser, how strangers from Kenya to Israel have given over $125,000. Quinn's game face, courageously worn so far, shatters and falls. "I did a stupid thing, and people are helping me and it's pretty amazing. So, thank you very much."

We muster smiles. Offer encouraging words. But the tension won't break till we stop our perverse well-wishing and finally sync up with Quinn, with all our dread and jagged edges. And the inexorable sundown of feeling hits home for all of us whose partners and friends have fallen through the net, leaving gaping holes, which stir with the doomed and the missing.

As the past breaks out in our hearts, the Oval Room is a house of catharsis. Scattered applause breaks the trance, and none too soon. I'll give the crisis this palliative minute, as a tribal rite. But I'm not yet ready to discover where I truly stand—about Quinn, speed climbing, any of it.

I peer at the clouds, brushed on the ceiling. Legend says that circa

1905, after John Singer Sargent finished the murals in the iconic Boston City Library across the street, he dropped by the Oval Room and painted an angel on the ceiling. I can't find it. Searching around, I find the next best thing: Libby "The Liberator" Sauter, with her bucket-full of freckles and a smile off a toothpaste ad. She's one of Quinn's partners from way back, and spent much of that first month at her bedside. Libby splits time between cutting-edge adventuring (a skilled slackliner and ultrarunner, she had concurrently held speed climbing records for *The Nose*, Salathé Wall, and Lurking Fear routes on El Capitan—the latter bagged with Quinn), and working as a war zone cardiac nurse in places like Benghazi, Libya. Libby Sauter never plays it safe.

My smile feels like a clown mask as Libby and I join the mob swarming through the exit. What is this, a celebration? A wake? By what crazy fluke are we even alive to be here, especially the alpinists and big mountain folk who dominate this crowd. Seen from the perspective of my Venezuelan-born daughter, a Latina pediatrician who donates her time to Doctors Without Borders, what gives with these callow white yahoos and their hoary legacy? What would all the dead say to our back-slapping and tequila shooters in their honor, as those left bereft ask why for the rest of their lives?

"My West Point class must have a thousand man-years of combat at this point," former soldier and Patagonia climber, Gregory Crouch, emailed me that morning, "what with Panama, Desert Storm, and all that shit in Afghanistan and Iraq, and we have one person Killed In Action. Of the people with whom I've shared the rope in my thirty-five years of climbing, seventeen of them are dead. It's like the Somme."

Most mountaineers venturing onto big, technical mountains have repeatedly feared for their lives—but many charge regardless. Climbing as fetish. But I'm a rock climber, where the risks are fewer. Unless you travel to stormy venues like Patagonia, in southern Argentina, talent and technology have largely brought the hazards under control, especially in pacific areas like Yosemite. To peer over the edge, a rock climber must solo or speed climb, or intentionally chase other dangers. The stated goal, as it goes for most alpinists, is to reap remarkable experiences, or perhaps, set a record, capture the public's eye, and get a sponsor. Or keep one. But every avid soloist or speed climber has, at some time, seen God.

I have a place in the hotel and Libby and Quinn will use it as a staging area before the gala dinner that evening. I let the pair into my room and lift Quinn from her chair and onto the bed. She can't weigh more than 100 pounds, her once-strong runner's legs now as slender as reeds. Her vacant eyes betray the incomprehensible disillusionment of going, in seconds, from a flower with a cannon inside, to . . . this.

Here's a conflict I can only square at the open bar downstairs. Better head over to Copley Square and the renowned Boston Public Library, a few blocks away. I'll admire Sargent's portraits, duck into a shady booth and eyeball the pictures in *Surfer* magazine.

Libby walks me back to the elevator. We both occasionally work for the same outdoor clothing brand, but we haven't spoken in months. She's still climbing, and harder than ever, she says, but on short sport routes, bolted and secure. Nothing like her halcyon days when she set all those speed records on El Cap, including the one with Quinn. Watching a soulmate go from able-bodied to paralysis "makes speed climbing a whole lot less cool."

The last time Libby went trad climbing and got way off the ground, she visualized bodies tumbling through the air. When one of the best of them all sees this in her mind, all that giddy valorizing we sometimes ascribed to speed climbing feels bogus as Halo Jones and Spiderman.

Libby will later write in *Rock and Ice* that she had been "guilty of having spread the bullshit narrative that there is a way to speed climb safely. At my peak of speed climbing on *The Nose*, I would do fifteen pitches on ten cams for the first block and, while it 'felt safe'—it sure as shit wasn't. I'm not telling people not to speed climb, but that kind of climbing isn't for me anymore."

"That kind of climbing" involves the leader and the second climbing concurrently ("simul-climbing") on opposite ends of a sixty- or seventy-meter-long rope. Once the team goes live, it's a blood oath. If the leader falls, or the second falls and pulls off the leader, the team is saved only by whatever protection they've placed between them, rarely more than one piece, since placing gear takes time and carrying it takes energy. Any fall will likely be 100 feet or more, prompting the universal credo that "you cannot fall while speed climbing." Advanced techniques, like short-fixing (quantum mechanics is easier to explain), are faster yet sketchier still.

Fact is, belaying at an anchor (at the end of a given pitch, or rope length) is where a climber recovers, however briefly. Now it's like a boxing match with no bell between rounds, because there are no rounds. It's a slugfest start to finish. What's more, climbing so much technical rock requires holding a surgeon's focus for hours on end; but hold it you must, between the short span of our fingertips and a sloping edge, or the climb can undo your life.

Libby's cautionary drift echoed through the adventure world at large. In an interview for *The Nose Speed Record*, Gobright said, "chasing The Nose record is absolutely dangerous. There's no getting around that." In a piece for *Outside*, writer and alpinist, Kelly Cordes, no stranger to danger himself, noted that, no matter how you play it, the techniques used at hyper-speed are complex and potentially lethal, a process he likened to redlining a Ferrari on a winding mountain road without a seatbelt. "Everything's fine—unless you crash," wrote Cordes. "But to embody the physical and psychological competency to race up the most iconic wall on the planet in a couple of hours must feel like flying."

The flying metaphor struck a chord with Tommy Caldwell, Cordes' neighbor and amongst the greatest large-scale rock climbers in history, whose free ascent of the Dawn Wall on El Capitan in 2015 became a worldwide media event.

"Man, I think of the wingsuit community," Caldwell said to Cordes, "how at first people were like, 'If you only fly in these conditions, only fly in this terrain, it's actually safe.' And now, everybody knows that it's just dangerous, no matter what. I wonder if speed climbing is the same."

Not the same, but equally addictive. I half-seriously coined it the "Icarus Syndrome," in light of what happened to Hans Florine, who'd climbed El Cap 178 times, breaking The Nose speed record eight times. Yet at fifty-four years old, he still needed more. On May 3, 2018, roughly six months after Brett's podcast in Boston, Hans started up Pancake Flake, 2,000 feet up *The Nose*, during a scheduled one-day ascent. A nut blew out and he crash-landed on a ledge, breaking his left tib/fib in two places and shattering his right heel.

The indomitable Alex Honnold was terribly sorry for Hans, who he'd partnered with two years before to capture the speed record from Dean Potter and Sean Leary (both perished wingsuit flying), only for Gobright and Reynolds to snatch it away the following autumn. Now Florine had an external steel fixator bolted onto his leg and Honnold wanted his record back. He enlisted Tommy Caldwell's services a week after Florine's crash, and the two began running laps on *The Nose*, perfecting their systems and teamwork with each ascent.

"I've never been the danger dude," said Caldwell. But after a few swift burns up the Big Stone, he understood Florine's trademark refrain, that The Nose speed record "is the most badass competition there is."

The fact that it's also dangerous as hell, even for El Cap master Tommy Caldwell, struck home a few days later during another training run, when he logged a monster fall off the relatively easy Stoveleg Crack. Alex fell a half an hour later, burning his hand and losing a chunk of flesh while grabbing the rope. It could have gone far worse.

"It was at least a hundred feet," said Caldwell of his fall. "I was like: I'm still falling. *I'm still falling!*"

"Hope nobody saw that shit," said Honnold, on top of El Cap, after their ascent. "Kind of horrifying."

America had never fielded a better big wall squad than Alex Honnold and Tommy Caldwell, and yet both had broken the golden rule to *never fall* while speed climbing. This didn't auger well for setting records. But once the adrenaline washed through and they slept it off, they both put their falls behind them.

On May 28, Honnold and Caldwell clocked a "relatively casual lap" in 2:25, only six minutes off Gobright and Reynolds's record pace. Two days later, they brought it home in 2:10:15, smashing the record. Might they possibly reach the "mythical milestone" and log a sub-two-hour ascent? This meant going a full five percent faster than their quickest lap, which increased the risks exponentially.

At the velocity top speed climbers were traveling, with the margin for error so thin, and with even the best logging monster falls in the process, many felt speed climbing was a game of chance, that it was impossibly lucky that a team hadn't straight-up died. Several days later, on June 2, 2018, that all changed.

≜

Tim Klein, 42, and Jason Wells, 45, had climbed together since their early 20s, and had nearly two hundred ascents of El Cap between them, including a mind-numbing forty one-day ascents of the Salathé Wall (the other El Cap route regularly speed climbed). Their accident occurred on the lower reaches of the Salathé, on moderate climbing above a prominent feature called the Half-Dollar, where the pair had passed another party attempting to free climb the route. No one is certain what happened, but whatever protection and anchors they had failed after the leader fell, and the partners experienced a terror no human needs to know, taking a 1,000-foot ride into the dirt.

Tim Klein and Jason Wells had no truck with record times. They simply loved climbing fast, and had more experience doing so than any team alive. But they still simul-climbed, still carried as little gear as possible, and placed it frugally. Since they intimately knew the route, and their own limits, so long as they kept their speed a hair's breadth below maximum, what did they have to fear? They'd already managed one-day ascents of the very same route approaching four dozen times. They had this.

Climbing magazine waxed that "speed climbing is the inevitable expression of our basic human yearning for transcendent experience." Maybe so, but *Climbing* had taken the dramatist's prerogative to milk the glory and skip the body count. Quinn was paralyzed, Florine was laid up in traction, and Klein and Wells were dead, both leaving wives and young children behind. The adventure world, smarting from a moral whiplash, could not so easily unpack this. Many insiders knew the fastest teams, like a conquering army, claim everything in their path. Since only elapsed time mattered, speed climbing has very narrow meaning, and could quickly become a force so misleading that even the greatest send was a pyrrhic victory. Stunning performances were happening, but gallant depictions of speed climbing sounded tone deaf.

Several weeks after the Salathé Wall tragedy, while cragging out at Joshua Tree, I ran into a young high-desert climber from the party Klein and Wells passed on the Half-Dollar. He had watched the pair hurtle past (and so close by that, fearing impact, he violently sucked himself into the wall, jamming his head onto a crack) as they cartwheeled 1,000 feet straight into the ground. A gruesome experience still haunting the climber and which, for me, knocked the shine off speed climbing forever. The effects ran deeper still, but my ostrich-like avoidance of my own feelings kept me a stranger to myself. Caldwell, being Caldwell, knew he had to get back on the horse, but he did so with few illusions.

"With all the carnage this past year," said Caldwell, "it makes me hesitate . . . a bit."

But the enormity of the two-hour barrier, and the thrill of the hunt, trumped his fear. On June 6, 2018, four days after Wells' and Klein's accident, Alex and Tommy started up *The Nose* at 6:00 a.m. and topped out one hour and fifty-eight minutes later.

Kelly Cordes got hold of Honnold and Caldwell on his cellphone shortly after they reached the summit. Listening over the speakerphone, he asked Caldwell if he had designs on going even faster.

"Totally done," he said.

Tommy is only an acquaintance, but I take him at his word. Meanwhile, Honnold, floating over Yosemite's scorched earth, was looking past the "mythical milestone" and into the future, as only Honnold can. He later wrote he believes the true human potential for speed climbing El Cap is 1:30. Or even 1:15.

≜

Two blocks down Boylston Street, the Boston Public Library heaves into view. First the red tile roof sloping into a green copper cornice, flecked with seashells and dolphins above a frieze of classical figures— winged horses, an eagle on a branch. Below this lie thirteen arched bay windows faced with wooden Roman grillwork, painted dark to appear as iron.

Soon I'm in Copley Square, gazing across at three high arches trimmed with wrought-iron lanterns, which form the library entrance. Out front, two allegorical female figures, cast in dark bronze and glistening in rainwater, sit on rusticated pedestals. One hooded figure, on behalf of Art, holds a palette and a paintbrush. The other, examining an orb in her hand, represents Science.

I sit on an icy park bench, trying to shake my funk, staring across at architect Charles Follen McKim's "palace for the people," a hulking Historic Landmark faced in pink granite, as though McKim built Boston their own El Capitan. Like Mecca, like Yosemite Valley, many come to pay homage. My eyes tilt up and I read the names chiseled in stone panels below the bay windows: Zeno, Plato, over to Praxiteles, on to Kepler and Laplace, settling on Da Vinci, Spinoza, and Bach. A board of trustees first envisioned this library in the 1860s, as a Renaissance-style monument to those who kept dreaming and getting-after until the world reimagined itself.

I'll never see my name chiseled in granite, but the getting-after has sustained me when nothing else could. And I've loved the fiery questing of it all. Having a raison d'être. Being the first human being to do *something*.

From my late teens onward, my strongest sense of meaning derived from flying close to the sun, knowing that with speed climbing and soloing, as with art, politics, and crime, it's what you get away with that counts. But every Icarus has an expiration date, and friends and family squirming on the ground, so questions lingered.

When does a competitive spirit become a reckless fling with death? When does ambition mutate into a selfish crusade for fame? There's more to the game than these thorny dichotomies. And no question, dreaming and getting-after are as tightly woven into some of us as the apocalyptic elements of life. But even the incomparable Tommy Caldwell, who heard the rattling chains, drew a chalk line on the rock and is "totally done" with speed climbing. Otherwise, danger becomes a granite-hard drug mainlined in a haunted house with no value beyond itself. There lies No Man's Land. There lies the black hole of coming back to consciousness and saying, "I can't feel my legs." But if I had it all to do over again, I would, in a heartbeat. It's a conflict I could never live without.

Quinn was barely out of rehab when *living without* became a global mandate as the coronavirus locked us down and swept 3.3 million souls off the face of the earth. The pandemic dragged on and our communal fear and neuroticism seemed to blot out the sun, as society reorganized along our fault lines. Most of us also had those take-stock moments that a crisis hand delivers; speed climbing was in nobody's thoughts. Yet as the hospitals emptied out and the world opened up once more, many realized that without challenge, life lacks carbonation. A point made clear in *The Greater Fool: Brad Gobright and the Blinding Shine of Originality*, Lucas Roman's superb biography (penned during the pandemic) of former Nose speed record holder, the late Brad Gobright.

"The Greater Fool," wrote Roman, "is the one who turns into the storm when all common sense and foot traffic points the other way. Intrepid and unwitting as they may be, they're also the ones we need."

Despite losing her husband to speed climbing, Becky Wells still says she would never tell Jason not to go to Yosemite and do what he loved. "He called El Cap the Magic Stone," she said. "It gave him what he needed to be the person he wanted to be. It fed his soul."

"Had I summited that day [of my accident]," said Quinn Brett from her wheelchair, "I would probably still be speed climbing. I mean, it's a pretty awesome feeling."

And this feeling, this experience, has little to do with records. It's a reckoning with our limits and our capacity to act with skin in the game, against all odds, on a vertical stage known as the ne plus ultra of natural magnitude. We rightfully ask why, as the sun sets over the valley, but answers give us nothing.

WHEN ICARUS FALLS

My phone chirps. A text from Chantel, an American alpinist and solo big wall climber whom I love and admire.

"John Long! My bros Kyle and Scott are overdue in Pakistan. I'm hanging with Kyle's mom in Salt Lake and my partner Jewell, Kyle's girlfriend. Keeping fingers crossed for improving weather."

That doesn't bode well. Two of America's best alpinists gone missing like that. Chantel didn't give much to go on, but who can blame her, biting her nails with mom and the girlfriend. I log onto the web and skim a dispatch from Kyle's gear sponsor.

A week ago, Kyle Dempster and Scott Adamson started up the unclimbed North Face of Ogre II in the Karakorum range in Pakistan. Their headlamps were spotted halfway up the face at the end of their first day on the mountain. Then a storm rolled in and nobody'd seen them since. With the clock ticking and the storm raging on, family and friends set up a GoFundMe site to help finance a search.

I have to text Chantel back and say something, just not what she has to be thinking as well—that it's 6,800 miles to Kyle and Scott, but they might as well be on the moon.

Whatever food and fuel they had is long gone after a week. Searching with binoculars is pointless in a storm. Maybe you check likely descent routes if the boys topped out and got stranded getting down. Doubtful, but I hold out hope, not wanting to jinx them. A rescue team might traverse the base in case the climbers got blown off the wall by rocks or avalanche. Nobody wants that job, with all that debris raining down. No helicopter (if there's one for hire) will fly anywhere near the mountain. Not in a storm, on a beast like Ogre II.

But just maybe they had a shot . . . Who can forget the photos of British crusher, Doug Scott, crawling off Ogre I (just west of Ogre II) in heavy weather?

Doug Scott. Make that Sir Doug Scott, now that he's been knighted. I was a reckless teenager when I first met Doug, c. 1973, in Yosemite, and we tried to cross the Merced to climb the North Face of the Rostrum. Except the river ran like the Ganges in flood and we couldn't clear the current, hopping rock to rock, like I'd promised. Finally I said, "Fuck it. I'm roping up and swimming across."

Doug laughed and said, "No you're not. You'll drown."

Doug was older and looked like Moses with his beard, plus he'd just bagged a new route on Everest and had that clout. So I forgot it and we hitched over to The Cookie and climbed Meat Grinder.

I surf around the internet looking for updates, backstories, a link to Google Earth. But there's nothing more about Kyle and Scott, so I dig out an old *Mountain* magazine with Doug's end-all survival story, "A Crawl Down the Ogre."

A photo of Ogre II shows the wall soaring off the Choktoi Glacier like an ice-encrusted fist. The North Face, says the caption, covers 4,600 feet of rock and ice. Tops out at 23,000 feet. "Futuristic."

Then an editor calls from *Nat Geo*, asking for my thoughts about Kyle and Scott.

A week, I agree, is forever. But what else can I add? Never been to the Karakorum. Never climbed a real mountain. Never laid eyes on the boys. Came close to meeting Kyle last May, at an American Alpine Club awards banquet organized in part to honor Kyle and Hayden Kennedy's first ascents on K7 and Ogre I. Only Kyle showed up, in a gray shirt he must have slept in, jeans, and sunglasses, looking amused to get a plaque the size of a STOP sign for climbs he'd bagged four seasons earlier.

Kyle read his acceptance speech off the head of a pin: "Thank you very much." Then he stood there in wrinkled glory, till a crowd gathered round and herded him offstage to hear all about it. By the time I made my way over, Kyle had left the building.

≜

That night, I text Chantel that I sent a hundred bucks to help with the search. Wishing them the best.

"Hey. Thanks so much," she writes back. "It's kind of a logistical nightmare trying to get a helicopter in there with search capabilities. But these guys are real good and real lucky so I like their chances."

She forwards a trip report about Kyle and Scott's first attempt on Ogre II, a year ago. A good story gets gripping just below the summit, where Scott took a 100-foot fall and fractured his leg. Kyle and Scott can only start roping down, the story continues. A few rappels from the base, they rip an anchor and toboggan 300 feet onto the glacier, escaping further injury. That's like the rope breaking when they're hanging you. More than lucky.

A brushfire of updates burns through the night, which is morning over in Pakistan. Army helicopters have joined the search, but weather keeps them grounded in Skardu. Porters are heading up the Biafo Glacier to the backside of Ogre II, where Kyle and Scott might have descended. No word yet from the porters.

Thomas Huber, a legendary German climber, is an hour down the glacier with an Austrian team prepping for an attempt on Latok 1. They're anxious to help but can't get near the wall due to gale-force wind and avalanches. A report out of Karachi says the storm might pass tonight. Or by noon tomorrow, at the latest.

In the time it takes to eat breakfast, the weather report has 7,300 shares. The GoFundMe site shows $97,734 raised from 1,965 donors.

We're twenty-four hours in and the crisis is arranging random pieces of a human jigsaw puzzle into a community rarely seen during slack times. The hope is that Kyle and Scott will return and take their places in the puzzle, once the pieces converge. I picture 2,000 candles across the planet, lit for two Americans lost in a storm. In a moment that calls for decisive action, there's little else to do but watch those candles burn.

≜

They call it "kill time," waiting for news from people gone missing. Like when my buddy Marty Navarro paddled into a canyon in Uruguay and I heard nothing for a month. Or the time my Yosemite pal, Alan Rouse, charged for the summit of K2 and vanished in the clouds. And Charles Rincon, disappearing on the Blue Nile. I doubt these guys ever met each other, but they all loved a sharp edge, and left us hanging in kill time. Not one of them ever came back.

The GoFundMe kitty has $123,000, plenty to launch a search mission. Chantel emails me an update. A Global Rescue helicopter has joined the hunt, though once again, low clouds on the mountain leave the aerial search team pacing in Skardu. But the barometric pressure is rising and Pakistani military choppers are ready to fly, soon as the weather clears. Porters have trekked up the Biafo Glacier from Askole to the backside of Ogre II. "We hope they can see something by day-break," writes Chantel.

I scroll down the GoFundMe site to a live chatroom, where hundreds chime in.

"You still owe me a quad-shot Americano, Kyle," writes a friend from Colorado. "Get home soon!" Below the text is a cell phone pic of Higher Ground, Kyle's coffee shop in Salt Lake City.

"This is not mountaineering. It's selfishness," writes another, call him Bart, who feels it criminal to crowdshare a preventable jam. The comment feels smug and malicious. But everyone has a voice nowadays, so we get the story in the round—the frenzied, schizophrenic jigsaw puzzle, not just the gaudiest pieces. Only fair. But fuck you anyhow, Bart.

Another update drops around noon: No break in the weather.

I'm boarding a plane in a couple hours to cover an ultramarathon in Aspen, Colorado. I jam stuff into a day pack and start wondering if Bart's fear of risk is his fear of being wrong, which keeps you from trying anything original, afraid to cash out the big dream. But I'm reciting only half the story. The shiny half with the bones left out.

When we set down in Aspen, I check my phone for updates. A confirmed weather window is opening tomorrow morning, the first break in the ten days since Kyle and Scott were last seen. Two Pakistani military helicopters will start searching in the morning. The next twenty-four hours are critical.

I roll out of Aspen and drive half an hour past Basalt and El Jebel to a bar-food restaurant in Carbondale, where I meet *Rock and Ice* publisher Duane Raleigh. Another Yosemite refugee. We order some food and a text arrives from Chantel.

"Weather is clear at base camp. Hopeful for the search to start at first light."

Duane's staff is posting updates about Ogre II on their website fast as word comes in.

"You know, Kyle was supposed to be a student in the last symposium," says Duane.

I had no idea. For the past three years, we've hosted a writer's symposium in Carbondale. Finished the last one just three weeks before.

Kyle had plenty to write about. He'd won the Piolet d'Or and multiple Golden Piton awards (the adventurer's version of the Nobel and Pulitzer Prizes) for pioneering climbs all over the world. He'd looked forward to honing his writing skills at the symposium, but all ten slots were filled, says Duane, who arranges the enrollment for the class. He'd had to tell Kyle, "Next year."

"Then a student fell out," Duane adds, "so I called Kyle back and said, 'You're in.'" But Kyle had already made plans to return to Ogre II, so it'd have to be next year after all.

Yet again, I'd come that close to meeting Kyle Dempster. As it happened, when that tenth slot opened up, Duane gave it to a girl, call her Wendy, who in her own way was also up against it.

Halfway through my burger, another text from Chantel.

"Helicopter finally took off. Good weather and they just landed in base camp to pick up Thomas Huber. I'll keep you posted."

I ask Duane what chance he gives the boys and he says, "Not much on such a technical face. But remember *Minus 148*..."

Minus 148, a classic endurance epic, chronicles the unlikely survival of author Art Davidson and seven others during the first winter ascent of Denali, way back in 1967. The team survived six days in a cramped snow cave when temperatures dropped to minus 150 and winds howled at 150 miles per. Suddenly, Kyle and Scott seem all but saved.

"Davidson lives around here," says Duane, "and he just had a barbecue to celebrate the fiftieth anniversary of the climb. I was there and we talked about Kyle and Scott."

The far-flung, random pieces are filling in the jigsaw puzzle. People I haven't thought about in ages and faces known and only heard about are racking into focus, all eyes trained on Ogre II.

Later that night, at a dumpy motel in Glenwood Springs, I brew coffee and start trolling the net for more of Kyle's writing, waiting for word from Chantel. The coffee's rank. No towels in the bathroom. A baby's screaming next door and the bed feels like Chickenhead Ledge. I know nothing about the ultramarathon I'm there to cover tomorrow morning, and I couldn't care less.

"I dreamed of a solitary adventure on a remote Karakoram peak," wrote Kyle in *Alpinist* magazine, "as a way to siphon off distractions and to answer the question of how much I was willing to give to the mountains."

Another text from Chantel. "First flight around the mountain . . . no sign of them."

That's dire, and plays like a dirge in my head. I drown it out by returning to Kyle's story about another climb, Tahu Rutum, seven years ago.

"After running out of food, I spent four days rappelling the wall and hiking back to base camp. Each time I fell, I had to find another memory with enough power to return me to my feet: the faces of family and friends; the sounds of their laughter . . ."

I read every word I can find by Kyle, and only pass out when the coffee wears off. The next text from Chantel comes in the wee hours, when the chirp on my phone wakes me up.

"Fuck, man. No bueno. No sign of the boys. One more fly-by after refuel."

I fumble to punch the letters on my phone. Good they're sticking with the search, I say. You never know.

My alarm goes off at 6:00 a.m. and another text is waiting from Chantel.

"No sign. But Huber feels confident in the search so don't let Duane publish anything in the magazine."

I sit up on the bed, vividly awake, clinging to the lives of people I've never met, in a place I've never seen, which feels greedy and secondhand. I pound down some toast and watery oatmeal at the breakfast spread in the hotel office, then motor toward Aspen Mountain. The thoughts are quick and ruthless:

What is the Ogre, really? Some ice-encrusted peak in Pakistan? Or the beast inside who binges on risk and excess? Maybe the Ogre is also the hero, strip-mining life for a dopamine fix. And the Ogre rolls with the crowds as well. At a NASCAR track, say, all of us jolted awake when the lead car flips and burns? Or the thousands following a search in Asia, all of us wanting to feel something. What's money, sex, and beautiful thoughts to people with dangerous appetites? Even God is wanting. We need a cannibal. We need an Ogre.

I'm making shit up, just to goose myself, which is the problem right there. Blame it on kill time.

I wheel into the grassy park below Aspen Mountain and start shooting 156 ultra-runners finishing the Icebreaker Grand Traverse, a forty-two-mile run along the mountainous ridge stretching from Crested Butte to Aspen. It starts raining around noon and the park is a swirling mudhole. The runners are crushed. Several fall face down in the muck as they slosh across the finish line. Some weep and laugh at the same time, as if their last and greatest wish is to run themselves to death. I know the type. I *am* the type.

My phone has died so I can't check updates on Kyle and Scott. When the last runner stumbles home at dusk, I race back to the motel, shower off the mud, power up my laptop, and read how late this morning, two Pakistani military copters made a close-proximity search of the North Face of Ogre II, flying to within 100 feet of the wall. They also searched the entire northeast ridge, where Kyle and Scott planned to descend. And scoured the glacier between Ogres I and II. No trace of the climbers was found.

Chantel's text is respectfully short: "They called off the search."

≜

Nearly two weeks have passed since the team was last spotted on the mountain. Further aerial sweeps, chancy at such altitude, hold out little hope. Whether a fall ripped Scott and Kyle off the wall, or the storm glazed them onto the face or some descent gulley, ten days' worth of snowfall would have buried all signs of the boys, till the mountain owned them entirely and they only existed in the memories of others.

I lay back on the lumpy bed and listen to the baby crying through the pasteboard walls, wishing for a second that I hadn't stopped drinking.

JOHN LONG

I've been here before many times.

Condolences float across cyberspace as pieces of the jigsaw crash to the ground, describing a new order, a new picture. Kyle and Scott are not on it. I try cooking up some fitting words for Chantel. Thanks for keeping me in the loop. Then just blurt with my fingers, jabbing at the letters on my phone.

"I'm sorry for Jewel and Kyle's mom and you and all of Kyle's friends and the same for Scott. But you're a stand-up person for seeing your people through this."

Seconds later, Chantel texts me back.

"Thanks, John Long. It's been some wicked heavy times, but there is a ton of support. Kyle was so obsessed with the Ogre II and obsessed with being in the mountains. Since it happened, it's kind of beautiful to think that he is now part of that landscape forever. Watching his mom has been tough, though. She just lost her husband one year ago. It crushes me to watch Jewell too, but they will be okay."

Then this on the GoFundMe site, from Robert L, I'm guessing from New Zealand:

"I smash a pile of pikelets with strawberry jam and cream when these events happen—it's bittersweet. Then try to do something nice for a stranger; to feel a little better about how tragic, beautiful, and forgiving life can still be."

The labyrinth of the human heart. I got nothing.

Back in LA, I log onto the GoFundMe site. They've raised $198,885 from 4,980 donors, a big chunk of it after the search was abandoned. Wordsworth quotes, rants, and small talk stream in as people rattle out of kill time, writing the chapter that doesn't fit magazine length, that doesn't develop or pay off as needed, that doesn't even properly end; rather, it dribbles forward out of habit, rudderless.

In a righthand column is a roll call of names and numbers. A running timeline listing who has donated, and how much.

I toggle down, studying the names of people who might never have heard of Kyle and Scott till they read how the pair were in trouble. I stop at a name that I do know: "Wendy," the girl from the writer's workshop. She donated $150.

Wendy started climbing two years ago and found her people in the "fellowship of fools," whose partnership she swore had saved her life. Then she made her way to our writing symposium, dragging along her craziness and runaway addictions that she'd recently reined in. Somewhere during the seminar, she had a boundary experience, returned home, and got a job. Working in a restaurant. Little money, but that didn't stop her, a few days ago, from signing over her entire paycheck. Hoping to save two members of her tribe who were fighting for their lives.

I remembered the video, saved on my desktop, of when Kyle "took off alone on his bike across Kyrgyzstan with a couple of mostly accurate maps, a trailer full of climbing gear, and a vocabulary of ten Kyrgyz words." The title card shows a panorama of snowy mountains. In the foreground, bearded, in a tattered puffy and wool beanie, Kyle stands tall on some mountaintop, holding a handwritten sign: I LOVE You!

Love. As usual, I take it only when it serves me. Like now. I picture Kyle, peering down from the mountain at Wendy, who gave him all her money, and him saying, "That's what I'm talking about!"

But an Ogre unchained is a cannibal. That's what gets lost in translation from the coffee shop to the wild places, where people run themselves into the ground to break from the snares of the world, and stand with the legends among the white clouds.

Several weeks later, I got a text from Kathy D., former cover girl for *Climbing* magazine who, after her marriage went bust, moved back to her hometown near the Florida Keys and started cave diving, one the most frightening and dangerous adventure sports going.

"Out here in the woods," she wrote, "sitting here—cave divers are overdue. But don't say a word to anyone. They tried a long push, are ten hours into the dive. No sign of them. Fingers crossed it's just a delay . . ."

ADVENTURE TRAVEL

DREAM ON, IRIAN JAYA

by Dwight Brooks (D.B.) and John Long

Dwight:

We flew 1,000 miles past Jayapura, the capital of Irian Jaya, to Jakarta. Both of us (John Long, a historic crossing of Borneo behind him, and me, heading to remote Indonesian locales for the fourth time) were well aware of the bureaucracy involved in getting permission to enter the unexplored areas of Irian Jaya in 1984. Indonesia's most troubled province, and ethnologically the most primitive place on earth.

If you don't have a Jakarta-issued rag of paper called a *Surat Jalan,* you can't even enter Irian, let alone catch a bush plane to Wamena, where mountain (as opposed to swamp) fun begins. While astronomical sums might part the bush for a full-scale expedition, there are no guarantees of free and easy access.

In 1982, for example, a large American film crew was deported on arrival, despite approval from Jakarta, due to expanded efforts by the Indonesian military, or ABRI (Angkatan Bersenjata Republik Indonesia), to "pacify" various reactive mountain tribes that were angered into battle after learning they were no longer Hirn-Yals, or Sibilers, but "Indonesians."

We heard that rather than try to bribe every soldier we met, being polite, patient, and, most importantly, fluent in Bahasa Indonesian were the most effective tools for covering ground. On the other hand, journalists had been shot at and smugglers shot, but most of those people acted clumsily, or foolishly, around soldiers, and by the time muzzles barked, they knew why.

No matter what your Irian itinerary, you must enter through Jayapura, formerly Sukarnapura, Hollandia, and Kota Baru. It has degenerated shockingly since the Dutch were forced out in the early '60s. This once-idyllic tropical outpost is now a floundering coastal dump, where most civic amenities are defunct and decay is the rule. Migrants from other provinces funnel in, asserting a hereditary right to Melanesian West New Guinea, which stems from the marginal control exercised on its coasts by the Tidore Sultanate in the seventeenth century. Raw sewage flows in the streets, Manado prostitutes abound, buildings are either patched up with rusting tin or engulfed by jungle, and the military presence is strenuously pronounced.

With no reservations, we left this sweltering commode for Wamena, a scenic mountain village in the pastoral Baliem Valley, which has become increasingly accessible to tourists. Once-feared Ndani warriors, naked save for the penis gourd, or *koteka,* stare absently, ask for cigarettes, and gladly agree to porter loads for smokes or crumply red dime-value notes. Less than a generation ago, they sat atop forty-foot bamboo watchtowers, scoped raiding parties, and met them in battle with fifteen-foot lances.

Warfare once defined power structures, and payback raids ensured economic stability. Today, such activities are brutally suppressed by ABRI with bullets, burning of villages, and, reportedly, torture. Old ways persist in some areas, however, and the cordillera running through Irian Jaya features a staggering array of valleys, ravines, caves, sinkholes, and forests that far exceeds the administrative scope of the government.

In 1984, Stone-Age people still existed in certain parts of Irian Jaya, and there was a broad range of acculturation. Many had seen airplanes and electric goods and were quite accustomed to them. Others had seen these things but thought they were forms of magic. Still others had seen white men or Indonesians only occasionally and were unsure what or who they were. In a few torturously isolated places, it was still possible to make a first contact.

John and I were lucky in this regard because we applied rock climbing skills to jungle-shrouded limestone, giving us access to remote plateaus and sinkholes. These features, densely green from the air and too airy for foot patrols, were the best bet. We looked for hunter-gatherers who moved their villages frequently, and who were never seen unless they wanted to be. We reached some very primitive places and neither of us could say where, exactly, those places are located. We could guess within a map grid, but we felt it best to keep specifics on the low-down, especially with the occasional soldier we encountered.

For weeks, we traveled light and fast with hunters who meandered extravagantly through excruciating bush. We spent nights in many obscure places: caves, trees, and declivities where wide-eyed inhabitants occasionally regarded us as other-than-human. We had tremendous luck making friends with many people who weren't sure whether we were ancestors or ghosts. Maybe this ready friendship was because we opened the packs and gave things away: food, tobacco, medicine.

My best guess is that they picked up immediately what a charge we got from seeing them in the first place. They liked that. All vibe. We were big, we could hike as fast as they could, we chewed plenty betel nut, and we laughed a lot, bossed no one around, and acted no better than anyone else. No big deal—most of the time.

Trekkers wander the Baliem and some go to Illaga to climb the Dolomitic Puncak Jayawijaya, aka Carstensz Pyramid, which, at 18,023 feet, is the highest mountain in Oceana. But few engage in systematic deviation from the maze of central foot tracks linking the various large villages of the massif. Traveling with the locals on their own circuitous routes, doing things their way, will position a person for discoveries. Most big villages have an Indonesian administrator who'll direct you along, as well as pointedly dissuade you from visiting certain hot areas. What worked for us was to go, discreetly, right to the most forbidden area and start from there.

If you are willing to take the time to confront the hazards involved, you may win the confidence of someone who will slash routes over dozens of 10,000-foot ridges, share bugs with you for food, pick a tenuous descent down a limestone face, slide down lianas into a sinkhole, and point out a hidden village. Usually, there is a sort of password for each region. You shout it out. If it is shouted back, you're in. If not, you push on. We did both.

Grim things can happen, obviously, but it isn't likely, unless you chop down a papaya tree or kill a pig. The guys you're with will read the bush signs, maddeningly subtle ones that say, "Come on," or "Shove off." Our first "first contact," twenty-two days out of Wamena, was with a group of Uhundunis, who had heard about white people but had never seen them. After each male had pinched our skin to ensure we were there, we watched them hack up a giant cassowary, a flightless bird whose talons are quite capable of disemboweling a man.

In order to communicate with the various tribes, we had accumulated interpreters as we progressed. To greet an Uhunduni is not simple: Justinus, our Ndani (pronounced *Donny*) friend, could speak to Itthips, a Woogi. Itthips, a Yali, was conversant in Jinak, and so spoke a good deal more with Ekjinak (tribe unknown) than Justinus could ever dream of. Ekjinak however, spoke no Uhunduni, nor did Ombaipufugu, a Korowai tribesman who did indeed speak Jinak. Without the bilingual Ombaipufugu, we wouldn't have been able to express our good intentions to the band of Uhundunis.

As it went, they sacrificed the cassowary on our behalf and proved hospitable, though guarded, hosts. They didn't so much cook the stringy meat as draw it slowly over the fire. I was uncertain about this. Not so John, who hovered over Chief Kabatuwayaga and his minions as they apportioned servings.

A premature reach for the banana leaf on which his serving lay nearly cost him his hand, which was blocked by a swift stone axe stroke.

They screamed and jumped about, getting very clearly across that he should hold his horses. Scarcely deterred because he was starving, John squatted back and looked on with determination. Then Chief Kabatuwayaga summoned his sorcerer, Tebegepkwekwe.

Tebegepkwekwe smiled at John benignly, and spoke to Ombaipufugu. Our four interpreters put their heads together and Justinus explained in Indonesian that Tebegepkwekwe wished to reassure John that he knew John hadn't intended to reach for the food. Surely, he wouldn't have been so reckless. A *mogat,* or major bush spirit, had impelled his hand, and if it seized him again, Tebegepkwekwe volunteered sterner measures to ensure it would leave him alone, so long as John didn't mind being suspended upside down with thick blue smoke purifying his head.

Tebegepkwekwe declared the *mogat* had probably been following us for days, and asked if we'd bathed in the bend of any river. Well, we had, actually. He rested his case. Then Tebegepkwekwe withdrew from a snakeskin sheath an eight-inch cassowary quill with a tiny white egret feather lashed to the tip. Feverishly, he waved the quill over each serving. None of the Uhundunis could believe we didn't know what he was doing. Of course, it finally came through: lesser spirits, *sulumilewolebalabats* by name, must be carefully shooed away from the food before it would be safe to eat.

Instead of eating a second portion, as John did, I asked Justinus to find out where they got their axe heads, which were made of a deep blue stone. Eventually, it was explained that several times a year, they met Monis, with whom they traded women for blades. The usual price was three for one, and I haven't the heart to spell out which went for which.

Apparently, the axe heads were obtained swimming among fish in a secret stream, whose location was jealously guarded. We were fortunate that a Moni was then among them. The terrible scars he had on his knees and ankles, these from the adzes that had slipped his grasp, validated his claim about swimming axe heads.

John:

After adventuring nearly continuously for a decade, things that once seemed unimaginable were now barely noticed and rarely remembered. Then the Uhunduni sorcerer waved a plume over the grub and it was like I'd never been out of Los Angeles. I imagine few Uhundunis had strayed far from their private grotto, and our persons, and the things we had brought, seemed as novel to them as their arrow wounds, *kotekas,* and porcine financial structure seemed to us. We decided to hang out— for a while anyway—with the Uhundunis, if only to rekindle the old stoke that had started us adventuring in the first place. Two days later, the old stoke burst into flames.

We'd spent the afternoon fishing in a deep lagoon, caught a few, and watched curiously as an elder told fortunes by analyzing a carp's entrails. Around sunset, it started raining, so about twenty of us packed into a squat little cooking shack. Elbow to elbow, we fooled away several hours chewing betel nut and smoking cigarettes hand-rolled from green jungle tobacco strong enough to gag Vulcan.

As with most whose lives are hard and unforgiving, the Uhundunis were devotees of tomfoolery and wackiness, a fact proven when, every so often, a tribesman would let fly a shaft of betel nut spit into the wee fire. The tribesmen would all righteously curse and wail and make a great show of it all, smacking the perpetrator upside his bouffant as toxic fog welled off the coals.

The grumbling would slowly die off and several minutes would pass in silence as we huffed our rank cigarettes, the tension building as all eyes stared expectantly at the flames. Shortly, the native who, with sovereign dignity, had just dressed down his neighbor would himself spit into the fire, then laugh himself to smithereens as we all screamed and smacked him around. It was a riot.

I thought about some of the anthropologists I had read, and their artistic interpolations of tribal life. Then I thought about us slackers in that hut, squatting on our heels and spitting into the fire, and wondered what an expert might read into this.

D.B. rolled another smoke but couldn't get it stoked off the soggy coals. He rooted through his pockets, drew out a Bic lighter, and lit up. You would have thought he'd pulled a flying pig from his hat for the reaction of the tribesmen. In turn, they all snatched the magical lighter from one another and, marveling, made fire. The lighter eventually ended up in the hands of a senior elder, old as Aesop's granddad. A deft and passionate orator, he delivered a five-minute homily on the lighter and concluded by pitching it into the fire.

D.B. and I both dove and I fished out the melting article seconds before it blew us all over the Papuan border. We tried to explain by way of our various interpreters, but before the message rounded the horn, the senior elder snatched back the lighter, harangued D.B. and me for another few minutes, then pitched the lighter into the fire again, and again D.B. had to roast his hands digging it back out. The tribesmen perceived this action as usurping the elder's authority. Or they perceived some transgression on our behalf because the dwindling fire now burned in their eyes and they were all yelling at us.

We needed some diversion to diffuse this rhubarb, so I fished out my Walkman, pressed PLAY, and, in a moment I'll regret forever, slipped the little headphones over the ears of the senior elder. He froze. His features screwed up, his eyes went out on stilts, and he fell into an absolute paroxysm. D.B. quickly nabbed the headphones.

"Christ, man. They're going to think we're practicing black magic on the old fart."

In a flash, one tribesman wrenched the tape deck from D.B.'s hands, slipped on the phones, and began pawing and slapping himself as though army ants were marching all over him. Another donned the phones and broke into jungle scat. Twenty other warriors jumped about with uncontainable curiosity, anxious to get their turn. The senior elder continued ranting. The scene escalated. Eager tribesmen crowded around the listener as veterans all screamed about the experience to no one in particular.

Suddenly, a shriek, and half a dozen tribesmen dove for the exit, damn near bringing down the hut. The eyes of the current listener bulged like a rock cod, due in part to the volume having accidentally been cranked up to 10. The searing jazz fusion tape was chaos in musical form, and it totally mastered the listener. He droned and screamed, both hands clutching his adze, which he whirled wildly, splintering this, shattering that. Then he rose off his haunches, twirling his tool at speed, screaming, limbs flailing, his face seized with who knows what.

The remaining tribesmen didn't bother with the tiny horseshoe exit, now log-jammed with diving black bodies. They simply blasted headlong through the hut's thick grass siding. This decimated the shack's superstructure but did nothing to check the hatchet of the crazed Uhunduni.

Fiendish howling poured from the hut as firelight seeped through the exits, outlining two dozen jumpy tribesmen, whose glassy eyes alternated between the sacked hut and us. We squirmed, our four interpreters rattling in terror, their heads lowered and shaking, lips quivering.

"I think we go now . . . I think we go now," volleyed about in four languages.

Suddenly, with the crack of adze to wood, the shack shifted wildly left and collapsed, the crazed tribesmen groping free just before the reed roof burst into flames. The resulting bonfire played across a crowd of glowering Uhunduni faces, all staring at us.

"You know," D.B. said, "my dad hates jazz as well."

But the joke found no traction with our little group, especially with Justinus, who trembled horribly. The Uhundunis had been traditional enemies of his clan, and he stood on hatchet blades owing to our crimes: affronting a sorcerer by grabbing food prior to having the ghosts exorcised, spurning the senior elder by twice snatching the butane lighter from the flames, and now causing a native to lose his mind and destroy the communal cooking hut.

Several tribesmen prodded us into a hogan-like structure where, once again, we faced the senior elder, who fingered the bright yellow Walkman while his teary eyes burned holes through us. First, who was responsible for cramming all those people into the tape deck? Second, how did he know those imprisoned were not the souls of his dead relatives? Third—and this he voiced with gravity—who had tortured those souls enough to make their voices sound like music from hell (trumpets and electric guitars).

To be accused of torturing the souls of the big man's dead kin put us at a disadvantage. Aesop's granddad and our four interpreters carried on, always acquiescing to the thunderous elder. Once the old man's drift trickled down to Justinus, we had great difficulty understanding his pidgin Indonesian and pre-Cambrian English. Justinus wisely capitalized on this, telling the elder it would take all night to explain the question and decipher an answer.

The elder wouldn't give us all night, but he would wait until the moon was overhead. With a flick of his hand, he ordered us to our assigned hut to work on some answers. We quickly exited past thirty savage eyes. One hundred yards away lay our hut, luckily isolated.

"Think we can talk our way out of this one?" I asked D.B.

"Nope."

"You want to try?"

"Nope."

We rifled our packs, pitched non-essentials, and cinched the straps. Ekjinak snatched up a narrow stone and began sharpening his canines. Itthips hopped about in a cross-legged position, probably to avoid the arrow trees Uhunduni are said to be able to make spring from the ground.

"We wait much longer and that sorcerer's gonna be waving an egret feather over us," said D.B. This was more fun than fact but I got the point and shouldered my pack, listening to the arguing roaring from the elder's hut. Then we slunk into the darkness, at first slowly, till we hit the faint trail at full stride, reversing by daybreak what previously had taken three grueling days. And damn near the whole time, Justinus was saying, "I think we go now . . . I think we go now," till even he was laughing about it.

They almost certainly let us escape, probably hoped we would so they could be done with the whole problem. Roughing up outsiders usually meant a visit from the military—probably some bored Javanese flunkie with a uniform and a rusty .45, who regretted the long hike. I'd bet money that no soldier had ever been there, but if we found it, so could they. And who needed that?

And in all likelihood, we could have redressed our crimes with some form of payback, the value of which could not possibly have exceeded those things dumped from our packs. At worst, we would have had to sacrifice Justinus, which D.B. suggested in jest, though the native didn't laugh, anxious as he was to put further miles behind us.

We joked some more but this was a gut check for two rock climbers clueless about jungle decorum and who'd handsomely bungled a rare encounter with the roots of humanity, with the people we all had been long before Walkmans and Bic lighters.

D.B. and I went on to spend memorable days with so-called primitive people, always keeping the fiasco with the Uhundunis in mind. We never managed to keep out of trouble, but the trouble was our own and not caused by accidentally tanking a native's cosmology with a gadget from an incomprehensible future. Of course, polluting ancient cultures is a confounding subject, and we fool ourselves by thinking we, as outsiders, can control how it ever plays out. But we'd done nobody proud barging in on the Uhundunis, and we knew it.

We gained the Sungai Pit (*sungai* = river) and jogged its banks to its confluence with the great Sungai Baliem, which would lead us back to the government outpost of Tiom, completing this stretch in three days, taking in sights and sounds only the Ndanis could supply.

Through open terrain, we passed startled natives, saying "*Nyak*" to the men—lithe, greased, plumed, and empty-handed—and "*Laok*" to the women—slumped under cords of firewood, lips stained from betel nut, bark-thread bags harboring either infants or dozens of sweet potatoes swinging to and fro, a dire metronome of their tired dance.

Gardens extended from river line to lofty ridges miles above, each neatly parceled and slaved over by wizened mothers, hunched, mechanically chopping the cobalt soil with stone trowels. Below vine bridges, shiny-skinned youths swam cold, swift rapids for sport while lanky bystanders skipped wafer rocks from one bank to the other.

We worked along thin trails carved into 45-degree slopes—up, and down, and up—stopping to munch molten yams and steaming greens, cooling them down with crystal water from thin bamboo tubes offered by pert-breasted, ebony-skinned girls looking so fine in their reed dresses before their years of childbearing and raw labor.

Rain came and went with rainbows arching across rumbling skies. Back on Justinus' native turf, a gardener spotted him. A hoot followed, then another, and another, until the whole valley thundered with mirthful yelps, hundreds of voices volleying from the water to gardens in the sky. Later that afternoon, we stumbled into the bumfuck government outpost at Tiom, and the world came rushing back.

The administration at Tiom proved thin—one military man (armed), two policemen (unarmed), and a government official, his wife, and seven kids. We had no permission to visit Tiom, but this requirement was waived for a pack of clove cigarettes. We were led quickly to the home of the Indonesian official (who had never seen an American) and soon we were eating buckets of rice and fanning our mouths from the torrid *sambal* sauce. Two days later, a Mission Aviation Fellowship bush plane landed on the grass airstrip. Seventy bucks after that found us in Wamena, where we caught the daily flight back to Jayapura and its repugnant brand of "civilization."

It took some local currency and several dollars to get permission to cross the volatile Irian Jaya-Papua New Guinea border, but money always wins in Indonesia, and we soon found ourselves flying for Vanimo and phase two of our expedition.

PART TWO: BIKPELA HOL

Dwight:

The thorny business of entering Papua New Guinea (PNG) from Irian Jaya involves leaving a police state, where the colonial administration's main activity is contending with the daring guerrillas of the OFM freedom fighters, and crossing into an independent nation, booming and upbeat. PNG welcomes visitors, has ethnological and topographical diversity surpassing Irian's, and places few, if any, restrictions on those keen to explore the wilds. Many have done just that. The twentieth century had crept in nearly everywhere, largely due to aggressive missionary activity, but a few pockets remain so isolated that no outsider has yet climbed up or down into them.

The problem is to find out where these pockets lie.

While kicking around a bottle shop in Goaribari, we befriended a towering Papuan with a boar's tusk through his septum and a steel axe in his belt. Describing himself as an assistant to the sub-assistant district commissioner, he accommodated us with a wide-ranging elucidation of why the Enga Province was the most barbaric, least developed in Papua New Guinea. Following this conversation, we ran out into the street, hopped a Public Motor Vehicle (an aging bus), and hung on for two days, hell-bent for a census post called Birip in southwest Enga.

We spilled into the little bush village only to learn that the provincial government had been suspended due to its failure to control the constant tribal fighting. A disgusted Tasmanian anthropologist told us there were no "first contacts" left in Enga, everyone there having been chased from a battle scene by the police chopper at least once. True, there was a certain allure to the plan of photographing Enganese against a backdrop of arrow showers, but we hung on to our initial goal of seeking out unexplored areas.

We did take the time to insinuate ourselves into the Official Satellite Record Bureau of the Suspended Provincial Government. Alone in the office, we read through volumes of patrol reports, apprising ourselves of the current situation and devouring the exploits of forgotten explorers. The name T. Sorari came up again and again, this officer chronicling an unforgettable spate of hair-raising escapades. Assigned to routine village tours, Sorari repeatedly contrived farfetched pretenses for heading off his designated patrol routes into what was then (late 1960s) practically impenetrable bush. We daubed our brows, packed our mouths with nuclear white orbs of betel nut, and excitedly agreed that this guy was worth meeting.

Much later, we were unpleasantly rousted by one angry Mr. Clementine Warulugabibi, informed by his secretary, Ululiana, that "two pela in de" (two fellas in there) had been rifling government files for more than three hours. He ordered us out, stiffly, threatening to "rifle and shoot" us. John whirled and asked, "But, who is this man, Sorari?"

Several Enganese gathered at the shouting of that name.

"Sorari?" said Warulugabibi, amazed, ejecting his quid of betel. "How would two breadloaves like you know about . . ." He paused, sternly. "I take it that you have been looking at Sorari's reports. How would you like to sweat it out in the hot-box and eat *sago* for a month?"

"We ate *sago* and less for nine weeks in the Strickland Gorge," said John.

Here was the macho back-and-forth that sustained life in jungle outposts and established just how far, or not, a person might go in these parts. The wacky drama was enhanced by frontier Australian shadings, which most native administrators—and Mr. Clementine Warulugabibi was clearly one of them—had picked up at school Down Under.

I had a Biami *sago* pounder inlaid with fine slivers of human bone that I produced and invited Mr. Warulugabibi to examine, hoping this might win his regard. It did not.

"So you think you're a couple of real bush *kanakas*, do you?" Mr. Warulugabibi said, flipping the pounder in his hand. All along, the number of steel axes in the immediate vicinity continued swelling.

"Pretty much," said John. "Besides, those bare feet of yours look plenty soft to me. Where you been lately, *wantok?*"

"No place you'd stay alive very long," Mr. Warulugabibi howled, then suddenly cut himself off, pausing a moment to consider something.

I'd spent a night in the swamp jail at Daru the previous year and had no interest in sampling a highland facility, and I told Mr. Warulugabibi so in plain English. He laughed.

"A service to Papua New Guinea, yes, yes. I've changed my mind," said Mr. Warulugabibi. "You'll find Sorari in the Gulf Province, our Siberia. That is where the board that drafted his last reprimand sent him. A patrol post called Kantiba. Of course, to get in there, you may have to face Kukukuku along the way. You'll need more luck than I can wish you, but," he looked up at the blackening sky, "I am not going to wish you any luck!"

The door closed. We knew about the Kukukuku. Once a feared highland tribe, they were still treated cautiously by the government, and isolated groups of them were rumored to inhabit nearly inaccessible nether regions of the Gulf Province.

We'd just missed the bush plane that made weekly flights to Kantiba, so we snagged a ride with a road crew to the malarial coastal village of Moveave, and started marching, swallowing gooey *sago* and side-stepping *puk-puks* (crocodiles) along the route. We saw no one.

Kaintiba gained, we made for the village men's house, inside which were stacked two dozen cases of South Pacific Lager, the pride and joy of District Commissioner Tsigayaptwektago Sorari.

The fifty-year-old commissioner, barely five feet tall and reeking of drink, was initially surprised at our arrival. Then he welcomed us emphatically, inviting us in to inspect the hang, and in particular, its trove. The vestibule was guarded by a Sergeant Wanyagildlili, who brandished an M-1 rifle of Second World War vintage. While in no way inclined to refuse the ninth bottle offered him, purchased by us from his stock, the Australia-educated Sorari proved himself an astute, witty, and fascinating conversationalist.

He sized us up quickly and began talking about various patrols he had made in the surrounding bush. Although cutting a deceptive pose, grinning wildly, bottle in hand, he had noticed the rising enthusiasm in our voices the further out his narratives led us. After several minutes, we were grilling the man for a unique destination.

"First of all, boys, no guarantee. You may go a very long way hunting down what may be only rumor. But, I'll tell you, I think there's something to this one. For many years, stories have trickled back here about a cave called the Kukuwa Wantaim Kapa Ston, a very gigantic cave; very, very gigantic. Truly a *bikpela hol.*"

"*Ya-Wa! Nogat! Nogat!*" shouted Sergeant Wanyagikilili, who belted out a torrent of winding syllables that raised Sorari's brows, then thrust the rifle into Sorari's hands and bailed.

I dropped a kina coin into the skull-bank and withdrew another bottle for our friend as John asked what that was all about. Sorari laughed, pried the cap off with his teeth, handed John the rifle, and took a long pull.

"Well, that's the problem. The local people are afraid of the cave, the *bikpela hol* (big fella hole), and not one of my officers will patrol out to determine if it exists. Word is it lies ten days' walking from the nearest habitation, and that place, about seven days from here, is not a village, only a *liklik plies,* or small place. Most everyone there has died from malaria and sorcery." Sorari shrugged.

"Now, Sergeant Wanyagikilili said there is a ghost in the cave, and a snake. The snake is a thousand feet long, with six heads and five tails. He said he is going home because he and this talk about the cave cannot sleep in the same village. His home is about twelve miles from here. I am a civilized man, but I do not know what to think. I would love to go, but I can't get away. They'd catch me absent, and I'd be sacked. I'm chained to the radio nowadays, relaying messages from outstations to Moresby."

The next morning, Sorari drew up papers making us temporary Government Patrol Officers (which he had no authority to do) and provided us with a guide (which we had to pay a day rate) willing to lead us as far as Hapayatamanga, the last Kukukuku village before the *liklik plies*, but not one barefoot step further. In Hapayatamanga, we were to seek out Irtsj, who was under government employ and who would lead us on to the *liklik plies,* Imanakini.

"Irtsj is a sort of a good-for-nothing," said Sorari. "He won't want to lift a finger, and you have my permission to be as firm with him as you feel is necessary."

From Irnanakini, we would have to rely on an elusive individual called Ofafakoos, who lived with four wives and many children, some of whom, it was said, had recently been killed and eaten alive by unknown tribesmen during a payback raid.

We stomped out of Kaintiba on a muddy track that snaked wildly along the contours of a luxuriant ravine. Soon, we were trudging up and down wearisome inclines choked with skin-slashing vines and seething with primordial leeches. Walking on newly fallen *dipterocarps* trees was fine. Those recently fallen, still hard though shorn of bark, were slick nightmares indeed. Trees long fallen usually looked recently fallen, which meant we had as good a chance of enacting cartoon cartwheels as we had of plunging into rotted pungent trunks to our knees, and mingling with the translucent larvae of rhinoceros beetles, discreetly squirming in the friable wood.

Mazes of steep rivulets ran everywhere, and were soothing to climb or descend. Moss, orchids, lianas were everywhere, large flying things constantly startled us, and our evasive dives were monitored by intelligent lizards. We slogged up to Hapayatamanga after only five days.

The enthusiastic reception the machine-gun-speaking Kukukukus gave us was encouraging. That good-far-nothing Irtsj, a gangly beast with a walking stick on his shoulder, earnestly translated as much talk as we cared to hear, but he flatly refused to march on to Imanakini, a dangerous place, he said, where the people were controlled by vicious bush spirits who made them harm each other.

But Sorari had sent orders for him to lead us.

"Samting Nating!" (Don't mean nothing to him.)

But we had hiked 200 hours to get there.

He laughed.

We had trade goods with which to pay him.

He said he was sure we would leave Hapayatamanga without them, and laughed again. We didn't, and only after John had threatened his very hide did he agree to roust a couple of bolder village boys to lead us off.

Nippongo and Timbunke, perhaps fifteen and seventeen, had just returned from a forty-day cruise in the Western Province, apparently all the way to the Irian border, and maybe a little farther, since the ragged clothing they returned with bore labels reading *"Dibuat di Jawa"* (made in Java). They did backflips when their fathers cut them loose again so soon. They didn't want money, just *buai* (betel), tobacco, and any excuse to get right out into the bush again.

These guys were unbelievably industrious. They'd lead, chattering and laughing, boosting exotic fruits and sweet nuts we wouldn't have found in 100 years. They built rafts in minutes for the gear, then swam the rivers four or five times each. Of course, they'd also have to run half a mile up the bank to ride the river down, and all this only after they'd speared a string of *barramundi* and whipped up an impromptu barbecue. Rice? They'd rip the bark off a certain tree, fold it into a sturdy wooden trough, build a fire, and boil it up. The trough never caught fire.

We began to see there really wasn't any limit to how resourceful one could be. They were having so much fun maxing themselves, they got euphoric. The going was treacherous, no doubt about it, but Nippongo and Timbunke completely transformed our way of looking at the jungle.

During the last twenty minutes before the *liklik plies,* irregular snaps and rustlings convinced us we were being shadowed by men with stealthy gaits. John was tense. Anyone watching the execution strokes of his bush knife could plainly see it. We paused a moment together and strained our ears. Nothing. John made it clear he had little interest in establishing a listening post, and blasted off anxiety by screaming up the last incline like a cruise missile. I couldn't match the clip, so I brought up the rear wide-eyed.

Then we hit Imanakini—all two huts, four men, thirteen wives, and nineteen kids of it. The people were jittery, freaked by us, we thought, but soon realized it was something else when no one had relaxed a bit an hour after our arrival, and every kid old enough to run was kept prowling the perimeter.

Whoever the stalkers were, we never saw them. They might have been a group of raiding Kukukuku spooked off by the odd double-white sight. Fatigue eventually supplanted anxiety, however, and we took turns sacking out beneath a teetering lean-to on a bed of fronds, food for every fly, mosquito, ant mantis, beetle, scorpion, spider, and kissing bug in the whole territory. One old fellow, betel-eyes out in the Crab Nebula, sat up all night chanting protective spells and exorcizing his horrendous hacking cough. Another, his toothless mouth a blood-bin with red betel, was so paralyzed by fear he never suffered himself to move, save for the spasmodic demands of his frame.

The women, meanwhile, did all the work. John and I swapped watches, slapping bugs, eventually giving up, hosting all arthropods, desperate by turns to doze. As the night wore on, we convinced each other no one was out there, each of us fully aware that in the Asmat, headhunting raids usually took place right before dawn.

Then we both went to sleep. Worse, however, than falling victim to any skull hunt was putting up with the infuriating gibberish of a cock pecking tediously six feet behind our heads. Once home, I would buy a rooster for the sheer pleasure of shooting it.

We slipped out of Imanakini before dawn, following Nippongo along a twisting brawl of rotting trunks that gave passage through hectares of flora deep enough to swallow a hiker whole. Eventually, we arrived at the bush hut *(haus bilong bus)* of Ofafakoos, the bitter end of habitation. Queried about Kukukuku raiders, he acknowledged they did sweep through there from time to time, but usually harmed people only when fruit trees they considered their own had pieces missing.

Upon being offered six kina per day to lead on to the cave, purportedly eight days away, Ofafakoos grinned extravagantly, thick lips framing a mighty red orifice and two rows of black teeth. He said betel nut offerings tied to certain trees would assure the Kukukuku of our good intentions. He snatched up his bow, six types of arrows, his bush knife, and *bilum* bag of *buai,* chatted with each of his four wives in turn, glanced askance at John's hand ferreting out several stimulant bulbs for the white man's consumption, then took off through the dripping blade-like leaves like a track athlete.

The unrelenting flurry of machete slashes plied against the untracked jungle by this superb bushman filled us both with enthusiasm and distracted us from the starchy, spice-less, boiled gunk of forest tubers we'd gagged down at Imanakini.

Six days followed, during which we traveled in great arcs and weaves, typically climbing gooey walls dripping with flesh-blistering poisons, needle-like vines, and invidious foot-snaring creepers. We'd top out on choked razorbacks, rest the duration of a smoke, then improvise descents down walls where pitching off meant a 100-foot fall. The only outsiders who had ever been within fifty miles of these locales were the bold Aussie patrollers who'd slogged around from Kerema,

Kikorl, and Malalaua during the 1960s.

Ofafakoos would lead a knee- or waist-deep wade for an hour or so, only to step out with spooky acuity and start up another hideous wall. We were truly amazed by his sense of direction. Fathom it? *Nogat!* Wall, ridge, wall, river; over and over and over. Timbunke and Nippongo had met their jungle brother with the man Ofafakoos, and the jungle seemed made for their enjoyment.

Understandably, we both began to wonder if he did indeed know where we were going, other than into unfrequented reaches, laced with odoriferous bogs and impenetrable clumps of pink lotuses, fourteen inches across. Day six gave us a view of a forbidding limestone escarpment, a sign that rejoiced us, hinting as it did at cave territory.

Next day, after scaling a mud wall on which ice tools and crampons would have been sumptuous aids, I looked at where Ofafakoos had elected to descend. Two ten-foot-high Urama Taboo Goblins—human haired, hornbill-headed, pig-tusked, red spiral-beaded eyes frankly terrifying—were staked out as an explicit warning not to continue.

Ofafakoos spit out a nervous riptride of pidgin, then spun around convulsively at what proved to be only the loud, chugging *huff-huff* of a hornbill. Apparently, the people who made these effigies were all dead now, having succumbed to the raids of the Kukukuku. Nipongo didn't believe a word of this talk about furtive raids and cannibals. With an upward flick of his blade, Ofafakoos severed the fibrous weave linking the eerie totems and bolted through.

John:

We hurtled down, legs moving like pistons to avoid cartwheeling toward the glint of water 1,000 feet below. Slipping, bashing, and heel-digging through ripe mulch, we slid the final 100 feet on our backsides, sailed off a mud bank, and splashed into the creek. After plodding downstream for an hour, under triple canopy, Ofafakoos zagged left into dense thicket. Twenty paces and we ran into a limestone wall stretching overhead for 500 feet and melding into a tilted mesa carpeted with ferns.

Around us loomed the strangest topography imaginable, as though some giant had grabbed the craggy jungle and twisted it into a green jigsaw. The land flowed in and out of itself with such confusion that getting a bearing was futile since one's other points of reference appeared upside down or backwards. Huge trees grew askance from cliffs and buttresses teetering at impossible angles. Waterfalls looked to fall sideways, creeks ran the wrong way, and grass hung down from the ceilings of mottled grottos. We'd be lucky to cover a mile a day in such terrain, and likely would end up where we started.

We skirted right along the stone wall, finally gained a clearing, and collapsed. Ofafakoos pointed to a tiny black hole. The cave entrance? Hardly the Gothic job we'd expected. More like the entrance to a dog-house. Native eyes peered in for *sineks* (snakes) as we wiggled out from underneath our packs, glad that, for a while anyway, the trudging was over.

D.B. dug out some dried swine from his pack as Nippongo, who never tired, laid his bush knife into a sixty-foot tree, showering us with wedges of meaty wood. Timber! He ran to the high bough and plucked just the right leaf with which to roll his black tobacco.

"Nogat," said Timbunke: too green. Nippongo shrugged and layed into a 100-footer, felling it after a pumping ordeal.

"Nogat," said Ofafakoos: too dry. Running sweat, Nippongo smirked, then went for a mammoth hardwood, stopping only when I tossed him a pack of Djarums, ferried with much devotion from the Indonesian pirate port of Ujung Pandang. We all howled. Nippongo bounced a pebble off my head.

After twenty minutes, when our legs stopped cramping and we had some food on board, we couldn't wait any longer. D.B. and Ofafakoos dove into the little cave entrance as Nippongo stared, carping about the 1,000-foot *sinek*.

"Nogat!" echoed from the chasm. Let's go.

Nippongo and Timbunke queued up behind me. We wiggled in. The tight entrance immediately gave way to a stupendous tunnel, where many branches shot off into velvet nothingness. Thousands upon thousands of startled bats swarmed into wayward flight. And the huge ochre walls, stripes of red and orange, swirling dikes of Pan-Ethiopian ivory.

Down, down we went, through crawl-ways into vast dripping arenas where fang-like columns, seemingly half-melted, loomed enormously. The Papuans—trying to spook the other guy—acted forever on guard for the *bikpela sinek* or its traces.

Onward, we squirmed past clusters of golden stalagmites, crawled through odorous guano under a two-foot ceiling, treaded around oceans of vicious quick-mud. We long-jumped over clefts, hooking into warehouse-sized antechambers and dead-end vestibules. I paused at a clean pool, pointing wistfully. Confused, Nippongo trained his gaze, just long enough for me to boot him in.

We'd been inside six hours, wandered two, maybe three miles. Though the way meandered, sporting many aberrations, all now explored, we invariably returned to the principal shaft tunnel. The tunnel ahead looked uniform, extending beyond eyeshot, but in 200 feet it started shrinking, the corrugated floor angling down at a 10-degree rake. The bats were gone, likewise the guano, so our little passage was hospital clean.

Bubbling potholes appeared—little carbonated springs—with the overflow racing down the incline into pitch darkness. Water dripped from the seamless roof. It was probably pouring outside. We washed off layers of mud from sweat-soaked bodies. The beastly humidity made our breath thick as the smoke from the hand-rolled cigarettes Nipongo kept twisting for all of us. The cave was vast all right, but a squall could trigger an interior flood. Just how far were we willing to push this. Nobody wanted to be first to bail.

We'd marked strategic bends with chalk—about forty marks so far—

but now everything was too soaked to hold chalk marks, so we simply pushed on, the rays of our flashlights disappearing fifty feet beyond.

The shaft angled down sharply, maybe 15 degrees. Worse, the ceiling was now only eight feet above and the walls barely ten feet apart. After 100 yards, the water ran knee-deep, with wall fissures belching blades of clear juice into our dwindling passage. Nippongo stepped into a pothole and disappeared.

Ofafakoos shrieked, *"Bikpela sinek em i kai liklik Nippongo!"* The big ass snake just ate little Nippongo!

Nippongo popped back up, laughed, pointed down the tunnel, and said, *"Yumi* go *now."*

This kid Nippongo—we wanted to slap him silly half the time. But in fact, Nippongo was the gamest person I had ever seen and a source of confounding amusement guaranteed to lighten us up when legs grew weary and the leeches too thick to bear. The struggles we had in that cavern might someday fade to black, but never Nippongo.

Nippongo led down the dark corridor. We followed.

In fifty feet, we were chest-deep, and in twice that we were treading water, the walls six feet apart and the ceiling only three feet overhead. Just beyond, the ceiling curved down to the water line.

"Fudge," I said. "Dead end."

"Lot of ground we covered just to bail," D.B. said. "I say we try and swim for it."

"Swim for what?" I asked.

Nippongo and Ofafakoos must have caught the drift because they started spewing incomprehensible *tok ples* (place talk dialect), afros flush to the ceiling, mouths taking in water. A novel sight, all our bobbing heads, like apples in a barrel.

"I don't know about any swimming," I said. "We got no line and no idea where the thing heads, if it leads anywhere. Plus, once you're under, you can't see shit."

"I'll just have a look," said D.B., who drew a deep breath and slipped into the underwater tube.

D.B. re-emerged five seconds later, wild-eyed and rambling.

"Man, is that spooky! We'll have to work it out five feet at a time. Just draw your hand along the wall so you don't lose direction."

I guess that meant it was my turn. Nippongo shouted that the tube was the gullet of the thousand-foot *sinek,* then laughed.

Glug, glug, and into obsidian. Free-floating in liquid space. When my stomach turned to stone, I reversed.

"I don't know about this one!"

But in half an hour, we'd ventured out a dozen times each. The shaft ran straight ahead—simple to reverse so long as we turned around with enough air. But we weren't really getting anywhere. We needed another approach. *Yes, forget feeling the wall*, I thought. *Put in a few big strokes and see where it puts you.*

"Okay," I said. "I'm going out ten seconds, taking two big strokes, and coming back."

One stroke out, gliding directionless through this ink, and I freaked, clawed for the wall, then groped back to the fellows.

"That's it. That's my threshold. I think I'm finished here."

Ten minutes later, we'd both gone in twice more, taking three strokes each. Still, we were only staying under about thirty seconds, max. I decided to push it a little more.

"All right. I'm going for four strokes."

I dove back under. Ten seconds, one stroke, two strokes, three, gliding blindly, untethered in space. My arms dovetailed forward and I pulled hard for this last thrust, bringing my arms to my sides, knifing farther. Then—*Bonk!* A stalagmite.

My hands wrapped my ringing head, and for several seconds, I drifted on the shadow line between consciousness and coma.

I grasped for the stalagmite, which was nowhere, then for the wall, which I found. Except I didn't know which way was up, or which way was back. With seconds of air left, I stroked out right. My left hand felt odd, different, and my head raised instinctively into an air pocket, black and soundless. I broke down, gasping, hyperventilating, rubbing my dazed head.

Sweet Jesus, I've done it now.

I'd known some lonely places in thirty-two years, but that air pocket—dark as the Devil's heart—made the North Pole feel like Trafalgar Square.

Then a thought. *Find the stalagmite!* That was my best hope, believing as I did that the air pocket was past the stalagmite. Finding it would at least point me in the right direction. A sound plan, but even brief exits from the pocket were terrifying. Again and again I ventured out, only to return to the pocket and hyperventilate in the darkness till I finally calmed a notch.

Finally, I found the stalagmite, fifteen feet away. Then back to the pocket. After a minute of big breaths, I glided out, slithered past the stalagmite, hand dragging the wall—but flashed on the fact that I might still be going in the wrong direction, panicked, and started stroking for all I was worth.

My arms shot out and heaved back, then out again; but with this last pull, I hit something—something moving. It's alive! The *sinek!* Some massive freshwater eel! I reflexively grabbed the snake—which turned out to be D.B.'s leg. I was seconds away from sucking in water when he hauled me to the thick air.

The oxygen and headlamps were heaven attained, but my nerves were shot, and not until grappling to a dry porch and gasping for minutes could I start talking.

Nippongo thumbed a thin trickle of blood from my forehead, then rolled me a smoke, which I zipped in about four draws. D.B. reasoned that since the air pocket was so close to the stalagmite, he'd go have a look. I was too whipped to argue. The few minutes waiting seemed like an hour, and my mind cooked up all kinds of crazy things. Then D.B. burst back, his face awestruck.

''It's there! It's true! No myth!'' he shouted.

Ofafakoos' face was a study, thinking D.B. found the *sinek.*

"The shaft ends just a few seconds past the air pocket—inside the *bikpela hol!* There's a river the size of the Mamberambo flowing through the bottom of it. You gotta check it out!"

"Just give me a minute."

I had no idea what I was saying, and wouldn't till I was fixing to swim back into the black tunnel.

Without hesitation, D.B. swam back under. Ofafakoos, Nippongo, and Timbunke set off immediately to find their way out, for the water level was rising by the second. I wasn't entirely sure I'd talked myself into going back under. But now I was alone, which is so spooky in such a place that you're urged to action, however crazy.

Finally, my mind went blank and I dove back into the inky tunnel, too frightened to stop at the pocket, finally popping up with a swift revivifying lunge to the flash of D.B.'s Nikon, feeling like I'd just been born.

We were clearly inside something very large, yet the cave was full of diffused natural light. Where was the light coming from, I wondered out loud as we scrambled from the pool. A little easy climbing over mossy blocks led us onto solid ground.

The *Bikpela Hol.* That first open vista defied words. This is how the Spanish conquistadors must have felt when first gazing into the Grand Canyon, or when ancient Miwok Indians first trekked into Yosemite Valley and gaped up at El Capitan. A million years means nothing to these places.

It took many looks, this way and that, to fathom the size, later calculated at eleven million cubic feet. We'd been treated to the rarest find—a natural wonder of the first magnitude.

Several years later, once the word got out, a New Zealand team battled to the cave and conducted a proper survey. The following year, D.B. and I were credited with "discovering and exploring the world's largest river cave." Nippongo, Ofafakoos, and Timbunke were not mentioned. Not that they would care. For D.B. and me, the real payoff was that first view.

The river, some 150 feet across, entered through a 400-foot arch, flowed through a half mile of open cave, and then exited through a 200-foot arch. Between the giant arches, the versicolored ceiling soared to an apex of 800 feet above the water. A 100-foot maw slashed the roof at center-point, rife with flying foxes maintaining a clockwise circuit between the dark ends of the massive gash.

The swim had gained us a balcony of sorts, 300 hundred yards long and extending at a gentle angle 100 yards ahead, ending sharply at a suicidal plunge straight into the river, slow and wide, hundreds of feet below. Light flooded through the colossal entrance and exit, taking us back to the Stone Age. Never before or since have I felt the force of eons like I did inside the *Bik Pela Hol.*

At the balcony's far right margin, D.B. discovered a tree-lined tunnel exiting to the original limestone buttress, a quarter mile downhill from our entry point: we could walk in and out of the main chamber easy as climbing a flight of stairs.

"Too bad," I said. "Everyone should have the pleasure of swimming in."

After an hour's gawking (and trundling boulders into the river), D.B. and I exited into a downpour for the forty-five-minute trek back to the entrance. After two nervous hours, Nippongo, Timbunke, and Ofafakoos emerged, battered, with horror stories of their own.

Constant rain had made for treacherous flooding, and twice they'd nearly been whisked into oblivion by rising currents. By the time they battled back to the light, only Timbunke's headlamp was still working. I quickly dressed wounds more painful than serious, then we charged for a bivouac in the main chamber, vast and dry. En route, we marveled over how the terrain could mask our perception of both the cave and its river.

The river, so distinct a quarter mile upstream, flowed through a twisted maze of upheaved crags and ledges overgrown with trees and shrubs so thick that even the huge cave entrance was noticeable only if you were looking straight at it.

Later, stretched out on pads in the titanic chamber, I told Nippongo if he didn't rustle up some food, he'd soon find himself diving into the river several hundred feet below. He said if I could find so much as a seedpod, he'd give me his widowed sister and her four daughters.

The starved march back to Hapayatamanga thrashed us into hallucinations and slurred speech. The kids could find food anywhere, but not in the pounding rain, which never let off from the moment we left the cave. The final hours were hateful uphill battles, our only aid the knowledge that we'd stashed four tins of Torres Strait mackerel in the hut of a Hapayatamanga sorcerer. One tin lay conspicuously open: Nippongo's sister told us that some of the men had been dipping their arrow tips into the uneaten fish. The other three tins went down faster than we could wince.

The Gulf Province averages twenty-plus feet of rain a year, and I swear we got half that in the following days. Bivouacs were sleepless disasters and the food was long gone. When we finally plowed into Kaintiba, we literally dropped, not rising for 24 hours. We later snagged a lift on a Pilatus Porter from a Kiwi mate bound for Lae, a coastal haven, and spent the next three days at a ritzy expat yacht club, eating and drinking and drinking and eating, yet strangely missing trundling footpaths and blue-shadowed caverns, the jade plait of the jungle so far overhead, and all that mud below.

IMPROBABLE MARKSMAN

None of the native Ibans could remember a longer drought. The air felt like fire in our mouths, and all living things, withered into a state of great tension, cried out for relief. Twice we were startled by horrific cracking sounds and ran for cover as centuries-old hardwood trees exploded, fragments tearing through the canopy like falling skyscrapers. Rather than track the overgrown jungle trails, we followed the streambed, normally gushing and now cinder-dry, skating over river stones submerged for a thousand years.

We were miles into the Sarawak jungle, Malaysian Borneo, five people, led by Bilap (who resembled Sitting Bull in the old daguerreotype prints), a native Iban chief I put at about fifty, though he could easily have been sixty or more. His torso was a tattooed cavalcade of deer and snakes and impossible animals. He'd never worn shoes and his feet were wide as fronds and so calloused he could jog over river scree like it was beach sand.

Two Iban hunters—mid-twenties, like me—carried our food in huge rattan packs. Like most Ibans, they continually chewed mouthfuls of betel nut, and every so often let fly salvos of spit that stained the river stones bright red. And Hassam, a young Malaysian soldier assigned to us because the government suspected all foreigners, especially those partnered with Ibans.

Since the early British colonial days, the Ibans had defied assimilation. During the 1950s, a good way for an Iban to turn up in a gully with bullet in his head was to sound off to officials. But this was decades later and Hassam had the starry-eyed enthusiasm of a scout on his first campout. Always tripping over creepers and stumbling through streams, he somehow managed to shadow Bilap and keep his ancient single-shot Browning held across his chest.

I rounded out our five-man crew. The aim was to film a documentary on the nomadic Punan Dayaks, the renowned kings of the jungle and source of tales so exaggerated that the TV folks wanted proof that the Punans actually existed before committing six figures to a film project. I had three weeks and $1,500 to complete my scout.

We weren't an hour into the tall trees when Hassam started in with his stumbling, slowing our group to a crawl. Rather than trying to force him along, Bilap began schooling Hassam on just how to swing the machete, pointing out dire insects and critical plants. The young Ibans, addled by the nut, spat their mouthfuls and trudged on. I didn't have much of a pack and kept pace okay.

We never saw sky through the tangled green canopy, but rain was so long overdue, we expected and prayed for it. When rain still hadn't come by the fourth day, we rose early and fell in behind Bilap, who seemed to float along the intricate riverbank, with Hassam staggering an arm's length behind, but moving faster than before.

The leeches were bad, drilling every inch of exposed flesh, which was most of us, stripped down as we were in the heat. Even Hassam was hiking in shorts, swatting all bloodsuckers.

The rain held out and I noticed everyone but Hassam glancing at the surrounding terrain, where black crags soared from stark lime bush. The return of the monsoon worried us, for the river could flood in minutes, forcing us into the spiked, squelchy hedgerow that climbed from the flat river passage.

In late afternoon, we camped on a sandbar that hooked with the river's sharp bight. It took the young Ibans and me thirty minutes to clear the scrub and limbs washed there during high water. Meanwhile, Bilap and Hassam, laughing and clowning, collected twigs for a fire in the lee of an ironwood trunk that we couldn't budge.

We spent an hour damming the river. But no fish ever came. The next morning, it still hadn't rained, so we broke camp at sunrise, eager to cover some dry miles and close the distance between us and the Punans. We could thrash out a roundabout route through the jungle, or follow the riverbed through a steep ravine. Bilap chose the riverbed. We'd have to move fast, for the march through the ravine would take six hours, and if it started to rain hard and fast, we might get flooded out. Once committed, there was no escaping the ravine into the jungle— just too steep. Bilap held up a hand vertically and nodded, as if to say, "This steep." Hassam had found his jungle legs, but if things got tight, I doubted he could put on much speed.

We entered the ravine after an hour. Overgrown walls rose sheer from the river. I couldn't throw a rock across the streambed, so I figured it would take even a deluge several hours to fill the canyon. But it could and often did, judging by all the splintered logs teetering atop twenty-foot river boulders. I flashed on another time and another canyon, when the sky cut loose and a wall of muddy water and uprooted trees tore past, taking our rafts and a New Zealand boatman along with it.

The first few miles passed quickly. On both sides, dripping red orchids spangled the vertical walls. Furry corkscrew vines spiraled down, looping and crossing the shallow river, then sweeping back up the opposite bank. Dawn vapors crept up the cliffs to form a steamy nimbus, broken in spots to expose the canopy's green weave far overhead. The air below was gummy, still, and furnace-hot, the river so low it barely made a sound. We stopped.

Bilap gave a short speech, his outstretched arm waving to one canyon wall, then the other. He emphasized words I could not understand. Hassam nodded quickly, sweat pouring down his face. He twice-checked the safety on his rifle, making sure it was off. Bilap resumed his march, his dark eyes traveling between the canyon walls, Hassam's eyes burning holes through his back.

Bilap barked and Hassam closed the distance between them to a rifle's length. On both sides, the young Ibans flanked out.

Bilap stopped and raised his hand. The young Ibans froze, but Hassam jumped, and for the first time, moved the rifle away from his chest. His knees flexed. His face twisted with fear and excitement.

Ever since he'd set boot into the jungle, Hassam had shadowed Bilap with his silly rifle, and every couple miles, Bilap would stop, turn around, and instruct Hassam about something. Maybe chiding him about being so slow. Or fanning his fear about the Punans, who scare everyone and who some say ran Michael Rockefeller through with a spear, lopped off his head, then ate him. (If this happened at all, it was by Asmat tribesmen, across the border in Papua.) More likely, Bilap was warning about sudden rain, so long overdue.

Whatever his point, Bilap meant it, repeating words till Hassam nodded quickly and made some small adjustment with the way he wielded his rifle or the distance he kept behind the Iban. Then Bilap lighted off again and Hassan stumbled behind just as before. Whatever this all meant was lost on me and was Hassam and Bilap's business. Curious as all of this was, I only wanted to get clear of the canyon.

The heat and humidity hung on us like a curse. I tramped on, staring at Hassam. A thin drizzle began bleeding through the canopy.

Bilap started hiking fast. In another hour, the vapors had burned off and shafts of blistering sunlight gleamed through holes in the canopy, intermittent with sheets of scalding rain.

Bilap's attention returned to the cliffsides, which slowly eased in angle. I panned up the left wall—it looked like the same verdant brawl from water line to sky. Meanwhile, Bilap threaded silently from shadow to shadow. Off to each side, the young Ibans did the same.

When Hassam stumbled, Bilap shot him a glance and Hassam nodded bashfully. His rifle shook in his hands. The river, in spots, covered most of the riverbed.

We moved through a cut of sunlight. Bilap treaded lightly along a spit of gravel, three creeping shadows playing across the moving water to our left. I froze. *Punans! Fuck!* But the shadows were our own. It took several panicked gasps to remember why we were there in the first place: to find the goddamn Punans. The tension kept rising with the river.

Bilap's gaze lingered high upon the right-hand wall. With a last step so slow it took some balance to perform, his hand came up; with his eyes still riveted up and right, he froze. Hassam froze. Spread out on both sides, the young Ibans froze. I froze, and could feel my heartbeat in my hands.

Bilap wheeled around. Hassam extended the rifle at arm's length, one hand clasping the middle of the barrel, the other, the butt of the stock. In one motion, Bilap snatched the rifle, shouldered it, turned, and no sooner had the barrel settled on a spot high on the right-hand wall than a flash leaped from the muzzle as the report banged off the canyon walls, volleying up and out through holes in the thinning canopy. A dark object rolled down the wall, tumbling with greater speed till it plunged over a last, vegetated ceiling and splashed into a pool fifty feet away.

The Ibans were instantly on it, machetes drawn. But when I raced over, I saw it didn't matter because Bilap was a deadeye: a gaping hole right through the deer's head. A brain shot.

I'd read about Daniel Boon shooting eagles from the sky with a flintlock, but Boon had nothing on Bilap, who'd nailed that buck from 100 yards, easy. With the river rising fast, the Iban hunters didn't pause to dress out the animal. The biggest one just threw it over his shoulder fireman's-carry style and marched on.

I turned toward Bilap, but he had already wandered off downstream, his eyes probing high on the left wall. Hassam fumbled to thumb a new shell into the chamber, looking up to see how far ahead Bilap had gone. Gun loaded, safety off, Hassam stumbled after and took up his position, walking quietly and in step behind Bilap, the chief.

In fifteen minutes, the storm shot through the canopy like a blast from a fire hose, and we all began charging downstream, half jogging, half fording through the rising current. When the ravine opened up an hour later, we'd been bodysurfing a waist-deep torrent for half an hour and were barked and bashed all over. Nothing dangerous, since the river was so wide, but the young Ibans had lost the deer and Hassam had lost his old Browning. And we never did find the Punans.

Fifteen years later, while reading a magazine on a Singapore Airline flight to Kuala Lumpur, I thumbed across an article about the history of Sarawak during the Second World War.

In 1942, the article ran, the Japanese secured the island, the fifth largest on earth. A year later, owing to their harsh treatment of tribes-people, the Japanese started losing significant numbers to native Iban sharpshooters. The situation confounded the Asian invaders, who were unaware that shortly after their invasion, Australian paratroopers had penetrated the jungled interior, hooked up with various nomadic tribes, and trained a handful of young males as snipers. By war's end, the article stated, many of these native riflemen had become "remarkable, if improbable, marksmen."

ADIOS, CUEVA HUMBOLDT

Squawking guacharo birds darted round us like swarming locusts, whizzing past our heads and careening off stalactites in a high-vaulted cave corridor large enough to park the Goodyear Blimp. We continued ducking, hunched under packs, shuffling down the tourist path we'd picked up after entering the cave through a limestone arch, a mile behind us.

Just ahead, the passage pinched down to a keyhole. We shimmied through and into a freezing thigh-deep stream that quickly rose to eye level where the ceiling dropped down to a little inverted V-slot known as "the Channel."

Delgado, a local Caripito caver and guide we'd hired to lead us to the climbing, waded in to mid-thigh and started gasping as D.B. trained his headlamp down the Channel. That was the way, straight down the slot—cramped, but there appeared just enough space to move through without drowning. A quick pant, and in went Delgado, whose teeth started clacking once his chest went underwater. He pushed on, grinding his pate against the top of the slot to keep his nose above water, his limbs churning for minutes. Then, "*Es facil, amigos.*" It was easy.

I drew a breath and waded in to my chin. The V-slot looked a mile long and the moment I crammed my head up against the little roof with the waterline right at my nose, I buckled from the bolt-like impulse to turn and clear the hell out. But I could hardly beg off the Channel after conning D.B. to come all the way to Venezuela to go climbing in this very cave.

The Cueva Humboldt, known locally as Cueva de Guacharo, tucked far into Venezuela's jungled interior, is the most celebrated cavern in South America. The name comes from the itinerant German naturalist, Alexander von Humboldt, who first explored the area in 1799. The Baron conducted a comprehensive study of the rare guacharos, as well as some basic ethnology on the local Indians. Two hundred years ago, Humboldt suggested, the horrible warbling of the guacharos (one who cries and laments) likely discouraged the superstitious Indians from exploring the cave. (D.B. figured it was their dive-bombing, not the bird's sad chorus, that kept the Indians out.)

Considering the remote location, it amazed us that a German naturalist had made his way to Caripe in 1799. What kind of man would leave his home two centuries ago and travel thousands of miles on a leaky ship to go caving, study a bird, bone up on the local natives, and become a celebrated naturalist by his own resources? The impersonal, soporific style found in Humboldt's memoirs paints a third-person portrait of a fantastic world, though with the explorer himself, his fears, passions, and dreams, absent from the canvas.

There was always a chance that under his cummerbund, Humboldt was someone much like ourselves, rafting though life in the wild places, doing his science. Except me and D.B. were pretty lax on the equations, didn't know ethnology from square dancing, and, standing buck-naked except for board shorts and approach shoes, probably looked more indigenous than Teutonic.

Just outside the cave entrance stood a bigger-than-life statue of the Baron, with his noble face, flowing beard, and aquiline nose. The work drew heavily from classic statuary depicting Neptune. The smart money said it *was* Neptune, a copy of a piece chiseled out in 1744 by German sculptor Johan Christoph Petzold, recently knocked off in plaster by Chinese artisans, with a period appliqué brushed on in Caracas. According to the guy running the little food counter near the cave entrance, the replica was christened and renamed there in Caripe during a historical gala several years before. True or not, the trident was an odd appliance in mountainous jungle. But the Baron opened the door.

In the early 1900s, a century after Humboldt's first visit, a second German group survived the first keyhole crawl, but got held up at a curtain of stalactites. Returning, they punched through with a sledge-hammer. The chilling waters rose with each step, and oral tradition says the Germans withdrew, just short of the Channel when, according to explorer Bernhard Graff, their testicles froze "like gemstones of the purest water."

Fifty years later, during a photo-documented exploration led by Remus Octavio Philippi, an Italian team slipped through the Channel to venture another ten miles, encountering a maze of passages and fabulous chambers. These were all awarded Italian names, which were rendered into Spanish in 1964, when a team from *Sociedad Espeleo-logicolia de Caracas* explored, surveyed, mapped, spray-painted, and fumbled their way to cave's end, fifteen miles into the mountain.

Aside from the Arctic waters, the Channel, and a few rock steps, it was a safe and sane trek to the Virgin Room, where progress was checked by smooth, featureless limestone, and where a small brass idol of Mary now cradles baby Jesus in a blanket. For each of the four or five (average) annual expeditions, it had become the custom to buff up Jesus' face, giving it a penetrating sheen under a headlamp. Recent parties had produced a cartographic map, which park superintendent Leopoldo de la Rubia had shown me on my first visit.

An ardent caver himself, Leopoldo fetched a stack of maps, then a photo of a gigantic *golina,* a Slavic word for "circular valley." The photo showed a huge uniform crater, ringed by jungle, as though a posthole plug had been pulled from the escarpment. Leopoldo pushed several maps together on the cement floor, gushing out Spanish while pointing to various contour intervals, erosion features, and alluvial fans on the overlapping charts.

D.B. and I were not master navigators, but we knew our way around topo maps and we couldn't get the numbers to jibe with the features in quite the fashion Leopoldo kept insisting. Rather than making things clear, Leopoldo raised his voice, swearing that the *golina* lay directly above the Italian Room, half a mile short of the cave's end. The Italian Room is a wonder of the world, he said, and is roofed by a great maw, so big that no light can reach the zenith. Nevertheless, he felt that a crafty climbing team might link the cave with the *golina*—somewhat like scaling the interior of an open hourglass, working through the breach, then popping out into the glorious jungle crater—the kind of thing that cavers and fools dream about. But why would Leopoldo tell as much, unless he, too, expected to go?

He did. But when we returned nine months later, he was stuck at a symposium in Maturin. There was nothing else for us to do but to follow Delgado through that freezing channel.

It was no great challenge, that Channel, if you didn't mind raking your head and face across the limestone while fearing the ice water might stop your heart. We stayed where the air was, and it was tight. We made four laps apiece to drag all our gear through, one pack at a time. On the last haul, our 600-foot static line snagged at mid-channel, so we took turns going underwater to feel for the hitch, later to lurch up and bang our heads on the rock. We almost left it.

I finally stopped shivering after stooping and crabbing beneath a low ceiling for most of a mile, just as we gained the first rock step, where a greasy rope hung over a vertical tongue of flowstone. Delgado hand-walked up without a word. D.B. followed, muddy shoes scrabbling under his sixty-pound load, variously scattered between soaking ropes, racks of pitons, and two unwieldy packs. I followed, wrestling the 600-foot rope. We pressed on into darkness.

Considering the cave's great size and the countless aberrations, the going was pleasantly direct, mostly scrambling, a little groveling over and around hazards, with limited crawling through thick mud, a murderous job with our loads. Colossal chambers bore square, milky boulders and telephone-pole stalagmites. Diaphanous crystals studded the walls, twinkling like rhinestones. Only a troop of spotlights could reveal the cave's secrets. Struggling with loads in 100-percent humidity was a cruel contrast to the glacial waters in the Channel. But what did we really know about caving? We were climbers.

I had puttered around a couple of easy caves in the California Sierras and D.B. and I'd nearly died in a Papuan cavern. Otherwise, we had no caving experience at all, and after about five hours of slogging, I started getting spooked. *It's just the darkness and misery of these loads,* I thought.

When we finally arrived at the Italian Room, seven hours in, we were mud-covered and bushed. A glance at the labyrinthine ceiling showed us that the climb looked anything but the direct affair that Leopoldo de la Rubia had promised. We'd expected as much, though perhaps not this much, and had brought along a Yosemite-style big wall kit.

"This thing looks pretty grim," D.B. said, peering up into the blackness.

We dumped our loads and started scanning the huge roof with our headlamps. We had a big police-style torch that cast a beam like a tugboat light, but the void seemed to swallow it whole. D.B. said he felt like Tycho Brahe, the ancient astronomer who had worked mostly with the naked eye and who was often entirely wrong. The ceiling was a confusion of twisting tunnels, spiraling arêtes, gaping shafts—like a dome of wormwood—and we didn't have a clue where to start.

"This thing looks totally horrendous," said D.B.

We went with a ramp-and-gully system that appeared to gain the upper wall most straightforwardly. Without a couple 4-K lights nicked from a film set, any choice was literally a shot in the dark. As I rooted through the climbing gear, Delgado wished us luck, then left, promising to return in two days. Delgado hadn't said ten words the whole day, so we had little idea about his reliability.

"Think we can find our way out of here?" I asked D.B.

"Guess we'll find out," he said. We didn't expect to see Delgado again.

D.B. climbed up to what we had hoped was a generous ledge below the first ramp, but it turned out to be a "big-ass sump," the bottom bristling with stalactites. Hand-traversing to the ramp would require skirting the sump, and finding some sound protection so D.B. wouldn't get shish-kabobbed on the stalagmites if he ripped off. He banged in several poor pitons, clipped the rope through, then shuffled across the ramp on sloping holds, fighting the rope drag.

The lead rope, soaked from the Channel, easily weighed forty pounds, and the 600-foot trail rope handled like a ship's cable. We were mud-covered, steamed like smudge pots at the first exertion. Things were getting real in a hurry.

"Watch me close!"

D.B. scraped the mud off his shoes and headed up, splaying his legs on the offset walls, blasting in pitons and grunting. After eighty feet, D.B., now just a faint glow, said he needed some "testosterone poisoning" to give him a needed boost.

I rooted out an old ZZ Top tape and plugged it into the box. Owing to the cave's fantastic acoustics, my two-bit Indonesian tape deck roared. The rope snaked out smooth and steady till D.B. yelled down that he'd reached an alcove.

As I ascended the fixed line, the pitons came out all too easily.

We walked thirty feet from the alcove to where the gully resumed, quickly giving way to a rubbly slot leading to a bulging, geological wonder—huge ivory horns, horizontal purple spears, teetering smoked crystals, and countless stone roots twisting in bizarre, electrified patterns. My pitons sucked, but tying off an organ-pipe crystal offered no help. Too fragile. The holds were crumbly or detached, and when treading them grew too nervy, I burrowed deep into the vertical gully.

Just above, a huge chockstone blocked passage. A mystery held it in place, and a whisper might dislodge it. I hadn't set a decent piton in 100 feet and clawing over that chockstone wasn't an option: too big and too loose. So I started shimmying up behind it, holding my breath. I stretched up for a big hold, then started yanking my hips through the wee space between the chockstone and the main wall, when the chockstone suddenly pivoted, then popped, roaring down the gully. D.B. dove for the alcove as the glittering stone exploded into fifty ingots.

"Nice shot!" D.B. yelled.

There was a big powder mark close to where he'd been standing.

Six hours and 300 feet later, I tiptoed left to start free climbing up a loose flake. After twenty feet without protection, the wobbles came on and I just managed a piton before my muddy boots blew off the holds and I wrenched down onto the peg. From there, I found continuously grim artificial climbing, gingerly clipping my three-step stirrups into a creaking string of pitons. I ran out of gear after 100 feet, whaled in the last pins—which were piss poor—then set up a hanging belay.

D.B. came up, re-racked, and led off. By the sound of the pitons and his constant cursing, the rock quality was not improving. Two hours and three tapes went by, as the *thunk-thunk* of pitiful pitons bandied about the pitch blackness.

"Hey, there's a cave up here!"

"We're in a cave."

"Okay, a hole in the wall, a tunnel, a cleft, whatever. How much rope left?"

"Twenty feet."

"I'll just make it."

I turned the tape deck back up and smiled at the notion of escaping these hanging stances, if only momentarily. After another few songs, I got word to ascend the rope nice and easy since the only anchor was "a sling looped around a schist gargoyle."

I tested the rope and started up. Some of the pitons had already fallen out, and the bulk of the others didn't require a hammer to remove.

We hoped to find the bottom of the *golina* soon, or some escape. We'd better. My conservative estimate had us about 500 feet off the cave floor. The rock had devolved into flaky trash, and the prospect of more artificial climbing was hateful. Fifty feet shy of the curious anchor, I started yelling for details, got none, and arrived at the subway tunnel with D.B. absent.

That bit about a schist gargoyle was a gag. The rope was secured to a cluster of solid chockstones. I dumped the gear and made my way down the flat tunnel, banking that it led to the *golina*. D.B. appeared just as the subway opened and turned snow-white with reflected light. From nervous release, or amazement, we both started laughing.

What could ever match this passage, decked in thick, alabaster crystal? For all of creation, this little patch of space and rock had been here in dark silence, and with a flick of a headlamp, a fantastic world was struck to life. What, I wondered, did our gratitude mean to the mineral world? What is beauty—or anything—if it's never perceived?

We crawled, shimmied, and walked another thirty minutes. A porthole-sized slot veered off our ivory tube, but we kept on, hoping for something direct, and more importantly, one beam of light from overhead that would mark the bottom of the *golina*. Soon the subway angled down abruptly into what our headlamps claimed was another big chamber. We'd need a rope to descend, which entailed a long round trip to the gear and back.

When we'd returned to the edge, I peered over the lip of the subway, gazing straight down into the void and the climbing we had done.

Over the last decade, D.B. and I had banged our way up hundreds of rock walls, though never inside a cave. Exciting, for sure, but we were in no hurry to resume that blind, hideous aid climbing. We hustled back to the new chamber, set an anchor, and roped down—not into another gorgeous room as we'd hoped, but straight into a small mud pit. The walls were featureless, the air dank and heavy.

Then D.B. spotted a little tunnel at the mud line. Our headlamps revealed that it opened up to a bottomless hole or perhaps another crystalline ballroom—we couldn't tell. I crawled in feet first, boring the chest-tight slot with my feet churning like a backhoe.

Once we could snake in two body lengths, we started talking about a rope; but that rope presently hung over the rappel and wouldn't quite stretch to the crawl. D.B. wallowed back in. A muffled sound, silence, then a distant *splat!* Wild cussing fired from the hole.

I quickly snaked in headfirst, an inconceivable concept a minute back. The floor had collapsed just short of the new room, plunging D.B. into a quagmire below. Closet-sized, the new room led nowhere. D.B. was knee-deep in primordial ooze and didn't look pleased. He raked his hands through the gumbo, vainly searching for his headlamp. He could no more claw out of that mudhole than he could swim through the La Brea Tar Pits. And I didn't have a hand line to pull him out.

As a fearful dog circles, my mind raced, unable to grok our no-exit jam, the whole thing made worse by D.B.'s flailing down in the sump. There had to be *something* I could do. But I couldn't jump down in there or we were both finished. I couldn't lower down and offer my legs to grab because my gooey stance offered no such purchase and my shoes would still be a dozen feet shy of D.B. I couldn't tie together my pants and shirt and lower those like they do in prison escape films because all I had on were gym shorts.

We were, quintessentially, fucked. I blathered out some crap about options, my breath fogging in the humid air, but there was only one thing I could do and we both knew it.

"Go get the goddam rope!" said D.B.

That meant grappling back to our packs, a long ways away, to fetch our remaining free line. We didn't have a second to lose. So I left D.B. in the darkness, knee-deep and sinking in a sewer, twenty feet down a mud closet, a mile into a virgin shaft, 500 feet up a limestone wall, over ten miles inside a cave, in Caripe, Venezuela, South America.

My headlamp started flickering just past the white room. Considering my breakneck pace, my guess had the gear only five, maybe ten minutes away. I started moving as fast as possible, which wasn't fast at all. When my headlamp tapered to a candle, I raged. I'd paid twenty-eight bucks for the special lithium battery in my headlamp (LED headlamps were several years off), said to be good for twenty-four hours, and now the bastard was failing. I slouched back and checked my watch. Damn, we'd been going strong for almost thirty hours. Then my headlamp died.

A wave of terror snapped me upright. My head banged off the low ceiling. I screamed and sat back down. My cigarette lighter was more psychological relief than anything, since I could only keep it going for twenty seconds before it felt like a meteor in my hand. The journey to the gear, probably 200 feet, took an age of fumbling, bashing, falling, and raging, during which I discovered every ankle-wrenching slot.

When the lighter finally melted, I was close to the gear, but took to crawling to avoid a free-fall exit from the subway. At last, I stumbled over the packs and played blind man's bluff rooting for the spare lights. Then, with a click—light was reborn. We had four extra headlamps and loads of batteries. I grabbed the essentials plus the spare rope and bolted for D.B., pressing for greater speed, paying the price in contusions.

Once down in the mudroom, I tied the new rope off, clipped on a pair of ascenders, stuck a bight of rope in my teeth, and burrowed back into the pit. D.B., sunk to mid-chest, was so unresponsive that minutes passed before he came around, squinting and mumbling.

Shortly after I'd left, he'd flipped his lid and started churning the mud, clawing for his headlamp and sinking deeper. When he couldn't move at all, and submersion felt imminent, he plunged into a fugue state and started hallucinating.

I crawled back into the mudroom. Soon the line came taut, and when D.B. re-emerged, wild-eyed and covered with mud, he looked like something from a Japanese horror film.

The hump back to the gear was slow going. When we stumbled into the one and only aberration, the little porthole walkway, I joked that we should immediately explore it. D.B didn't break stride. Back at the gear, we swilled a gallon of water and started rifling for food, but we both slumped back unconscious before the first can got opened.

When we woke up ten hours later, I was ready to quit the Cueva Humbolt, but after wolfing down most of our food, we psyched for a last jaunt back into the subway to inspect that porthole passage. If our estimates were remotely accurate, we had to be close to the bottom of that *golina.*

With three headlamps apiece, plus pockets bulging with batteries, we powered past the white room, gaining the porthole crawl soon enough. I headed in. Once through the stricture, the shaft merged into a massive, multi-layered catacomb of meandering tubes. I quickly retreated for a guideline, and we spent the next hours questing through the vast arteries, pursuing independent lines.

After half an hour of belly crawling, my knees and elbows were raw. I'd kept praying to see that little shaft of light that would indicate the bottom of the *golina,* but apparently no god was listening. We might spend years groping through, in, up, and around this cave, never finding that damn *golina.* On the crawl back to the subway, my headlamp flickered, and I cussed. Later, my chest got stuck and I nearly wept.

"Get me the fuck out of here!"

We lumbered back to the gear, resigned to give the climbing one last shot.

The wall above the subway overhung gently, but a flared crack reluctantly accepted gear. After forty feet, the crack melted into a rounded groove, with no crack and no chance to place any kind of pro. The rock degenerated into loose mortar, and, as before, it simply flaked away when drilled. Free climbing was out of the question. I swung around, looking for options. Then the top piton popped and I dropped twenty feet.

"That's it," I said. "I'm done with this."

"Color us gone," said D.B.

I lowered back into the subway. In one minute, we didn't care that we had come all the way to Venezuela and still failed. It was get out or go mad.

The descent was tedious and dangerous and took hours. On the long trudge out of the main chamber, we were amazed to run into Delgado. Throughout South America, "Your tire will be repaired in this afternoon," usually meant they might get around to fixing the thing in a week—if ever. It was unfair to paint Delgado with the same brush, but we had anyway, so his returning like this, as promised, made him a saint in our eyes.

We reached the rock step knowing only two miles remained to open air, food, girls, and sandy beaches. Once down into the main shaft, we made good time because Delgado knew all the shortcuts. Then, in the process of dragging our packs through that blasted channel, Delgado went and got his foot stuck. After about ten minutes of wiggling, yanking, and freezing, we were not only hypothermic, but confused. It didn't seem that Delgado's foot was all that lodged. He could wiggle it around but it still wouldn't come loose.

An absurd idea occurred to me, and finally Delgado admitted as much: he wouldn't pull so hard as to lose his shoe. When D.B. told him he had thirty seconds before we left, his foot slid out of the constriction just like that. But Delgado was heartbroken, so I swam back in, searching for his goddamn shoe. After another fifteen minutes, D.B. said he would buy him ten new shoes. No good. I finally found it floating just past the Channel.

We were all shivering convulsively by the time we made the tourist path, breaking into a jog and ducking the whizzing birds, hoping to warm up and possibly exit before dark. Soon the cave's ragged lip arched in faint relief against the darkening sky. Thousands upon thousands of guacharos swarmed into the twilight, where clouds and stars and moon and all kinds of open space kept my feet shuffling until I nearly tackled Humboldt's statue. For no reason whatsoever, I surveyed the Baron's face, actually touching his hair and beard and clutching his trident.

We trudged over to a little trailer that sold empanadas, coffee, and candy to tourists, all gone at this late hour. The trailer was shuttered and chained shut, but there was a hose beside it with some water pressure, so we stripped down and washed off the mud and grime and fatigue.

It felt like we'd narrowly escaped doom, yet standing there wringing wet, neither D.B. nor I had a scratch. None of our fears came true. We'd covered some sketchy ground, suffered intense uncertainties, but the telling adventure, as usually happens, occurred between our ears. We had been inside the cave for about sixty-five hours, had slept ten.

I dropped to my knees and kissed the ground: Adios, Cueva Humboldt.

A BEND IN THE RIVER

Black smoke spewed through holes in the ship's open deck, so gouged and corroded and cobbled with pig iron patches if a single spot weld ever let go, the entire quaking heap would stove-in on itself and sink. The pilot was all leather and bones and his gaze had the set changelessness that comes from years of silence and solitude. He rarely spoke. When the engine started clanking, he grunted to his caboclo (the mixed-race river people of the lower Arce) assistant, maybe thirteen years old, who once more ducked below. Hammering rang from the hold. The engine hit its clunky rhythm and the boy crawled back on deck, hacking from the smoke, smeared with grease and reeking of bilge and benzene. Whenever he wasn't toiling on the engine, he worked a hand-cranked bailer every waking minute. He had a long lick of shiny black hair and strips of tire thonged to his feet. He hadn't eaten a thing but saltines during our two days on the barge.

The deck overflowed with fuel drums, cases of Pepsi-Cola, canned foods, rebuilt outboard motors, rolls of Visqueen and sheet metal, even a plastic Christmas tree dusted with snow, ordered by the dwindling outposts, plantations, and native settlements upriver. The human cargo had thinned to the pilot, the boy, Dwight, and me.

This was my eleventh trip to the wild places with Dwight, who I'd grown up with in Southern California, who would go anywhere at any time and enjoyed discovering, somewhere along the way, why we had gone in the first place. Our last few adventures were our best because we started with so little, drawn to an obscure river by a sepia photograph in an old book written in Dutch, or by a curious-sounding village or tribe which nobody knew much about.

Family and friends were vexed why the moment we had time and funds we once more were getting typhoid boosters and Recombivax shots and scrounging visas to Kalimantan, New Hebrides, and now, Brazil. How could we, well into our thirties, disentangle ourselves from our peers, and the quest for significant stuff, and up and go? I was a nobody from nowhere. But Dwight came from money so big that abandoning the castle made him a traitor, betraying the ways and means of a life that mattered. We could never give them reasons why, in those moments, they didn't.

Late that afternoon, as the barge took on more fuel, we trudged through the mud, heading for the mine we'd read about in *Época*, a popular weekly magazine we'd filched from the bar at the São Paulo International Airport, on our flight from Caracas, Venezuela, to Brazil the previous week.

The pilot and kid stayed on-board, doing small repairs. The kid had spent more than a year mired in the mine, basically a child slave, before the pilot found him and pulled him out. Their business was upstream. We had an hour before the barge hammered on.

The miners had razed the jungle for five square miles, the fringe a jumbled chaos of bulldozed trees crackling with flames and hissing in the deluge. Raw sewage clashed with the ripe smell of worked earth as we approached a seething sump full of ex-cons, ex-barbers, ex-doctors, even ex-priests. The racket swelled and the smoke thickened as we trudged closer to the massive open pit and peered inside.

Two hundred feet below were an estimated forty thousand itinerant prospectors—*garimpeiros*—nearly naked, glazed in sweat and muck and rain, one thunderous livid mudhole of flashing shovels and writhing backs attacking a sloppy grid of claims averaging 20 square feet. A dozen men, hip to hip, worked each tiered plot.

We saw workers slither into holes while others were dragged out by their ankles, bags of dirt clutched in their hands as, all around, men shoveled, swung axes and mauls, and levered huge stones with pry bars. I watched a man turn to piss and get a pickax through his foot. The two men fought and one opened the other's forehead to the bone. A dozen others piled on, but the surrounding throng hardly noticed and never stopped.

A train of roughly five thousand men trudged through the mud in an endless loop, shouldering enormous burlap bags of soppy soil up a steep slope, legs shin-deep and churning, finally stumbling to the summit mound of tailings and dropping their bags and collapsing as if dead except for their heaving ribs.

Others, also by the thousands, hunched under huge wet sacks and practically standing on each other's shoulders, teetered up a web of creaky bamboo ladders, some fifty feet high, linked via crumbling terraces. They stumbled to the top and dumped their bags, the sloppy pay-dirt sluiced and panned by ten thousand other men while the carriers, sheathed in muck, rose wearily and joined the loop for another load. Each task done by hand, the toil and wretchedness heightened by taskmasters screaming at the workers, who had little chance of unearthing the big ingot, and no chance of getting paid until they did. Forty thousand muddy men sustained by jungle tubers and coconut juice and the handful of millionaires strutting around the mud.

One of them, featured in *Época*, was Guilhermino Caixeta, the twenty-three-year-old son of subsistence farmers from Cuiabá. He'd dug out a nugget big as an attaché case, somehow escaped the mud hole with his life and the ingot, and bought a *rancho* in Borba with twelve thousand head of cattle. Even gave his folks a job. As peons.

Guilhermino had since returned to the mine owing to *febre do ouro*, gold fever, a soul sickness healthy people streamed in from all four corners, hoping to catch.

Cocaine fueled the operation, and most everyone in it. Jacked by the drug, men could eat less and work longer. Narcos controlled the trade until the military took over the mine the previous Easter. Now it was open war between the two, the brass cashing in either by strong-arming their cut or simply confiscating the blow and having junior officers peddle it directly to the miners. Freelancers trying to deal the generals out of their cut were given two options: take a bullet to the head, or deal for the generals. But no matter, said *Época* in a lurid cover story. The blow would keep flowing over the Bolivian divide and up the river so long as there was a *cruzeiro* to buy it and gold to be had. "Guernica," without the bombs.

We paced along the muddy perimeter, peering into the sump, my eyes searching out Guilhermino Caixeta, the peon miner and multimillionaire. He had to be down there somewhere, laughing, colossal nuggets in both hands. But all the faces swam together into a mirror image of my own dislocation.

Out beyond the swamp and the blazing shoal of trees, Dwight shuttered photos of a spoonbill perched in a solitary jacaranda tree, peering at a wilderness no soul or god could endure. Only the *garimpeiros* could. Somewhere down there was their redemption. Somewhere down there was gold.

We forded back to the barge, trailing a string of caboclo kids—too wasted or broken to continue in the mine—and pushed on upriver, hour by hour offloading our cargo of young refugees. Most had been driven downstream by poverty, or curiosity, even indentured as the result of a father's dice game with the miners—and thrown straight into the pit. They were surrounded by strangers and a strange language, fed strange food, made to work like animals. Often they sickened, collapsed, were sometimes beaten. And since dying in the pit ruined morale, they'd get shunted back upstream, worse off than when they arrived and rarely one *cruzeiro* richer. They'd stumble off the boat at the vaguest shoals, find a footpath, and meld into the fastness, never looking back at the place where youth and laughter went to die.

Two days above the mine, we passed the last boat scouring the riverbed for gold. Another day and we passed the last miner and the final logging camp and forged into primary terrain.

The forest reared higher, the river narrowed, the current quickened, the boat slowed.

We hugged the bank against the current and plied through curtains of green light slanting from the trees. The caboclos called it *el salón verde*, the green room. Gnarled ropes looped down dangling in midair, flecked with black orchids and strangler figs. Bullfrogs croaked from fetid streams emptying into the river. Twice we passed mangrove coves bellowing the mad chorus of howler monkeys.

Every few hours, we'd chug past a small settlement marked by the sparse, meager homes of the caboclos. Their thatched hovels, set high on wooden piles, overlooked the river from above the monsoon line. Now and again the pilot would veer around islets of rushes in the river shallows, his hands slow dancing with the giant ship's wheel. I milled around the stern, smoking Brazilian cigarettes and staring into the trees.

This was likely my last sortie into the wild places, at least into the beating heart of it. The caboclos ventured downstream. We were going up, seeking a different life. If only we went far enough, we'd molt out of ourselves and fly.

The engine clanked like hell. The pilot, fighting the current, pulled over at a small, abandoned settlement half a mile upstream, and tied off to a cannonball tree at the waterline. Several decaying oblong huts stood on palm pylons in the small clearing. The pilot and the boy worked below while we panted in the bow, soon forced off the boat when the top end of a grimy diesel engine covered the open deck.

The pilot mumbled a few sentences, motioned toward the huts, handed me a sledgehammer, and went back below to the hammering. Portuguese was close enough to Spanish I usually caught the gist.

"He says the sun's going fast and they need a fire to work by," I told Dwight. "He's got to make Raul by Thursday and can't waste a day on repairs. We can get the wood off those huts."

"What about the people?" Dwight asked. I glanced toward the huts.

"The pilot said they all died last year. Measles."

We climbed a notched log and into the first hut, sobered by the wooden basin intricately braided into the reed wall, a carved stool, a manioc grater leaning in the corner, as if carelessly left there yesterday. We went back outside and laid into the hut with the sledgehammer. In an hour, we had a growing pile of bamboo, reeds, and hardwood joisting, and a fire licking thirty feet into the air.

The sky was dark and starless. All night the pilot and the boy tinkered with the engine, and all night Dwight and I worked the fire to keep the light high enough to slant into the boat, our shadows dancing over the somber screen of trees.

My eyes were occasionally drawn to the prow of the barge, where a brass nautical figurehead, one of Neptune's angels, was welded in place, her features so gouged by collisions and deep green rust she couldn't possibly see us. But I kept checking to make sure, feeling like a grave robber as we bashed away.

The wood gave out in the wee hours, and Dwight and I took turns sledgehammering the palm pylons until they worked loose and we could draw them from the gluey soil and roll them into the fire. The engine fired over and the pilot waved us back aboard.

Behind us, a mound of coals smoked and crackled. In a week, the rising current would claim the cinders and the jungle would creep over the small clearing. Rain and wind would salt the ruin and, in a matter of months, there would be nothing but a solitary pylon to tell a traveler that people had lived and died here.

Rain beat down from one black cloud, the blood-red sun beside it. Steam welled off the moving water—dull, hanging, and so thick I could taste my own hot breath. Thunder clapped through the green corridor, followed by sheets of blistering rain.

The river surged a foot in fifteen minutes, and fifteen minutes later the sun filled half the sky. The barge rattled on, the pilot's face pouring sweat and fixed upriver, like a man stalked from behind. Everything here was stalked from behind, from downriver. The forest grew close and immense and the slender aisles between trees darkened.

Towards sunset, the sky caught fire between rags of clouds and the river, flat and still, shined like liquid gold. A tribesman paddled by, a huge manatee in the floor of his dugout canoe. The tribesman's chin was smeared red with annatto and a tattooed streak ran from the corners of his mouth to his temple. He neither ignored nor acknowledged us, slowly riding the current downstream, the huge mammal's tail twitching and flashing in the light.

We walked along the barge all the way to the stern, watching the tribesman until, far in the distance, he fused with the flaming water. The day, hour by hour, seemed to dissolve into the river. I'd scribble in my journal, fold it shut mid-sentence, and stare into the forest gliding by.

≜

For most of a decade, since fleeing "The Ditch" (Yosemite Valley), my journal described a succession of exotic beatdowns consequent to chasing some feat or discovery: a first traverse, a first contact, an unexplored cave or uncrossed jungle or most any damn thing which sounded novel and risky and could affirm our repute as adventurers, as bolder than you'll ever be, as seeing things you'll never see.

But as the fog burned off, the slow realization dawned that I'd been living for some years in a bubble. My life spanned the globe—I had two ten-page extensions in my passport, with stamps from Bougainville to the North Pole—but my world was much smaller than I'd ever imagined. I'd have to learn how to stay put for my life to expand and burst the bubble. But I couldn't settle.

We made it to the outpost at Quejos early the next day. Another small, grimy barge onloaded fuel drums on its journey downstream. Dwight and I helped the boy roll off half their cargo, and the pilot steered the barge back into the current. The deck lay bare except for several fuel drums, three pallets of various foodstuffs, and the plastic Christmas tree.

Who ordered the thing? They must have come from where the love light gleams, which was always somewhere else.

We watched the little settlement recede. A bend in the river, and the world behind us disappeared.

Three miles upstream, the river pinched and steepened into a gutter of spume, roiling holes, and standing waves. We drove straight into the creaming tide, veering around sandbars and shoals, grating over river shallows as water-logged trees torpedoed the prow. In two weeks, the returning monsoon would raise the waterline five feet or more, but now, in low water, we butted boulders and battled swirling eddies, fighting for a precarious course.

A hydra of roots and lianas entangled the prop, and the pilot throttled down before the seizing engine blew apart. As the current plowed the barge downstream, the pilot dashed forward and threw off a huge, rusty anchor, which dragged and skipped along the river bottom and finally caught with a lurch, the straining chain nearly tearing the strut off the deck.

The pilot lashed a rope around the boy's waist and Dwight and I braced to belay him from the helm, our legs stemmed out between crates on the iron deck. The boy grabbed a machete, drew a lungful, and dove underwater. A faint ticking sound on the prop, and a mass of black vines floated to the surface and washed downstream.

The boy's head burst through the foam, and he gulped half the sky in panicked mouthfuls before the current pulled him back under. We pulled harder still to reel him back into the boat.

The anchor gave way and the boy disappeared underwater as the barge swirled sideways to the current, water gushing over the deck. Dwight and I scrambled back to the stern and hauled the boy in. He collapsed on deck like a big brown fish bound in roots and creepers, hacking and wheezing, water streaming from his nose. Dwight beat on his back until he heaved and hacked some more and started breathing right.

The pilot slammed the old barge into gear as I returned to the bow and cranked the anchor back on board. Onward we went, careening off rocks, grinding through snags, Dwight beside me at the bow, scouting and yelling out obstacles. The moment the boy caught his breath, he dashed below, hammering like a railroad coolie as the old pilot coaxed the rust bucket upstream.

And so it went the entire day.

Near sunset, the river leveled off, and on both sides the green hedge-row ran straight ahead—a long, hushed foyer tapering into the night. The pilot maneuvered to the middle of the sleeping river, now 100 feet across. Dwight lowered the anchor. A mile ahead were more cataracts, said the pilot, and the three hours between us and the next settlement were the trickiest yet. He'd need all the daylight to navigate this stretch. We moored for the night.

The whole sky fell all at once. Through the rainy gray pane, the land loomed void and dark. The deck swirled shin-deep. We stripped to shorts and stood in the bow, the hot rain streaming over us as we stared at rain pocking the water, and at the buffeting limbs of the plastic Christmas tree. The pilot took great care with the tree, checking its lashings several times a day, and never brushing its snowy limbs while offloading drums and crates. But after days of rain and wind and buffeting, much of the fluffy stuff was gone and the tree was scarcely more than a rack of white-washed sticks.

The new moon burned off the inky water. An electric silence fell around us and the feeling of pure duration. The pilot gestured toward the left shore and said, "Urupa."

Two forms came into focus, and we saw these ghostly shapes were alive, squatting on their heels, their faces cast in irrefutable sneers. Somewhere in the bush around them lurked their clansmen, the dusky, bleeding sacrifices to an industrial juggernaut adding nothing to the beauty of their land or the life of their souls. "Wilderness," which had always indicated the original and untrodden, increasingly suggested black magic acts of disappearance. In a few years, the world around us—the trees, the natives, *El Salon Verde* itself—would vanish forever.

Under a pattern of stars, the pilot broke into a pallet and opened two canned hams. We ate thick slices offered to us on the tip of the pilot's stiletto, and watched the boy devour the entire second ham with his bare hands, jellied fat streaming from the corners of his mouth.

THE HOWLING

The place was Pentecost Island, way down in the South Pacific, "where people wear bushes for clothes" (according to an in-flight magazine from Cathay Airlines). The subject was Timu, who had a toothache. And not a dull little pang, but a thunderous throbber.

Timu had scary red eyes and the frame of a black Achilles, and was a person of influence on Pentecost. But just now, his face had swollen shut, his hands shook, and he'd gladly have shot the nearest white man to ease the pain. D.B. and I were the only white men.

Pentecost Island, in the Republic of Vanuatu (formally British New Hebrides), is home to the legendary land divers, who built a bamboo steeple upwards of 100 feet high and dive off the zenith with ninety-foot-long liana vines lashed to their ankles. The practice derives from an ancient fertility rite, staged to ensure a plentiful sugar beet harvest. *National Geographic* ran a feature article on vine diving some years before, which gave it anthropological cachet.

Once upon a time—and probably even now—vine diving bespoke a tribal cosmology; but like many rituals in many lands, vine diving also provides local fellows a generational rush and a chance to impress the ladies. And it was this dynamic, not the gods, that got their motors running.

But the ritual has its risks. If a vine should snap during a jump, it's a head-plant into the turf. So every inch of surrounding jungle is scavenged for loyal vines, which the tribesmen select judiciously. D.B. and

I had joined a dozen or so would-be divers on an overnight vine search when Timu's tooth, troublesome for a week, finally took him down.

We forded a big brown river near the eastern divide and began slogging up the muddy bank when Timu's legs buckled and he dropped to his knees. D.B. and Taru, Timu's eldest son, helped him over to a boulder, where Timu put his hands over his face and rocked back and forth like a lunatic, but didn't say a word. A Pentecost man can betray no pain. That's bad form, a disgrace to himself and his clan. Whoever dreamed up that code never suffered a toothache. Not the kind Timu had.

When Timu's hands came away from his face, his eyes ran like a tidal drift and he mumbled something to Taru in dialect, who translated it into pidgin, but too fast for me to catch.

D.B.—who'd kicked around the South Seas for two years now and had a fluent pidgin—looked at me and said, "Timu says the tooth has got to go. Like, now."

"I got that part," I said, "But what about the last bit?"

"He says you're going to pull it."

"Me?!"

D.B. dropped his pack into the mud and said, "I'll get the tools."

"Hold on," I said.

"Well you can't yank the man's tooth out with your bare hands."

"Who said I was yanking anything?"

"Timu said."

D.B. opened his pack and rummaged around.

What the hell did his ancestors do when they got a toothache? I wondered as D.B. kept rummaging his pack. How come, in all my scattershot reading, I had never come across an antique dental epic. Not a single mention of it. What had Socrates done? And Joan of Arc? And George Washington? I read somewhere that George had wooden teeth, but who had pulled the real ones, and how?

"Pliers," D.B. said. "And we got a pair here somewhere."

He began ferreting through the side flap of his pack for our little tool kit and showing an eagerness I didn't appreciate. Tent poles, the stove, the ten-piece frame packs—they all required occasional tweaking, so we carried a tiny tool kit with a few nuts and bolts and screwdrivers, though I didn't recall any pliers. But there they were, a rusty pair of needle-nosed jobs. D.B. fired up the stove, boiled the pliers in a billy can, and declared the appliance "ready."

I cursed because I felt like it, but from the moment that Chinese junk had dumped us on Pentecost, I'd set myself up for this assignment. Over the last few days, hoping to get his endorsement so D.B. and I could try our luck at land-diving (strictly forbidden to outsiders), I'd done everything but kiss Timu's ass. When Timu got a headache, I fed him aspirin; when Timu's back hurt, I cracked it; when Timu's flashlight went dead, I gave him D.B.'s. So when Timu's tooth supernova-ed, the dental chores naturally fell to me. But the story ran deeper than that.

White folks were rarely seen on Pentecost before World War II, and during the war and after, the most jackass thing they ever did was to promote the old Kipling hogwash that it was the "white man's burden" to manage and better the tribesmen. Of course, they rarely tried, unless there was money to be made off native backs. Everyone Taru's age already knew the score. But some of the old farts like Timu still held out hope that the Caucasians might save the day. Taru, snickering like a thief, knew damn well I was nobody's savior and was no more qualified at dentistry than Donald Duck. But Kipling came from my group—that's how people saw it—and the guy kept shooting off his mouth about the white man's prowess. And since I couldn't take it back for the old Limey, I'd have to prove it, which is justice of a kind, minus the poetry.

But maybe I could swing this thing in our favor. If I handled the job gracefully, they'd surely let D.B. and me take a few dives off the bamboo tower. Not that I, or the President of the United States, could refuse Timu anything. When a Pentecost elder sires thirty kids, owns half a dozen long houses, forty canoes, and 300 porkers, his wish is your command or you find yourself treading water in the Big Pot. Not literally, of course, but you would never be invited to participate in a sacred ritual, which is the reason we'd come to Pentecost Island in the first place.

That's not quite true. Officially, we were down there to scout vine diving as a possible segment for the joint BBC/ABC show I was helping to cook up, based on the *Guinness Book of World Records.* The vine divers weren't breaking any acknowledged record, but the activity was so visually spectacular and little known that eventually, we just contrived a record and went down to Vanuatu to break it, our cameras running. That was still a year off.

This was our first look, in person, and as usual we fell in with the natives straight off, resolved to make a jump or two ourselves, since we were already there. After talking it over with D.B. for a few more minutes, we figured if yanking a native's tooth was the price of admission, it was worth trying.

I moved over to the boulder and peered down Timu's gullet. Sunlight flashed into his mouth and I saw a gaping cavity, deep as a well.

"It's badly abscessed," I said to D.B.

"Looks like your work is cut out for you then," he replied.

I wanted to ask what made any of this my work, but we'd already been through that. D.B. handed me the pliers. I grabbed the instrument and drew a breath. The natives' chatter suddenly died off. I held up the pliers and tapped them on Timu's chin as a conductor taps the lectern with his wand.

Timu opened wide and I began probing with the pliers. With the first clutch of steel on his abscessed tooth, Timu shot off the boulder like it was the electric chair, dropped to his knees, and rocked back and forth again, both hands pawing his jaw. This went on for several minutes, then Timu gushed out a few sentences to Taru, who translated it into pidgin.

Timu didn't trust himself once the procedure got underway, and wanted me to promise that I would finish what I started no matter what he said or what he did in the meantime.

"In other words," D.B. said, "you leave the job half done and we're all dead."

I told Taru he'd better get the boys to hold his father down or we might never resume the job. Whatever transgressions the big man had ever pulled on his fellows, here was the chance for them to get even, and several wore tight little grins as they sat on each limb. Taru locked Timu's head between his knees and pried his mouth open with his hands. I nodded.

"Here goes nothing."

That second grip of steel to Timu's tooth annoyed him every bit as much as the first one, judging by his reaction. To make matters worse, the tooth was of the wisdom variety, set so deep in his jaw that I might as well have been working on that punching bag at the back of his throat.

Taru's legs, clamped tight around Timu's head, flexed mightily, but the big man's head kept jerking about, leaving me to try and clasp a moving target, the pliers biting variously onto Timu's tongue, his cheek, then finally back onto the tooth. A quick reset and I got decent purchase and started cranking, gently at first, but the tooth wouldn't budge. More cranking got me nowhere.

"Okay," I said to D.B. "There's no coaxing the bastard out. I've got to try and muscle it, so have the boys bear down."

D.B. said as much in pidgin. The boys got set and I put all my 205 pounds into the work, twisting those pliers with a vengeance, torquing Timu's head side to side.

Timu started howling, his legs bicycling in the natives' arms. I tugged and wrenched till the pliers sang. But that tooth still wouldn't budge. I tried again, two-handing the pliers and twisting so hard my hands went numb. Timu thrashed and howled; the natives struggled to hold tight; Jesus wept. And that blasted tooth still wouldn't budge. I withdrew the pliers and stepped back, frustrated and sweating all over.

"Don't let him up," D.B. yelled to the men.

"I don't know if I could get that thing out with a pair of foundry tongs," I said.

"You'll have to stay with it," D.B. gasped, struggling to hold onto Timu's left leg.

"Oh, I'll stay with it," I said angrily. "I'll have that tooth if it's the last thing I ever do!"

"It might be—if you don't get it soon."

Timu's eyes begged for mercy but if I showed him any, I'd quit muscling that molar, and the chief could only howl. So it goes sometimes in the wild places, when empathy is forsaken just to keep it. I grabbed the pliers.

If suffering is the gateway to wisdom, Timu was a sage, although an angry one. How angry we didn't realize till, just as the business end of the pliers neared his face, he got an arm loose and started groping alongside his waist for his machete. He got it, too, and we all scattered for our lives.

Timu roared and nearly turned himself inside out twirling in ten directions at once, flailing the air with his blade, totally out of his mind. He quickly exhausted himself but kept spinning in place like a buzz saw, murdering the air till his grip tired and the machete whirly-birded over a native's head.

"Grab 'em, *bikpella!*" Taru yelled, and we all gang-tackled the big man—who went at about six foot, 220—and got him pinned back down on the boulder. Taru locked his legs back around Timu's head as he spat, writhed, and ranted, promising to slaughter every lifeform on Pentecost unless they let him up. Taru said he'd do worse things if we *did* let him up, so the natives held fast and I again bore in with the pliers.

This time I braced my knee against Timu's chest and started cranking hard enough to twist the top off a fire hydrant. I was really earning my money now, drunk with the dementia of the jungle dentist.

Suddenly, a dull pop. I removed the pliers, and gripped in the end was a gory tooth. Or rather, half of a tooth. It had snapped almost flush with the gums.

"Caramba," I grumbled, glancing at the crown of red tooth, then flicking it into the peat. "It's no good. I only got half of it."

Timu, his face just as runckled as the seracs on Makalu, was too far gone to hurt anyone. The boys let him go and he started rocking and sobbing and clawing at his jaw again. So much for the code of honor.

"Liquor," D.B. said. "The man needs strong drink or we'll never get through this."

It's not unusual to administer liquor before an ad hoc surgery, though I was no surgeon. The natives had a couple bottles of urgent jungle shine, and we'd have to pour it all down Timu's drainpipe if we were to ever carry on. Taru fetched a bottle and gave it to D.B., who put the bottle to Timu's lips, where it rattled against his buckteeth. Between pants and whines, perhaps half the bottle went down his throat, while the rest streamed out the sides of his mouth like the "red tide" you used to read about in Argosy.

Once Timu had slumped down in a daze of shock and drink, the men took his limbs again, Taru pried open his mouth, and I went back at it with fresh resolve. The clamp of steel to his jaw jolted Timu from his stupor and it took all hands to hold him, shrieking and thrashing and sweating rivers.

I worked on that tooth for a full hour before I finally broke its will and it came out. I poured some salt into what remained of the jungle shine, and after Timu gargled the concoction, the abscess was washed clear and comfort quickly followed, as it always does once a festering wound is discharged. Timu eventually managed a smile.

Several of the men had been kicked in the face and Taru's fingers were bitten down to the wood from trying to keep his father's mouth open. We were all glad the business was over.

We arrived back at the village the next day toting several hundred yards of prime liana vines. Timu put our case before the tribal executive board, but fearing our participation might endanger the spud harvest, they denied us permission to vine dive. Two days later, we snagged a ride to New Caledonia aboard a Twin Otter owned by a Dutch oil company surveying the island for black gold.

All told, it cost ABC about three grand for us to have the pleasure of removing a native's wisdom tooth with pliers. But our contacts were in place and the next year, our crew went back with thirty helpers and filmed vine diving for British and American TV. For reasons I can't remember, I didn't go.

SHOOTING THE TUBES

We planned on an early start but Carlitos got hijacked by a telenovela marathon about a young heartthrob named Figaro, who stumbled across a smashing nun named Roseanna. Then Roseanna's half-brother, the profligate rancher, Julio Del Monte, came to visit, having recently been swindled out of six hundred Belgian Blue beeves by Figaro's stepfather, Don Plutarco Monteverde. A fire broke out and the plot took off, but we didn't, not leaving the Hotel Maravillas until going on midnight, when we rolled out of Caracas in a rusty Chevy Biscayne.

Early the next morning, we sputtered into El Tigre, a ghetto town on the upswing, sprawled across scalding savannah carpeted in range grass and flecked with bushy Moriche palms. A decade later Venezuela nationalized their *petro* industry, but back then, the rigs were largely managed by *Yanqui* engineers holed up in vast, hermetically sealed *campamentos*.

The mercury sizzled at 95 in the shade, if you could find any.

The moment we arrived at Carlitos' family home, 300-pound Abuelita stopped kneading the *arepa*, quavered to her feet, and kissed Carlitos, her very grandson, on the lips as his arms went stiff and he bicycled his sneakers away. Niece Pepina, six-foot-one and thin as a cactus quill, rushed over with a tray of pig's feet *al carbón* as a dozen rowdy kids sprang from nooks and cubbies.

A home in Venezuela is rarely short on kids. The people pride themselves on getting married when they want, not when they should, and they quickly fashion a couple *niños* because they can. I was the first gringo to enter their house—or their neighborhood—during my first visit the previous Easter. But so long as I was Carlitos' friend, and now Teresa's fiancé, the house, and everything in it, was mine.

We slept till dinnertime, when brother Luis Manuel rushed in from work, cowboy hat perched just above his dark eyes, a chrome starter pistol in his hand. Thick, mustachioed, with a face off a post office flier, Luis Manuel worked sixty-hour-a-week shifts at the petrochemical plant outside Anaco to preserve the dignity of the household.

He bolted past Carlitos and me into the *jardín* to fire three glorious rounds (blanks) into the sky. Then he laid down several Creole dance steps, booted a sleeping dog, cracked his bullwhip, fired a fourth blank at me, and slapped my back till I gasped.

His black eyes narrowed. *"Matrimonio? Cuando?"*

When I mentioned a tentative date for the wedding, Luis Manuel hugged me, Pepina, Carlitos, finally Abuelita, and he broke back into his dancing, faster this time.

My first time in El Tigre, I swore Luis Manuel was putting all this on, like a crazy uncle in a Latino cartoon. Only when I spied him all alone and acting just as uncorked did I know he came this way.

He once more made for his pistol, halted by a bottle of *Doña Bárbara*—a bathtub shine that could strip the hide off a dinosaur—proffered in Abuelita's plump hand. He swilled a tan inch before Pepina snatched it back for Abuelita to lock in a chipped wooden cabinet secured with a single key, the silver skeleton Abuelita tucked into her black lace brassiere, a fallow acre no human, sober or drunk, would dare trespass.

We all sat down and feasted through flanks of *bistec*, fried plantains, *ensalada aguacate*, crunchy sheets of *casabe*, quarts of *jugo de tamarindo*, and various colorful tubers with impossible names.

Later, Abuelita got a headache, requiring a trip to the *farmacia* for headache medication, a journey of nearly five blocks. Luis Manuel could have walked there and back in ten minutes, but he took the pickup—because he had one, because it had a full tank, because he'd washed and waxed it on the weekend, and because, when he gunned it, which he normally did, it roared like the cannons at Pampatar. All this made the man appear all the more *magnifico* as he thundered down the street to the cheers of friends leaning in doorways and lounging on their verandas.

Going to the *farmacia* in the pickup was an event, and an event in El Tigre, no matter how big or small, is always performed in numbers. I wedged myself into the bed of the pickup among a dozen kids, several dogs, and Abuelita, whom Luis Manuel, Carlitos, and I conveyed there in an easy chair, and who would check the expiration date on the medication to ensure it was *bueno*.

As Luis Manuel gunned the truck down the road, frame sagging to the pavement, the great straight pipes belching three-foot flames and whoops sounding from every porch and open door we passed, I reentered the emphatic world of a people who lived like everybody would if they could ever stop worrying about life and just live it.

Back in the house, as I watched a red gecko creep across a peeling white wall, Luis Manuel laid out his plan . . . or started to.

"*Guacala!* What now?" Carlitos moaned. As I later learned, Luis Manuel's plans often ended in spectacular debacles, including bulldog-ging range donkeys, a stunt costing Luis Manuel several teeth and a fractured collarbone; salsa dancing with the mayor's wife, resulting in jail time and a flogging for Carlitos; and paddling a canoe after the truculent Yajiros, the local indigenous tribespeople, into the darkest jungle and getting lost for three days.

"*Disparando a los tubos*," said Luis Manuel.

"Shooting the tubes?" said Carlitos.

"*Sí, chamo.*" And Luis Manuel explained.

During construction of the nearly completed hydroelectric plant in Tascabaña, thirty miles outside town, the Cariña Indians had discovered tube-shooting through accident. The plant's cooling system required rerouting several surrounding rivers, accomplished via five-foot-diameter steel tubes piping water along a twisting path to a central aqueduct, where it drained into the plant and exited to a river below.

Disparando a los tubos involved intentionally performing what had mistakenly happened to a young Cariña boy who, while diving for crayfish, got drawn into a half-filled drainage tube and became a human torpedo, tearing in black passage for several hundred feet before his free-fall exit into the open aqueduct.

To give us a clear picture, Luis Manuel, who'd punished a covert bottle of licorice cordial for several hours, assumed various dive-bomb positions on the cement floor until he spotted a terrific *cucaracha* on the wall, a three-incher, black as sin.

He sprang for his bullwhip, but Pepina thrust out her pool cue leg and tripped him. The roach zipped into a chink in the wall and the roof nearly blew off for all the laughing, none louder than Abuelita, who farted like a big rig backfiring. The key to the liquor cabinet bounced from her dress and clinked on the floor. Luis Manuel dove for the key, but got only a handful of Pepina's moccasin. Grandmamma repositioned the key back in no man's land, broke wind once more, and we all just cleared the hell out.

Luis Manuel fanned himself with his hat and spit like a real man, pining that tomorrow's tube-shooting would be the last of it. Foundry workers would weld grates over the tubes' entrances before the plant powered up on Monday. Since Teresa wouldn't arrive in El Tigre till the following evening, tube-shooting sounded fine by me. The chickens were roosting and *Doña Bárbara* was finished. Luis Manuel grabbed his bullwhip to hunt for *cucarachas*.

≜

We headed out for Tascabana and the tubes the next morning, rumbling through a scattering of drowsy pueblos. On the outskirts of San José de Guanipa rose an adobe shack topped by a peeling icon, gaudy as a circus bill, featuring a ravaged Jesus dragging the cross toward Golgotha. Several Roman soldiers were whipping Our Savior who, under a crown of thorns big as a tractor tire, stumbled on, drenched in blood.

A long line, mainly children and old women in mourning, filed in one side of the shack and out the other.

"For fifty bolivars, you can get in line to see part of Jesus's genuine crown of thorns," said Carlitos.

"Is that a fact?" I said, craning my neck to study the grisly icon.

"But it's only a small part," Carlitos added. "Over in Falcón they got a whole one."

"Verrrrrga!" Carlitos yelled as Luis Manuel wheeled his pickup toward the mob at Tascabana. Easily five hundred people were already there. Some had driven from as far away as Ciudad Bolívar. Others had ridden burros for hours across blazing plains to shoot the tubes, or to drink, or both. The city council and the National Guard had decreed various safety procedures, all ignored, and a phalanx of soldiers stood by to try and enforce them.

From atop two jalopies parked on opposite banks of an Olympic pool-sized mudhole, the mayor of Tascabana (Don Armando Brito, renowned for reading nothing except Marvel Comics and the Bible) and one Lt. Colonel Juan Baltazar Negron megaphoned commands, sounding like crazed hyenas. Easily one hundred cars, stereos blaring, girded the sump in a formation so tight Luis Manuel, Carlitos, and I had to tread over trunks, roofs, and hoods to gain the mudhole.

At the waterline, local kids hawked sweet bread and bottled pop while, on small patches of surrounding dirt, people barbecued chickens, fatty sausages, and pig rinds for their beloved *chicharrones*.

The sun beat down like a hammer, and a fetid brume of sweat, charcoal smoke, burning pig fat, and toilet water (Venezuelans love their cologne) hung over the lagoon, which floated more trash than a World Cup soccer stadium.

Enriched by dollar-a-liter booze, the mob laughed, jeered, and shouted, anxious to go before their valor washed downstream. Bobbing pop cans, plastic wrappers, basketballs, a wiener dog, and dozens of humans

JOHN LONG

rapidly drained down the twenty-odd tubes, continuously replaced by roof hoppers on the rebound, bruised and frightened but ready for more.

Luis Manuel gazed suspiciously at the layer of foam in the water, grumbling something I couldn't understand.

"He wants to go to the highest launch," said Carlitos. "Faster tubes up there."

"Lead the way," I said.

Our bare feet made slurping sounds in the mud as we followed Luis Manuel a quarter mile to the highest pool. This one had a tenth the people, half the tubes, and five times more soldiers than the lower launch. I waded in and stroked for a tube, but—*¡Alto!* A young soldier would first have to take an official ride.

"*¿Por qué?*" asked Luis Manuel.

"*El gordo. ¡El gordísimo!*" said a private, knee-deep in the murky water and clutching an old rifle. Someone prodigiously large had apparently just taken off, so he would first have to flush the tube, for our safety.

Luis Manuel grabbed our arms and we kicked over to another tube and slipped in, me clutching Luis Manuel's ankles, and Carlitos, sheet-white and trembling, clinging on to mine. Logic said to go one at a time, but not in Venezuela, where anything worth doing is worth doing en masse. So we went all at once.

The turns were five-degree welded elbows, so at the first turn, we were jolted apart, as were half of Luis Manuel's remaining teeth and most of my vertebrae. Heavy flow meant mossy tubes and, in seconds, we vaulted into blackness and slammed through another turn. *If I hit another bend, I'll dent the tube*, I thought, trying to ignore the screams of careening bodies.

After a long minute and a few hundred yards, as my nuts had shrunk to chickpeas, light showed far ahead. We rifled out into free space, flailing to avoid hitting each other, and free-fell twenty-five feet into the turbid mud of the aqueduct.

We swam to shore, rubbing our barked hips and shoulders. Nobody could stop laughing and Carlitos carried on as though he'd just slain the Hydra with his bare hands.

"It takes a set of *huevos* to take that ride, *primo*," he yelled. We kicked back in the mud and watched for a while. Better than half the tube-shooters were women and girls, but Carlitos kept on about his *huevos grandes*.

An eighty-foot cement wall dammed the uphill end of the aqueduct, festooned with a dozen pissing tubes, whose positions varied from below the waterline to near the top of the wall. So far as I understood, the tubes were fed by nearby rivers and *lagunas*, and all of them emptied into the aqueduct, a fact that took several misadventures to establish. No one wanted to repeat the accidental feat of the Cariña boy, who got sucked into the inaugural ride, and verified where the tubes dumped out and that a body could survive the passage unscathed. But this was something that deserved double-, even triple-checking, so, according to Luis Manuel, a National Guardsmen got the wise idea to chuck stray dogs into the tubes and find out that way. The bit about feeding a black dog in one end and a white dog splashing down in the aqueduct—its coat blanched from fear—was, of course, bullshit, but Luis Manuel promised all tubes were vetted and ridden many times. And the exit was the best thing about it.

From tubes high and low on the eighty-foot wall, screaming bodies came whistling forth, backward, upside down, landing on friends who had landed on friends. Everyone howled as the human torpedoes, stunned and dumbfounded, hobbled over to the bank, collapsed into the mud, and licked their wounds.

"*¡Coooooño!*" shrieked Luis Manuel. I caught sight of a girl, maybe sixteen, rocketing out at the sixty-foot level. Her scream could have woken Simón Bolívar, and she pawed the air like a cat as everyone below dove for their lives. Whop! A 10-point bellyflop. But she quickly stroked to the bank and raced off.

"*Vamo, pue,*" said Luis Manuel, jumping to his feet.

"The *gaffo* can't let a girl outdo us," Carlitos said to me, white and shaking again.

We scampered after the girl, but lost her in the crowd. Just to our right, steady traffic staggered to and from a cordoned area surrounded by a dozen menacing soldiers.

"Oh, that?" said Carlitos, encouraged we'd lost the girl. "Liquor is forbidden anywhere near the tubes. Much too dangerous. But anyone willing to join that huddle can drink themselves half dead and go right back to the pipes. You figure it out."

Back at the high mudhole, Luis Manuel spotted some footprints leading up through the muck to higher ground, and we tracked them to a small rivulet, vacant save for the girl we'd seen delivered high above the aqueduct. Luis Manuel beamed as the girl peered into three half-submerged tubes.

"These babies look a little rusty," I said. Luis Manuel scoffed and, with a casual hand flick, said most of the pipes were old and repurposed to begin with. And it didn't matter anyhow because everyone knew all pipes led to *Roma*. Luis Manuel questioned the girl, who answered by slipping headfirst into the middle pipe.

"Oh, sheeeet," Carlitos said, as Luis Manuel waded over to the middle tube. "We best take this one feet-first, muchacho. Better to have your feet take those bends than your freakin' *cabeza*."

Sage advice, since soon after the entrance, the tube angled down sharply, slammed round a bend, and we shot into the darkness at speed. I tried to stay centered on the slime, clutching my gonads, praying I'd find no V-turns or sloppy welds.

The girl's screams died off. The pipe vanished beneath me and I tumbled through the darkness ten feet, twenty—who knows how far—and I splashed into some sort of tank. No sound from the girl.

I thrashed for Carlitos and we clasped hands and were whisked into a whirling eye like in a draining bathtub. We gasped what we reckoned were last breaths as the vortex sucked us down a thin, vertical shaft.

After the two longest seconds of my life, we splashed into a pool, bounced off the bottom, and were gushed out into a larger pipe, recognizable by the more gentle curvature beneath our speeding gams. We pitched down a ramp so steep our arms flew up and we were racing all over again, slightly reassured by the stale air and Luis Manuel's distant screams. His shrieks shortly gave way to something sounding like a drumstick raked across a mile-long *charrasca*—a stuttering, wrenching racket we soon matched when we ground across a corrugated stretch that tweaked and pummeled every joint.

The aqueduct loomed miles behind us and, in total silence, we whistled along for an age, regaining some wits and a numbing terror. Finally, I managed a scream, as did Carlitos, somewhere behind. And Luis Manuel and the girl, both well ahead.

We coursed through the darkness. My mind raced with images of the pipe forking into two, or getting extruded through a grate, or getting spit out the top of a 300-foot-high dam.

We bruised off a final bend and shot for a pinhole of light. I breathed again, bashed across a final washboard, and only half-felt my ten-foot free-fall before landing into a pool of mushy green slime. I wobbled toward moving water to soak and check injuries. The girl had a strained neck and didn't know if she was dead or in Paraguay. Luis Manuel rubbed his collarbone as blood trickled from a gash on his chin. Carlitos hobbled around in circles, ranting about *huevos grandes* and some matador named Belmonte.

The distant truck horns proclaimed the *autopista* a mile or so away. Hardly a great distance, but we'd have to hoof it naked since the tubes had stripped the suits off all four of us.

EL TIBURÓN

*None of us had religion, but the yuletide in Venezuela—synonymous
with Catholic voodoo, food to die for, and a regular downpour of booze—
is like found money. And we meant to spend it all.*

"Cousin" Marisol pulled into the long queue at the Conferry docks
in Puerto La Cruz, where an armada of giant blue ferries looped to and
from Isla Margarita, the "Pearl of the Caribbean." My wife Teresa's extended family was largely *Margariteños* who'd moved off the island but
still had homes there, or had relatives with homes and who'd always
return for holidays. We'd head over for Christmas and New Years and
continued this tradition till our two daughters left for college.

Around midnight, we joined the crowd rolling onto the ferry, climbing a steep metal staircase above the *motos*, jalopies, and big rigs overflowing with trade goods. Hundreds of passengers swarmed the upper
decks. We walled off a little square with the cooler and the twenty bags
we'd lugged on board, laying out thin foam pads for dozing.

In minutes, the entire deck, long and wide as a soccer pitch, resembled an emergency shelter during hurricane season, with laughing heads
jutting from hammocks strung off poles and port hole hinges, water boil-
ing on small camp stoves while hands snatched cakes, liter bottles of
Pepsi-Cola, *empanadas*, and colorful fruits off cloths spread over the
deck. Jokes were cracked, mosquitos were swatted as kids tossed balls
and frisbees. The *sibarita* from Caracas let her lap dog roam and it peed
on the purser's cowboy boots. Meanwhile, somebody's great-great-aunt

sat in a deck chair reciting the Rosary, her crooked brown fingers moving the beads on the string, as the ferry chugged towards open water.

The commotion slowly settled, the lights were dimmed, and the moment the women and children lay down, Carlitos said, *"Vamonos,"* and we joined the men crowding the open space near the prow, talking shit and watching the stars.

"It's forty-nine miles to Margarita," said Carlitos, my brother in law, "but the ferries are old and one like this capsized in Somalia a few years ago and killed six hundred people."

Carlitos loved to goose the facts. But no one could bolster this night, drinking *tragitos* of rum chased by ice-cold *cerveza* on board the MS Rosa Eugenia, which managed the trip across the water in less than five hours, landing at *Punta de Piedras* just as the sun came up.

We took a taxi to the shambling hacienda of Teresa's childhood friend, Luz, a Margarita native who had moved to Valencia after college. Her folks, Don Julio and Doña Rosalva, a retired schoolteacher, rarely left the island and had the two-story place in La Asunción, several blocks from the oldest church in Venezuela. Don Julio, also retired, had played valve trombone in the state orchestra and local salsa groups. Don Julio's son, Chico, drove a bus and drank the powerful local *caña* like water.

Margarita was renowned for accomplished drinkers. Locals had appropriately rechristened then Governor Fucho Tovar (Fucho = diminutive for Rafael), *Mucho Tomar*, or big drinker. That's how people rolled before the Venezuelan currency tanked in the early 2000s, when populist president Hugo Chavez (*"El Eterno"*) ran the country into the shitter and bankers and professors had to kill their pets for food. But at the time of this story, the bolivar held strong, so for this trip and many that followed, we drank.

Once we got the kids settled, we drove over to visit Kin Ting—that's the phonetic spelling, and I've no idea where the Siamese-sounding name came from since the man was Creole head to toe. Don Julio had known Kin Ting since grade school, going back seventy years.

Margarita describes an hourglass on its side. Most residents live on the more developed eastern half of the island, near the duty-free shopping in Porlamar. Kin Ting lived and fished on the western, leeward coast, where he and Don Julio were born. The single lane road passed through a narrow isthmus and slashed through jade hedgerow climbing right to a ridge, while plunging left straight into the ocean.

Just past El Manglillo, "which has more dogs than people," according to locals, we followed a dirt road to rolling sand drifts and terraced rock. Old builders had cobbled a few dozen cinderblock houses into stony hollows, reminiscent of the Anasazi dwellings at Mesa Verde. A tin-roofed A-frame, set back from the sea, covered a massif of nylon nets. We met Kin Ting, climbed onto his motorized skiff, and headed out over flat water.

Kin Ting had the far-reaching gaze you sometimes find in cowboys and Bedouins who live in open spaces. He stayed in the prow, mostly, stoically pointing directions to his grandson, Felipe, who manned the tiller with both hands and whose eyes never left his grandfather. Felipe wore his new Christmas trunks and a baseball cap for his favorite team, the Caracas Lions. The fishermen had the day off, but their lives belonged to the sea.

Only a certain kind of person, who fits in awkwardly most everywhere else, finds sanctuary on the big water. The ocean keeps them poor and exhausted, and gets chancy when the trade winds blow, so rational people don't normally work there. But they rarely have what the fisherman has: magic. Adrift in old rhythms. And drinking whiskey when they feel like it.

Kin Ting had a fifth of Glenlivet and he'd frequently pass the bottle around the horn. Then we'd motor on to no place in particular, never dreaming of being somewhere else. I'd been awake for days so, next time we paused, I dove into the water to clear the cobwebs. Currents I never saw swept me off toward Trinidad. I dog-paddled like mad but drifted farther to sea until Kin Ting motored over and hauled me in with a calloused paw.

"Forget about swimming in these waters," I said.

"You'd be right about that," said Kin Ting. "But *El Tiburón*—"

Don Julio stirred at mention of that name, which means shark in Spanish. *El Tiburón* remained a legend with local fishermen and, like everyone on this side of the island, Carlitos had suffered the stories so many times he could shoot somebody. Now, *El Tiburón's* name was heard less and less because he was going on eighty and had hung up his nets years before, though he still swam for exercise. And far, said Kin Ting.

In the days before motors, Kin Ting and friends would row the nets out to set their buoys. No one remembers when, but *El Tiburón* began swimming out the nets with a rope lashed round his waist. He could drag the nets for miles, sometimes towing the boats behind him, sometimes with a knife between his teeth—surely a poetic touch—and occasionally getting separated from the flotilla and having to swim ashore from way out there. One time, *El Tiburón* got snagged by evil currents that hauled him halfway to Curaçao, and his family feared him dead till, a day later, he washed ashore in Paraguachí, miles down the coast.

Glenlivet did the talking, but Don Julio and Kin Ting kept nodding their heads, saying, "*Es verdad*," as Carlitos related the old stories he grew up with, and which we immediately forgot as we drove back across the isthmus.

Next afternoon, during an afternoon jog by Playa Varadero, Carlitos and I noticed several trucks emblazoned with logos for *Cervecería Nacional*, a popular Venezuelan beer. Twenty day-hires and their boss, a Benicio del Toro look-alike in purple board shorts, worked like beavers erecting bleachers on the sand and inflating an arch serving as the finish and starting line for an open-ocean swimming race. Benicio said triathletes and watermen had arrived from all over to compete. An Olympic hopeful from the national team was favored to win, but local money was on a Cuban named Rubio.

Benicio grinned as he told us Governor Fucho Tovar would personally supervise the bikini contest. A big motor launch had dropped anchor a mile-and-a-half offshore—the turnaround point for the out-and-back swim—and a tethered *Nacional* blimp hovered above it. *Nacional* had donated fifty kegs of pilsner beer, so twenty-five kegs might get there.

"So long as the beer lasts," said Carlitos, "Mucho Tomar will hang around and so will the crowd. This could be legendary."

Helpers offloaded a long surf ski (a sit-on-top kayak) from the *Nacional* truck. Benicio said, as a promotional gimmick, they'd scheduled a local waterman—none other than the swimming fisherman, *El Tiburón*—to perform a short demonstration swim before the official race kicked off. The surf ski would follow the ancient angler in case he tired and needed a little something to hang onto.

I reminded Carlitos how The Shark swam nets out with a knife between his teeth and treaded water all night long in a hurricane.

"And was born in the ocean to a mermaid," said Carlitos, who went on to tell me how *El Tiburón* later washed ashore in Tobago, clinging to a snapping turtle, something even Don Julio thought unlikely. And now this Creole Poseidon would swim a few strokes for the crowd, who knew him from the classic stories, or not at all.

Back at the house in La Asunción, a handful of retired fishermen, all grade school pals of Don Julio's, had joined us to eat glistening loaves of *pan de jamón* (a smashing sweet bread-and-ham medley) and the traditional Christmas *hallaca*—marinated pork, raisins, capers, and olives wrapped in cornmeal dough, swaddled with plantain leaves, tied with twine, and boiled like a tamale. Interlarded with strategic shots of rum and a tidal drift of cold lager, the yuletide carried us far.

The women drank sweet Uruguayan wine and sang carols, and we men moved into the front room to play checkers. Someone produced a bottle of *Cacique*, a local rum, which drains straight to the migraine sink in your brainpan and sloshes around for days.

Carlitos put on some Dominican salsa music and mentioned their *paisano*, *El Tiburón*, would perform his demo swim at the comp the next afternoon. They must be excited to have their fellow fisherman representing at such a big event, he added. The fishermen never glanced up from the checkerboard. I mentioned the rescue kayak, in case *El Tiburón* tired, and they chuckled. Carlitos thought it reckless to have an old man out there battling those currents, kayak or not. Finally, one fisherman spoke.

El Tiburón always attended afternoon mass, he said, since he retired years ago. So why would he screw around with spoiled brats swimming in his ocean? If *El Tiburón* showed up at all, he'd swim the same race as everyone else. And he'll win. The others grumbled, *"Claro,"* and *"Por seguro,"* and moved the red-and-black pieces around the boards.

"Por favor," said Carlitos. As if some waterlogged grouper, pushing eighty years old, could keep pace with Olympic-caliber distance swimmers and triathletes.

I waved a hand at Carlitos—it wouldn't do to mock retired old fishermen who knew less about modern athletes than thermodynamics. One fisherman, built like a rhino, thrust the *Cacique* bottle at me and said, "Go over to Playa Varadero tomorrow. If *El Tiburón* shows up, you'll see for yourselves." The others said nothing, suffering us as fools, which felt quaint and wonderful.

Next afternoon, Carlitos and I jogged over to Playa Varadero and watched the crowd gather while a rock band from Puerto la Cruz threatened to blow out the sun. *Nacional* held good to their word about the fifty kegs. A dozen hostesses trimmed out in blue satin *Nacional* bikini tops brimmed tankards of beer as quick as we shoved them under the tap.

An athletes-only area near the start, below the inflatable *Nacional* arch, filled with swimmers small-talking and psyching each other. With *Nacional* giving real money to the first ten finishers, these guys meant business. Several women also came to race, including a pale-skinned giantess named Prima Doña, with close-cropped, bleach blonde hair and a wire-thin, creeping vine tattoo winding around her torso. We couldn't take our eyes off her. Rubio, the Cuban favorite, resembled a deep-fried James Dean. Even had the pout. With all this going on we hardly noticed the old man pushing a rusty bike across the sand.

"That's gotta be him," said Carlitos, elbowing me in the ribs.

El Tiburón, taller than I'd imagined, and more golden than brown, had barnyard shoulders and a Saint Anthony face as rucked and seamed as the floor of Lago Maracaibo. He set his bike against the arch, padlocked it, walked over to a portable spray unit, and stood in the misty curtain like a triton in a fountain, staring out to sea. As the fisherman had promised, *El Tiburón* came to race, something so incidental to the proper competition it barely earned mention over the loudspeaker.

We stood outside the roped-off area and had a clear view of the other athletes, who hardly noticed and didn't care about the wrinkly fisherman swimming in their contest. Three minutes and counting.

The competitors stripped to trunks and windmilled their arms, jostling for position at the starting line, a short ways inland from the *Nacional* arch. The crowd tightened at the edges. We elbowed around in order to keep staring at Prima Doña's marble corpus. *El Tiburón* stood motionless at the rear of the pack.

"Cuatro, tres, dos, uno—"

The gun sounded and the swimmers stormed across the sand and dove into the sea, surfacing in a flurry, their arms thrashing the water. All but *El Tiburón*, who walked toward the water on unsteady pins. To his right, a young man dragged the rescue surf ski, just in case. The main pack had built a sizable lead as *El Tiburón* duck-dove under the shorebreak and pulled his first stroke, which brought charity hoots from the crowd. The kayaker flipped in the surf but quickly crawled back aboard and stroked after *El Tiburón*.

Carlitos and I grabbed a beer and trudged up to a bluff overlook, where the bikini models preened, signed hats and t-shirts, and slapped a hundred traveling hands.

Out at sea, the pack quickly lengthened into a loose chain, churning past small breakers in the shallows and clearing a sea ledge where the ocean floor dropped off and the water went gray to deep blue. In open ocean at last, swirling currents yanked the chain apart, sending the pack in all directions, as a stain spreads out on a blue tablecloth. An on-shore wind and oblique rolling swells doubled their trouble. Even the lead swimmers only could pull a few clean strokes before the rip broke their rhythm and pulled them sideways. The stronger swimmers held a ragged trajectory, but they covered fifteen or twenty feet to gain ten on the motor launch and the turnaround, still better than a mile out there.

El Tiburón, far behind, swam at a casual but fluid clip. But once he pulled into open water, he looked little affected by the violent riptides, gliding through hidden troughs. Now he hitchhiked onto the off-shore edge of whorls, thrusting him out at speed, as if he and the currents were on speaking terms. Slowly, he closed the distance with the stragglers in the main pack.

"Old fart might make that boat out there," said Carlitos.

The kayaker, tired of fighting the currents, turned around. If *El Tiburón* couldn't gain the motor launch, we'd have a dead fisherman on our hands. The swimmers shrank to specks, waning to occasional white flashes, till only a working sea stretched vacantly out to the motor launch and the tethered Nacional blimp. Time for another beer.

The crowd defied gravity and flowed uphill to the bluff overlook, where the bikini girls staged a bump-and-grind dancing comp on a flatbed truck as the band played at 100 decibels. A trophy and two judges in matching *guayaberas* lent the contest a veneer of respectability. Then the generator conked out and we stood there, waiting for the swimmers to stroke back into view.

I headed over to the hot dog cart—and ran into Governor Rafael "Fucho" Tovar. Though I grew up with Spanish, locals always know I speak "the English," and Fucho's wasn't half bad. He'd learned by listening to Frank Sinatra LPs and watching *I Love Lucy*, he said. We both bought dogs and Fucho garnished his handsomely with mustard, onions, mayo, and croutons. I mentioned Prima Doña—not that the governor would have noticed—and I thought the man might weep.

Whatever else one might say about Fucho Tovar, he stood right there with the rest of us common Jose's, sans bodyguard and fanfare, the gazillionaire owner of Conferry, who once sold empanadas off a dog cart in front of his house in nearby Juan Griego, who later left for Caracas and worked in banking, went to law school, fought his way into the Senate, the governor's office, then dropped by the swimming comp there at Playa Varadero and bought himself a dog. I stood little chance of sharing a frank with such a man in an American or European country. And this wholesale disregard for hierarchy—even while they lie, steal, and kill for the upper rungs—gives Latin America, for all of its blunders and *basura*, a hallowed place in human culture.

"Holy shit," said Carlitos, glassing the open ocean with binos he'd begged off a Dutch tourist. The swimmers kept growing on the horizon and we moved in a crush to the edge of the bluff. A bikini girl tripped and took a nasty tumble to the sand below, and fifty hungry hands maneuvered her back to her feet.

Carlitos passed me the binos and I framed the first three swimmers, moving together, several hundred yards in front of the others. El Tiburón was one of the leaders. The Dutch tourist snatched back his binos and Carlitos and I scrambled down to the beach.

Word quickly spread, *"El Tiburón"* repeated a thousand times in thirty seconds. The great fisherman was pushed by unseen hands; only a fellow *Margariteño* could swim so wonderfully and, according to the man yammering over the loudspeaker, we were witnessing a *milagro*—a miracle.

El Tiburón could never keep pace with the other two in an Olympic pool. But traversing open ocean across the squirrely-watered, windward side of the island, *El Tiburón* was nonpareil, less swimming than navigating the rips and whorls.

The other two leaders—Rubio the Cuban, and Prima Doña—struggled to track the duffer's course. Lacking his feel for the currents, they tried to compensate with furious strokes. Slowly, they tired and fell back as *El Tiburón*, with the wind and swells behind him, squirted over the sea ledge, snagged a gentle comber, and bodysurfed onto the sand. Police and lifeguards fought off cameramen and the converging mob, giving *El Tiburón* a clear path to the beach, through the inflatable *Nacional* arch and the finish line.

But *El Tiburón* hadn't run in twenty years, so he shuffled toward the arch in no kind of hurry as Rubio and Prima Doña closed behind him. The crowd jumped and shouted *"¡Ándale!"* and *"¡Ir!"* as if their pleas might blow the old man to victory. Instead, we all watched *El Tiburón* stop like a boss and rinse himself off in the sprayer as Rubio and the giantess sprinted past.

Attention swung to the finish line, where Prima Doña out-leaned the Cuban by a nose. The mob crushed in and paraded Prima Doña around— ten boys at each elbow—as the band played "Tush" on the bluff. Carlitos and I jostled over to the arch, but *El Tiburón* had already left.

"Probably to Mass," said Carlitos.

THE RIDE

We pulled into Del Rio at high noon, mummified by dry heat till another Talon fighter jet streaked in from nearby Laughlin Air Force Base and startled us back to life. We came for the annual George Paul Memorial Bull Riding challenge—"The Toughest Rough Stock Event in Tarnation," according to promotional flyers tacked around the Texas border town.

The promo fliers, now collector's items, were Lone Star reboots of the *Return of Godzilla* movie poster—from the 1984 *Kaiju* ("strange beast") movie—where the scaly monster claws the air, swarming with Japanese fighter planes. The Del Rio edition had swapped out the monster for a fire-breathing Brahma bull, with supersonic talons jetting between its horns.

Many champions, past and present, had traveled to Del Rio, including the current points leader out of Henrietta, a five-time world all-around champ and the only cowboy on the circuit to ride each rough stock event: bareback, saddle broncs, and bulls. We'd come to shoot Jaime "Legs" Maldonado for Telemundo, a Spanish language TV channel I occasionally worked for in the late 1980s.

As the writer on a proposed documentary on Legs (which never came off), I had zero qualifications, having never seen a rodeo. My grade-school friend, director Ruben Amaro, filled me in about Legs, Del Rio, and bull riding during the flight from Los Angeles. Brazilian riders were climbing the world standings, said Ruben, worried the sport was getting outsourced. Diversifying, for sure; but most of this crowd looked "raw-hide"—white Americana—all the way, from the big Stetson "El Pres-idente" Cowboy hats on their heads, to the warty, hand-tooled, ostrich skin boots on their feet.

Several busloads of fans had spent the day just over the border, in Ci-udad Acuña, and many had a load on when the stadium lights clicked on. The Texas heat hung on the bleachers like a saddle blanket. A water truck rolled through the arena, dampening the dusty sod, and made a second pass with one hose turned on the stands, where bare-chested men hooted and cuffed each other as skanky brown reservoir water washed over them and into their open mouths, blowing the hats off their heads. The an-nouncer, who went by the stage name of Ferris Irons, shuffled around the arena with a wireless microphone, and over a John Philip Sousa march blaring from the PA, in a drawl thick as linseed oil, gave a speech about "these great U-nited States."

Miss Del Rio—a moon-tanned Nefertiti in a string bikini—cantered into the arena on a haughty palomino and half the crowd leaped up whis-tling and punching the air. As Miss Del Rio circled, cargo bouncing and clutching a wooden flag pole as 'Ole Glory rippled overhead, the na-tional anthem sounded over the PA and everybody removed their hats, held them over their hearts, and sang. Ferris Irons eased us into prayer and everyone bowed their heads as he sanctified the riders, the stock, the fans, Yankee Doodle, Old Mexico, and all of creation.

I glanced behind the corrals at the cowboys limbering up and rosining their gear. Each had taken a knee, pulled off their hats, and closed their eyes. Their faces set like Rodin's *Thinker* as Irons, with the solemnity of last rites, bargained with Lord Jesus Christ about "being on the square" with the cowboys, and "protecting Our Father's champions," and a bunch of other blasphemies in this high kitsch theater.

Irons said, "Ahhh-Mennn," heavy-metal rock burst over the PA, and the crowd exploded.

Telemundo threw little money at these one-off shows, so we didn't have a remote video truck with real-time displays, meaning the two cameramen were shooting "iso"—in isolation. Since we didn't have an on-camera host, once he positioned the cameras to his liking, there wasn't much for Ruben to direct till the interviews after the show.

We climbed onto the catwalk above the chute, perched over the last partition, and peered down at the first cowboy, straddling the steel fence poles beside the first bull.

The stall could scarcely contain the colossal, slobbering Brahma bull, which snorted and rocked as the cowboy shimmied around on its bare back, trying to find the sweet spot. The bull hated being mounted and clearly considered it as an act of domination, made worse by several men cinching a braided rope around its torso, behind the bulbous hump on its neck. On top of this rope was a thong handle the cowboy clutched with a gloved hand, gummy with rosin. He wrapped the tail of the rope around his "business" hand and yanked it tight enough to pop his knuckles.

Meanwhile three other cowboys pulled a second "bucking rope" around the bull's belly, close to its furry, pendulous balls, yanking the line so tight the bull started jumping and jackhammering the stall with its rear hooves, its horned head rearing back trying to gore the rider on its back, savage eyes red as the sun.

"Coming out with Travis Pettibone on Skoal Psycho!"

The guy working the PA cranked the rock track. Travis Pettibone shoved down his hat, gritted his teeth, and nodded. The gate flew open and a ferocious chunk of snorting, bucking, chuck-roast-from-hell exploded from the chute. It spun left, kicking its back legs so high it nearly did a handstand, snapping its giant head straight back. This was no farm animal, but a highly tuned athlete in its own right. Travis was all flying limbs yet hung on somehow, and the crowd went off.

Skoal Psycho spun right and yawed into the fence, slamming Travis into a sheet-metal sign for Santiago's Steakhouse. The bull whirred away and Travis dropped limp to the ground.

The "bullfighters" faces were painted like clowns but their job was no joke. One raced up and lured Skoal Psycho toward a guy on a tall black horse, who hazed it to a gate opening to the back corral. The bull shot through the breach knowing another guy was waiting back there to ease the rope slip-knotted around its belly.

The second the arena cleared, paramedics raced in with a gurney. An ambulance with its tailgate open backed to the rear of the arena and they lifted Travis onto the gurney. He sat up and tried to get off, but a bullfighter gently pushed him back down. They loaded Travis up, the ambulance sped off, and another, lights flashing, backed into its place.

I ran back along the narrow catwalk toward the chute, my sneakers sloshing through pools of inky "tabacca" juice crooked old rodeo hands kept spewing onto the slats. Jimi Hendrix's "Astroman" blared over the PA and Irons yelled, "And it's Cody Lambert on Cajun Moon!"

The gate flew open, Cajun Moon rumbled out and jumped completely off the ground, sunfishing—kicking all fours, twisting and rolling—landing like a runaway train. The bull dug in its hooves, snapped its haunches almost vertical, and Cody Lambert shot off into the night, landing in a welter of elbows, knees, and trampled soot. He must have wrenched something, but he crabbed to his feet, sprinted to the fence, and clawed up it as the big black Brahma bull rumbled after. Cody looked safe enough, clinging fifteen feet up the chain-link, but Cajun Moon kept snorting and bucking beneath him, trying to loosen the rope throttling its gut. The bullfighters decoyed Cajun Moon around and the man on the black horse drove it back into the corral.

The bullfighters were, if anything, more athletic than the riders. One wore football pads and the other a knee brace and soccer cleats. Each time a cowboy ate dirt, and they did most every ride, the bullfighters jumped straight between the bull and the rider, diverting the beast from close range, circling and sidestepping with their bare hands palming off the Brahma's horned head. They occasionally got grazed or kicked and, when Cooter Bodine took a dive on the fourth bull out, the rearing bull's head got under one bullfighter and launched him through the air. That any bullfighter survived an entire rodeo felt like an act of God, and the riders showed their gratitude after every ride with back slaps and fist bumps.

"And give a big Del Rio welcome to D.J. Mulroon on Black Ratchet!"

The star of this match was not Mulroon—still futzing with his rope— but the bull, whose name brought cheers from the crowd and whose career Irons described with corny flair, ending with his buck-off rate: 96 percent over the last three years. Outside the stadium, several vendors sold t-shirts with silkscreen images of bulls, including Black Ratchet.

The bulls were the cowboys' dance partners for the night, said Ruben.

Black Ratchet vaulted out and hobby-horsed wildly in front of the gate, went airborne and "broke in two," uncoupling in the middle, hooves kicking, slammed back to earth, and spun like a cyclone. But D.J. hung on for four, five seconds, and the crowd went off again. Black Ratchet juked to one side and D.J. skidded off-center and slipped forward. The bull's rearing head slammed into D.J.'s chest and bashed him back to meet the monster's rearing flank, which drove him into the ground like a railroad spike—a hell of a one-two punch. The bullfighters raced up and drew the bull away, but D.J. Mulroon, bleeding from his mouth and one ear, didn't move. The cowboy lying in the dirt, limbs splayed and dead limp, reminded me of a body piled at the base of a cliff after a climbing or BASE jumping wreck.

"Guy's dead," I mumbled to Ruben.

"*No se*," said Ruben, who broke into Spanglish whenever he got excited. "These guys are *duro*, amigo. Give him a chance to get his wind back."

The paramedics jogged in as Irons likened bull riders to gladiators, slipping in Disraeli's words about courage being fire and Jeremiah's promise the Lord would restoreth. After a few minutes, D.J. came to. The paramedics fitted D.J. with a cervical collar and loaded him onto the gurney. D.J. waved a wilting hand to restless applause. They wheeled him off and into the ambulance, which roared away as another backed into the hot spot.

In the next fifteen minutes I saw two more cowboys body-slammed to the ground and another pitched into the fence and knocked cold. I saw a Brazilian cowboy from Dos Santos get kicked in the groin and another fracture his arm after an electrifying cartwheel exit off a bull called Hum Dinger, which got a standing ovation from the crowd as it rumbled around the arena.

Two other riders—the Fawcett brothers, who both looked about seventeen—went one after the other. Both got rudely chucked off but not hurt. They gathered their gear and stumbled to the dirt lot behind the arena. I traversed the catwalk and watched them slump into a rusty old pickup and sputter off.

Only top riders could afford to fly to rodeos, said Ruben, which, during the season, averaged several a week in cities often thousands of miles apart. The top thirty-or-so guys made their money from sponsorship deals, mostly with beer, chewing tobacco, and apparel companies. Champion-caliber riders often owned planes and might hit two rodeos in the same day, picking and choosing high-profile contests with full purses. But most riders lived closer to the bone, forming partnerships with other wannabe pros who followed the circuit in old pickups like the Fawcetts'. Win or lose, it was right back into the truck for another all-nighter to another rodeo in Tuscaloosa or Dodge or Tuba City. It was a tough go, but they weren't asking for pity and they wouldn't get any.

Buddy Dollarhide, from Checotah, Oklahoma, was the fifteenth rider out and, like most others, went at about five-foot-eight, was lariat thin, and wound tighter than a hair in a biscuit. We watched him swagger to the gate, a bantam rooster in calfskin chaps. He was only the fourth to ride eight seconds to the horn, but he couldn't get off clean, and landed with his legs crossed, flopped on his side, and one of the bull's hooves mashed his left ankle. The clowns got the bull's attention and Buddy Dollarhide hobbled off, the jagged white bone jutting through a hole in his boot.

They'd run out of ambulances, so Buddy slouched back on the stairs below the judge's booth off to our left, yelling, "Goddammit! Goddammit to hell!"

A couple other cowboys rubbed his shoulders, and a man with a face like a saddlebag pulled a half-pint of Crown Royal from his hip, twisted off the top, and handed it to Buddy. He gulped, hauled up his pant leg, and poured the rest into the top of his boot, screaming, "Son of a fucking bitch!" as the amber liquor streamed out pink through the hole in his boot and over the jutting bone. Buddy chucked the empty bottle and another ambulance wheeled up and took him away.

From the moment Skoal Psycho first burst from the gate, a tsunami of adrenaline kept flushing me outside my body. I'd spent a dozen years risking the farm in adventure sports but here, when things went south, a malevolent, two-thousand-pound antagonist wanted to stomp your brains out, which felt like a whole 'nother square dance. How did they ever make this legal? It felt like at any moment the Marines would march in and arrest us for crimes against livestock and humanity.

"Coming out with Waco's own Bobby Reeves on A-Bomb!"

I watched several cowboys limbering up on deck. One glanced back and straight through me, eyes fixed on the oldest drama on earth: man-against-beast. Jumping onto that beast's back was a direct deed hotter than Godzilla's fire, a fictional bugaboo made frivolous by mounting a heap of whoop ass, prefaced by hayseed salvation and jingoism, and enacted to a rabid crowd and a feckless few thousand surfing late night cable TV. Raunchy? You bet your ass. Lowbrow? Lower than a feeding trough. But when a bull and a cowboy thundered from the gate, it was real and it was thrilling and strangely transcendent. As if the limits that bound came untied.

After about three turns, A-Bomb chucked off Bobby Reeves and a clown helped him stumble away to "shake off the bad." Reeves sank to one knee and pawed at his back.

"Getting a few *golpes* is part of the fun for these guys," said Ruben, but this went beyond fun by a country mile.

Ruben clasped the railing, peered over and said, "*Mira*, John. Here's our *paisano*."

We shuffled over till we were directly above the gate and had a straight shot of Legs easing onto a big tawny bull. Legs, thick-necked and ripped, couldn't have been taller than five-foot-six. A couple boys yanked on the rope running across the palm of Legs' gloved hand till he muttered, "Yup" in that edging-into-Cajun twang you hear around Stephenville. Legs fiddled with the lash around his hand, folded his fingers, and thumped them with his fist for purchase.

"Boy's got his sand," said Ruben, referring to the gritty, self-contained mien that cowboys so prize.

Back then, Legs was one of the few Mexican-Americans on the pro rodeo circuit. Whenever a rodeo hit Texas, Arizona, or New Mexico, or wherever there were other Mexicans, many turned out to watch Legs ride. Only twenty-four, Legs labored to milk high scores from pedestrian bulls. But on rank stock, where even the best hoped only to stay on board for eight seconds (a qualified ride) and to escape without bleeding, Legs shone.

Legs slid forward so his rope hand was right at his crotch; he nodded quickly, and was gone. When the horn sounded, Legs reached down, loosened the lash, and let the bull's bucking action catapult him off. He landed on his feet in a dead sprint—a nimble, trademark move that earned Legs his handle.

Legs rode differently than the others. He was a little stronger, a little more confident, had a little better balance. When the tawny bull jumped straight up, twisting and rolling, and kicking Legs' center of gravity across the arena, Legs snatched it back with his free hand cutting the air for balance, rope hand clenched to the braided line.

Most of the Mexicans sat together on a bleacher off to the side, and they all whistled and clapped and shook each other's hands.

Legs' score wasn't huge—a seventy-four—because his bull wasn't as homicidal as several others, so it required less gumption to ride. But when a rider lasted till the horn, and if he got away unscathed, that cowboy had earned a great victory. No person who actually saw it could believe otherwise.

Once the first round finished, the arena cleared and the judges made the draw for the championship round. Of the thirty-two riders, only nine had ridden to the horn. Ruben and I climbed off the catwalk and wandered over to the Mexicans, ranging from Humberto Juarez, a multi-millionaire who owned a shoe factory in Tecate, to rustic *frijoleros* who had snuck in through a hole in the fence. In Mexico, *ricos* like Juarez wouldn't be caught at a funeral with most of us, but in the arena, they mostly hung together because they were Mexicans who had come to see Legs ride. I couldn't join the conversation because I wasn't wise to rodeo speak. Plus, I struggled to follow their rapid-fire Spanish.

Ferris Irons announced the draw and three thousand "Ooooohs" sounded from the crowd: Legs had drawn Vulcan. In the other bleachers, fans nodded their heads and shook their hands and whistled louder than when Miss Del Rio jiggled across the arena on her big paint.

"*¡Joder!*" cursed a man beside me, pulling at his mustache. "*Vulcan, pues!*"

"Who brought that bastard here?" Ruben asked.

"He'll kill our boy like he killed that gringo kid," said Humberto Juarez, shaking his fists toward the others.

"You think Legs will even try Vulcan?" someone asked.

"Sheeeeet yes, he'll try," Ruben said in English.

The Mexicans kept arguing over each other, not sure if Ruben's forecast was the best or worst news ever. Vulcan was a killer. Later, on the flight home, Ruben told me only three bulls in history had ever been more than five years on the circuit and never ridden to the horn. The other two were in the Rodeo Hall of Fame. In the past three years, Vulcan had killed one cowboy outright, and had maimed a dozen others. During the previous season, riders often suffered with groin pulls or bum elbows after drawing Vulcan. But this season nobody bothered feigning injuries: they refused to get anywhere near the bull. When word got out Legs was going to ride Vulcan, or try to, the mood grew ominous as we went to intermission.

Ruben and I climbed off the catwalk and walked to the food stands. The rider's score was accrued from both the bull's and the rider's performance, each having a possible max score of fifty points. The rankest bulls earned their riders high points, but also concussions, blown out knees and shoulders, broken arms, and buck-offs.

"Thinning the heard," as Ruben called it.

The crowd pooled around the beer vendors and I wandered off to a quiet bench out by the tack house and started scribbling ideas in my notebook, searching out an angle for the documentary we never made because, despite a loyal fan base and long tradition, mainstream media considered bull riding a sideshow. How things changed. This long-forgotten Telemundo show was an early iteration of the Bulls-Only rodeos that, decades later, would pack venues from Madison Square Garden to the T-Mobile Arena in Las Vegas.

Soon after the Del Rio event, twenty-one cowboys gathered in a hotel room in Scottsdale, Arizona, and threw $1,000 each into a collective pot to fund the Pro Bull Riding Circuit. If you were one of the original investors in Professional Bull Riders, Inc., your seed money is worth over $4 million. Now the sport is broadcast into more than half a billion households in fifty nations and territories worldwide. But this was three decades ago, when the overall winner took home a silver buckle and $2,500 cash money, and the bull riding clips were used as filler on late night cable, between cooking shows and *Bonanza* reruns.

They called it sport, even back then; but a proper documentary required some figurative theme to push Legs and bull riding into a larger context. Problem was, bull riding had no analogue because it didn't look, feel, or taste like anything else. The Roman Coliseum? The Great Pyramid of Tenochtitlan, where human sacrifices became an Aztec ritual? Maybe this Bulls-Only rodeo was a hayseed twist on a passion play, where cowboy messiahs faced life and death in the dirt? Jesus fought the Devil and was completed. The cowboys battled the cosmically rank bull, who had to be defeated, if only for eight seconds. I was reaching big, but this was Texas.

Ferris Irons announced the bulls were running in fifteen minutes, and I hustled back to arena, hoping I'd sorted out bull riding. I thought like that in my twenties.

The catwalk overflowed with photographers and a video crew from ESPN, plus a couple local news stations. The rock soundtrack kicked back in. Irons yelled, "Are we ready to rodeo?" and life was a blur once more, all streaking limbs and thundering hooves. A crash and burn, a perfect ride to the horn, another rider mashed into the fence, and the shrill wailing of ambulance sirens. No stopping now.

The ESPN video crew flicked on some lights, and the cameraman bent over the guardrail, an assistant holding onto his waist. ZZ Top's "She's Got Legs" came over the PA, and the crowd erupted.

"Dad-burned right," said Irons. "We're talkin' 'bout señor Legs on that son-of-a-biscuit Vulcan, rankest beeve since the Forest Bull. So curb the dog and hide the kinfolk 'cause here comes Legs!"

The gate flew open and the audience roared but, for several seconds, the crowd on the catwalk stood in my way. Then Legs and Vulcan snapped into view, the killer bull looking like a giant eel fighting a riptide: writhing flanks, head, and limbs all convulsing north and south, up, down, and sideways, with the violence of an electrocution. Corkscrewing in midair, hooves slamming into the dirt, pancaking Legs into its back. And Legs somehow stayed on-board.

The beast was chocolate brown streaked with black, a grim and rippling hunk of heart meat that bolted to the center of the arena and whirred into a flat spin.

After about five seconds, the cheering drowned out the music. Vulcan vaulted and reared his head, scalding bolts of snot firing from his nose.

Legs seemed nailed to the back of the creature. Once, both his legs flew over his head and his trunk doubled over so far to one side the bull's flank knocked his hat off. But Legs was still on-board, still over his rope hand, the bull and the cowboy melded together like a Minotaur.

The horn sounded, but Legs and Vulcan were only starting to dance.

Vulcan broke into a bucking sprint, and Legs' rope hand was hung up. He tried loosing the lash with his free hand, pawing at the cinched rope between bounds, his boots trawling gullies through the dirt. But he couldn't break free. Twice they circled the arena, Legs flopping wildly, clawing at his hand, lashed in tight. Vulcan dug in and plowed to a stop. Legs flew over the horns, somersaulted, and landed about thirty feet away, his limbs splayed all over. A bullfighter dashed over, and Vulcan turned and chased him up the backstop fence (the arena doubled as a baseball park). The bull wheeled and rumbled after the other bullfighter, who dove into a big red barrel before Vulcan's lowered head crashed into it; the barrel sailed halfway to Amarillo before thunking back to the dirt.

The guy on the black horse dashed in and Vulcan charged straight at it. The horse ground into a turn and galloped away, sailed over the retaining wall at the far end of the arena, and, unable to veer or completely stop, caromed off the Pepsi-Cola stand. The great bull pawed the dirt, shimmied, tossed its head, and finally hobbled off and slipped through the open gate into the back corral.

Legs lay face-down and didn't move. They cut the music. Everyone held their breath as the bullfighters raced over to Legs. Holding his side, and with a bullfighter on each arm, Legs finally teetered to his feet and stared at the sky, his mouth open and sucking air. Half the crowd clamored up the screen and hung by their fingers, screaming and rocking back and forth, nearly pulling the whole works down as the Mexicans stampeded over the rails and into the arena.

Someone jammed a sombrero on Legs' head and they paraded him around on shoulders to the strains of "She's Got Legs" cranked so loudly you could have heard it in the Yucatan. The other cowboys came into the arena and hoisted Legs in the air as well, and he tried to smile, though he kept clutching his rope hand, couldn't straighten, and mostly grimaced.

It took Irons ten minutes to clear the arena. They prodded Vulcan back inside where, despite favoring a leg, he snorted and feigned charges at the crowd, his savage breath mixing with the steam welling off his body. Every man, woman, and child pressed against the chain-link fence and gave the great bull a standing ovation.

Miss Del Rio, who'd changed into a gold lamé bodysuit, once more rode through the arena as the crowd, purged of a great tension, kept cheering. Irons put his MC hat aside and said in plain English he and all the rest of us had witnessed history.

But we hadn't watched a passion play, or man-against-beast, or any of the other five-dollar ideas I'd cooked up while surfing adrenaline in Del Rio, when crowds were small and the purse modest and the half a billion viewers of the future had never heard of the George Paul Memorial Bull Riding challenge, or anything like it. It was blood sport, no question, but also a ritualized chance to flout taboos and let our shadows rip, full-fuck-ing-throttle. Miss Del Rio and baby Jesus, the great devil bulls and stone cold crazy riders, blood on the dirt and ten beers in your gut, lust, violence, melodrama, machismo times fifty, and corn pone sentimentality for days. All those passions that can shame our refinement, yet strangely reassure us that someone, somewhere is embracing the whole cosmic shitshow, for the length of a hot Texan night.

A couple weeks later, back in LA, Ruben told me D.J. Mulroon, who Black Ratchet had driven into the dirt like a tent stake, had a Grade Two concussion and was done riding bulls for the year. Surgeons screwed Buddy Dollarhide's ankle back together and he vowed to ride again next season. All the other riders who'd ridden the "meat wagon" out of the arena were back and riding again. But not Legs Maldonado, who'd ruptured several vertebrae while flopping around on Vulcan, and who doctors advised to quit bull riding forever. Vulcan, "the Secretariat of bucking bulls," had torn the big tendon in his hind leg.

"They retired each other," said Ruben.

ADVENTURE
STORIES

THIRD MAN

By the time I staggered back down to the Bottleneck, the sky had greyed over and gusts were blowing me sideways. Dozens had died right here, pinned down by storms while descending from the summit. Like I was. I had to get lower down the mountain to have a chance. I hadn't stopped in nineteen hours and my legs kept buckling every few steps.

I post-holed down through the Bottleneck and traversed left below a headwall of ice, which formed a windbreak—and I saw the natty old North Face tent, tucked into an alcove of black rock, set on an icy pedestal they'd dug out decades before. Warming temperatures had melted the snow that for ages had buried the tent, which we'd spotted on the way up, but gave a wide berth because the late, great British alpinist Allan Bancroft was still inside it—and had been for twenty-seven years.

The tent flap was thrown open and I saw, or thought I saw, a hooded figure, waving a gloved hand and yelling, "Come on. Get over here!"

I was worse off than I thought. Seeing and hearing things.

"Don't get in here soon, you're finished . . ."

That got my boots moving. I was too far gone to question the figure, waving from Bancroft's old tent. I kneeled at the entrance.

"Get in and zip the bleeding flap, will you?"

I slithered through the small entrance and closed the flap behind me. That barely left enough room inside to sit upright with my legs outstretched, snugged up against the stranger who was lying flat in a sleeping bag, rimed in hoarfrost and cinched up around his chin. My eyes were so bleary I couldn't focus on anything.

"Drink. You gotta drink."

I still had a hydration bladder of unfrozen water strapped to my side, under my parka and close to my skin. After all that time above the death zone (26,000 feet), I felt dry as a rock. But the first sip caught in my throat because I was still sucking air. I got a couple swallows down, and my convulsive shivers started easing off.

"Where's your partners?"

It took many reedy gasps to say how Selma and Dan, my partners for the summit push, faded at the Bottleneck, around three that afternoon, and descended back to Camp 4.

"And you pushed on?"

I felt OK at the Bottleneck and was hell-bent on bagging K2, the second-highest mountain on Earth. I was only thinking this, in fragments—that if I had to solo up and down the 1,000-foot ramp to top out, I would. And did. That made our expedition successful.

"Not till you get down," he said. "And you never do if this tent isn't here. You did a daft thing. And I should know."

I coughed out a few words.

"—Keep drinking. You don't rehydrate, you die right here. Have any gel packs?"

I did. A dozen little packets of energy gel, stuffed into pockets.

"Keep that water coming or you'll gag on that shit," said the stranger.

I got several packs down, with little sips from the bladder. My head started clearing but my eyes kept closing. Then a cold hand smacked the back of my neck.

"Wake up!"

I snapped back. It was dark now. Wind lashed the tent. I could see my breath, but little more.

"No sleeping till you finish that bladder."

I was god-awful thirsty but my throat felt raw and every sip burned going down. Then a poke to my ribs.

"Finish the gel."

That went down a little easier. I managed another two packets. "Keep drinking! You're getting off this thing, mate. Don't forget Joshua Tree. And Christmas in Zermatt."

Joshua Tree was my happy place. And no way could I forget Zermatt for Christmas. Rhonda already bought the tickets. No idea how he knew that.

"Keep drinking," he said. "You got *plans*."

This back-and-forth kept on, with occasional ministrations from the stranger, till I'd almost killed the bladder. I don't remember passing out, only waking up at first light. I unzipped the fly and stuck my head out. A cloud draped the upper massif. Light snow fell, but otherwise it was dead calm. Selma and Dan's tracks were still visible, next to fixed ropes snaking down into the mist.

I sucked down my last two gel packs with my last few sips of water. Several inches of rime had settled over the stranger, still lying flat in his sleeping bag and not moving. I pressed a gloved hand against the bag, wanting to give thanks, but the body inside was frozen solid.

I wormed over and looked down at the figure, the sleeping bag cinched around his face— Allan Bancroft's face, white as marble, lips shrunken back in a yellow-toothed rictus, his glossy eyes wide open, staring at forever.

I bolted for the tents at Camp 4, down at 25,000 feet. Selma and Dan were waiting with soup and hot tea. Both were alert but spent. We needed to get off the mountain before the next storm hit. I passed out for an hour, then the three of us tromped down to Camp 2 and we bivouacked there. We made it to Base Camp late the next day.

We had a big mess tent and the cook made pizza and we celebrated. All the others—especially our Pakistani liaison officer, Colonel Kahn—were dying to know how I'd survived the night out in the open, at 27,000 feet in a storm.

"With difficulty," is all I said. I never returned to the mountains.

A decade later, work took me to London and I bought a big marzipan pineapple and planned to drop it off to Bancroft's widow, having no idea what I'd say. But I learned she'd remarried and moved to Austria, so I ate the pineapple myself—and kept the water coming to get it all down.

NINE MORE HOURS TO HEATHROW

She was the only person sitting in first class, coiled in a window seat. I glimpsed her as I was coming out of the bathroom stall up front, behind the pilot's cabin. When I paused in the aisle and she glanced over with her rowdy green eyes, I knew that it was her—which was impossible because she was dead.

I could picture it all from the moment we found her, and heard her voice, how she'd probed us with questions and grabbed arms till she heard true answers. I remembered her tattoo, barely visible under the reading light—a thin black line circling her wrist, like a delicate bracelet inked on, with a small heart stenciled in the middle. And I could still see her face as she'd died. I'd watched it happen. I dropped into the aisle seat, and she gazed out the window at nothing. It was ten p.m. and pitch-black outside.

"Eight or nine years ago," I said, "a woman tumbled off the Yosemite Falls trail and got banged up, and we carried her down in a litter. Her name was Hope."

She turned from the window, uncoiling a little in her seat. "I wasn't sure if you were you, or some creeper. Thanks for remembering my name."

She reached out her hand and I shook it, and she held on for one moment longer, in that way which changes everything. "You'd climbed one of the big rocks and got all sunburned and had white stuff on your face."

"Zinc oxide."

Hope smiled and said, "You looked like a radish with frosting on it."

She could say wonky things and make them sound normal.

"It's crazy you remembered that," I said.

"Who really forgets anything?"

Hope sipped a little wine from a champagne flute sitting on her tray table, and I imagined her springing back from the other side, straight into a SoHo loft full of cubist drawings and Kutani ware. She jumped straight into everything. No brakes. No filters.

"What about Bama?" she asked. "How he got all tweaky and kept fussing over me like Uriah Heep. And the muscley guy. The med student."

"Chet," I said. "He's a doctor now. Up in Vancouver. He thought you were leaking inside."

She hiked up her shirt, exposing a thin red scar rising off her belly button and over her stomach. "My spleen. They took it."

"Ouch," I said, and I clutched my belly. "I went back to school a couple days after the rescue, and never heard back about you. I thought you were gone."

"Three times," she said.

She'd twice been resuscitated in the helicopter, doctors had told her, and once more in the ER, where they transfused her with everything they had. She pressed her palms together, giving thanks. She talked a little more about battling back, how sometimes her knee hurt at night, her words coming slower and slower. She had bruises on those memories.

"You seem OK now," I said. "Better than I remember, and you looked good then—till the end."

She shrugged and said, "Well, I'm sorta rich and sorta famous these days."

"Congratulations."

She threw her head back and laughed. "Don't even act like you're impressed by that." She grabbed the wine but didn't drink it. "I'm allergic to lies," she said. "And I'm living one. I come clean with myself by the time we land at Heathrow, or I walk off this plane in rags."

She wasn't Cinderella. She was buzzed on Pinot blanc and so thrown open and bombs away that sitting next to her felt like camping in an avalanche zone.

"So, what about you and your wingman, Bama?" she said. "You couldn't even look at each other."

"How'd you remember that?"

She cracked a wintry smile, like I'd asked the stupidest question.

"Bouncing down the trail in the litter, there was lightning between you two. With me stuck in the middle, remember?"

"Pretty much," I said.

"I asked Bama what happened between you, and he lied and said nothing happened. So did you. Remember that too, Sunburn?"

There was laughter in her. And her razing felt like summer. But I had good reason to say nothing. I stood, and she took my arm.

"If you ever sort yourself out, tell me how you did it." She grabbed her wine and chuckled again, but the flight attendant frowned as he pushed the cart past us and saw me homesteading in first class.

"Just leaving," I told the attendant. I glanced past Hope, not at her, and said, "Glad you made it, Hope."

I hustled to the way-back, found an empty row and crawled into the window seat. Nine more hours to Heathrow. Bama ghosted in and lowered into the aisle seat. No telling where Bama actually was—I'd only caught the rumors—but I could sense his presence, all hate and grimace, imagined onto that seat by my guilt, him stewing with the intensity of a thousand suns. Hope was the second person we'd lost on a rescue, both in the same month, and some vital thing had flown from our lives and we could never call it back. That was my last full season climbing in the valley, my last rescue, and I hadn't seen Bama till now. What Hope said: We never forget anything.

≙

Bama kept blazing up the trail till he collapsed in the dirt at the elbow of a switchback. As soon as we caught him, he wanted to push on. An hour before, Ranger Reggie (the only name he'd answer to) swung by Camp 4—where all the climbers stayed, including us on the rescue team—and grabbed Chet and me.

We were smoking shag tobacco cigarettes and holding down a picnic table, peering through the pines at ragged flocks of birds. They were flying high, at rim-level, and heading south. It was last August, and our spring was gone, and our summer. The few of us still slumming in camp were running on fumes after three months climbing in the valley. But we couldn't leave till college started in a couple days. Even the birds knew better than to hang around. Served us right we got fetched for a rescue. We had to go. And we had to hit the Falls Trail, said Ranger Reggie. Full speed. Immediately.

We finally caught Bama, a mile above the trailhead, and we all doubled over, sucking air. All Bama said was that a hiker had skidded off the steep part of the trail, right below the rim, and she'd gotten scraped up.

"Well, hell," said Chet. Why kill ourselves sprinting after some hiker with a couple measly scrapes?

"The Juniors radioed down she blew out her knee," said Bama, annoyed, "so she can't hike out on her own."

"So we're schlepping her down?" I asked, cringing at the thought.

"You wanna try that shit in the dark?" said Ranger Reggie. "On this trail?"

I scanned across the rubbly north wall above us, and the narrow trail slashing across it in a ragged series of Zs. We'd never get the woman down this trail before dark. Bama shot off again. The trail steepened just above.

"What gives with Bama?" asked Chet, wobbling to his feet.

"He's a hick with a badge," said Reggie. Like we didn't know that. Reggie threw on his daypack and trudged off. Reggie always got along with us climbers better than he did with fellow rangers. For a hundred reasons.

We charged on, chasing Bama. The last heat of summer hung on us like a cloud without rain. After plowing up the initial slope, we cut across a ledge system, dunking our heads in a streamlet that pooled on the trail. Just above, the trail hooked left and climbed a ramp angling across a bushy granite wall. Then up through a maze of shale inclines and tiered rubble. A few hikers stumbled past, all rubber legs and sunburnt faces.

The rusty sign at the trailhead read: FOR ADVANCED HIKERS ONLY. Every day from May through September, hundreds tried living up to that sign. The Falls Trail rises 3,200 feet in a little over three miles and feels like climbing the stairs to the top of the One World Trade Center. Twice.

Out right and far above, Yosemite Falls pours through a cleft and straight off the north rim, free-falling into a bridal veil. Every summer day, down on the valley floor, thousands march a quarter mile up a paved access road toward the base of the gusher and get soaked to the bone, watching the white cascade. It seems to stretch out a hand to you. Miwok legend says when a tribal member approaches death, their souls travel to the foggy granite slabs below the falls, which locals call the Lost World, where swirling mist and water, streaming over stone, heal their wounds and their memories.

We jogged across the ramp and swarmed up the last 1,000 feet, covering about a mile over increasingly loose terrain. These final switchbacks formed an invisible barrier against everything below, and all that level ground represented. For anyone, at any time, the way could crumble underfoot. At 7,000 feet elevation, it took us a minute to catch our breaths and debrief the two Juniors—ranger interns—who Bama had sent ahead to fetch the litter chained to the footbridge on the rim.

The Juniors had loaded Hope into the litter, and she kept apologizing for causing all this trouble. Her left knee was red and swollen and she had some scrapes that the Juniors had dressed. She'd tumbled off the crumbling upper switchbacks and, with no secure place to put her, we could only cram together in a single file. Hope and her litter balanced on a strip of steep rubble. Bama eyed the queue piling above us, which snaked all the way up to the rim. Nobody could hike past till we got Hope to a clearing half a mile below.

"We best get you to lower ground," said Bama. "Then we regroup."

Hope's eyes settled curiously on Bama, tall and thin as a rake, with his wiry red hair and Baby Jesus face. Add in the plantation accent—leaning towards a higher register—and his tense decorum around women, and no wonder people felt they were meeting the Spider from Mars. Not Hope, who grabbed Bama's hand and said, "Thank you, sir."

"You're very welcome, ma'am," he said, as the worry lines between his eyes relaxed. "Now, let's get you outta here."

We scanned the switchbacks cutting across the hillside. On solid ground we could take turns and piggyback Hope down, but the gravel, shale, and narrow trail made a fireman's carry too dicey. Chet mumbled out, "The toboggan from hell."

Everyone groaned as we stared at the trail, trying to picture something nearly impossible to feature: four people carrying a woman across a crumbling balance beam. This could quickly go way wrong, but that was a problem for the future, and the future never felt real to me.

"I'll take the front," said Reggie. He'd suffer, which he liked.

I pulled on my climbing harness. Chet got a long nylon sling from the gear pack, tied it with two hand loops at four-foot intervals and clipped the sling into the back of my harness. Hope's eyes closely followed our moves, but we couldn't explain with a hundred hikers bottlenecked behind us. If only she knew.

The litter described a shallow, stretcher-like basket. Hope lay lashed inside it, face up. A thin, aluminum rail ran around a wire mesh bed, contoured for a human body. We'd normally carry this litter with six people, two on each side, one up front and one in back. But not on a trail barely a foot wide, with no room on the sides for the carry. A couple years later, they started making litters with a single wheel and an all-terrain tire mounted below the basket. We could have used one.

Bama reached into his day pack and fetched a small thermos of jet-black coffee. We each took a shot, which committed us to get going. We double- and triple-checked everything that might separate us from the accident report. I grabbed the rear rail. Bama and Chet locked their wrists through the hand loops on the sling coming off the back of my harness.

Reggie, facing forward, squatted and grabbed the aluminum rail with his hands matched behind his waist. Soon as we hoisted the litter, the weight nose-dived onto Reggie's hands, thickly calloused from hard service. But the shock load nearly buckled his legs as he plowed across the steep trail, heels digging into the loose-packed rubble, the three of us behind getting dragged down the slope like we were tethered to a runaway horse.

Lying powerless in a litter made wimps out of El Cap speed climbers, but Hope owned it. Even when we'd totter and the litter yawed sideways, she never lost her amused little grin, which made us believe we might do this. We were redlining from the first step, burning energy we couldn't get back. I knew that would cost us as we made our way down. It took over an hour of fifty-foot pushes to tractor the initial half mile, our bodies absorbing thought and feeling, condensing them into sweat. We collapsed in a small clearing above some fortified steps, cut into living rock. Waylaid hikers streamed past. One of the Juniors held out a water bottle and I gulped, then offered the bottle to Hope. Reggie beat me to it.

"I've been coming to Yosemite since grade school," Hope said to Reggie, "and you're the first black ranger I've ever seen. Can't imagine what it feels like to be you."

Reggie smiled thinly and said, "It's not so bad as all that."

"You're a lousy liar, Ranger Reggie. This place is as white as the glacier that made it."

"The Miwoks tell it differently," said Reggie.

An uneasy divide, wide as the valley, had always loomed between Reggie and us. He was so much his own man, maybe race only told half the story. Hope closed the distance in four sentences flat. Reggie was just people to her. They talked a little longer and Reggie laughed, and Reggie never laughed. He glanced at me and thrust his chin toward Hope, as if to say, "Who is this woman?"

Good question. I put her around twenty-one, likely a runner with her toned legs and the lug-soled trail runners on her feet. Straight black hair, cut stylishly short, and deep olive skin, like a Persian or a Turk, with eyes just as green as imperial jade. And the delicate tattooed line circling her wrist, with the small red heart in the middle. Back then, the only tattooed females I'd seen were biker chicks and convicts. Hope was the future.

Bama and Chet took a knee next to us and Bama asked Hope how she felt.

"Knee's pretty sore," she said, "and my side hurt at first. But it doesn't anymore."

"Better check," said Chet.

Hope glanced at Bama, who said, "Not to worry, ma'am. Chet here's a medical student."

"Only first year," said Chet.

Ever since high school, Chet spent all ninety days of every summer break climbing in the Valley. Never enough but, at that age, three months feels like a year.

Chet hiked up Hope's t-shirt and we grimaced at the purple hematoma on her abdomen, just below her ribs. Chet gently pressed his hand against the wound, and said, "Better get her down." Bama motioned his head for Chet and me to follow, above Hope's earshot.

"Some important machinery under that welt," said Chet. "She's three hours out from her accident, and her vitals check out but—"

"We're going," Bama cut in. "Now."

We lurched down the lower steps, taking short breathers to shake the sensation back into our hands, setting Hope on a patch of grass and monkeyflowers flanking the trail. Bama kept asking how she felt. Offering her water, raisins, fruit bars. Hope unclipped her straps, sat up, and asked, "What's your real name, Ranger Bama?"

"Bama's okay," said Bama.

"Stop your worrying," she said, grabbing his arm. "I'll be fine. But I still want to know your name."

I mentioned the time we didn't have, and Hope asked Bama about his name again. Injured people often binged on questions like this. A good connection can crush a lot of fear. But Hope wasn't scared. She was the stranger you meet on a plane or in the barbershop—or on a rescue—and you stamp the heat in your secrets through private disclosure, much as you douse a campfire before moving on. Then you pray to never meet that stranger again so long as you live.

"My name's Beau Dobbins," Bama finally said. His nametag read Dobbins, but "Beau" was news to us. Even the Chief Ranger called him Bama—as in Alabama, his home state—a slightly pejorative handle he lived with.

"Would that be Bocephus Dobbins?" she asked. Bama flushed a little. "That's world class," said Hope. "Family name, Ranger Dobbins?"

Bama paused, and said, "So they tell me. We gotta get this party moving. We're racing the clock here, ma'am."

"What's up with you two?" she asked, glancing at Bama and me in turn. "You guys act like you shot each other's dog."

The woman had a gift for asking awkward questions in a way we felt obliged to answer. Plus how do you ignore someone two feet away?

"He's a climber," said Bama, as if I weren't there. "And climbers only respect their own authority. That's the problem right there."

"Your pants are on fire, Ranger Dobbins," she said.

Bama peeled her fingers off his arm and we both said, "We gotta go."

The trail widened slightly so we could handle the carry with two to a side, one on point and another in back. We hoisted the litter and slashed across the middle switchbacks.

"I think you're a frustrated artist," Hope said to Bama as the litter pitched and rolled. "I'm sorta one myself. You play an instrument or anything?"

Bama mumbled, "A little piano, ma'am. But not very good."

Another lie. A big one. The previous summer, after the annual climbers-rangers softball game, and halfway through our second keg, we straggled into the backcountry ranger's cabin, which had an old piano in the corner. Bama sat and banged out a medley of ragtime tunes from Jelly Roll Morton, Fats Waller, and Lucky Roberts. All the classic stuff. The Billy Bob Thornton of the Park Service was a redneck who'd been touched.

"Pick it up, hilljacks," said Bama. "It's dark in two hours."

But racing up the trail and the toboggan-from-Hell had ruined us. It took Reggie two tries to even stand after our next break. We barely made it 100 yards before our hands went numb and our forearms pumped out, and we had to set Hope down on a flat-topped boulder in the shade. Spent hikers staggered by.

"Three minutes," said Bama. "Not a second more."

"The climbers and the rangers," said Hope. "How come you're working together?"

Enough already with the questions. Couldn't she see us cruxing here? She grabbed my arm, so I told her — that ambitious climbers needed the whole summer to round into shape and do their projects. But with the seven-day camping limit, the only way around it meant working on the rescue team for burrito wages. Climbers came in handy for technical rescues when they broke out the ropes and the tackle; but rescues were run like military operations, and climbers were never huge on taking orders. A few years later, all the rescue rangers *were* climbers. Good ones, too. But not back then.

"But you get to stay here all summer," she said, sweeping her hand across the valley.

"We make it work," I said. "Barely . . ."

"So what's up with you and Bama?" she asked.

"Nothing that matters now," I said.

It wasn't getting any lighter outside. But Hope was. The second we set Hope down in the shade we saw her skin blanching. Chet tapped the crook in her arm, checking the vein. She sounded a little dreamy when she answered his questions. Chet didn't pull us aside this time.

"She's bleeding inside," he said.

Bama went off. "You said she was fine an hour ago!"

"Two hours ago," said Reggie. "We're gonna need help."

My head felt heavy and my insides raced. An eerie freeze crept through me.

"Grab a few guys off the trail," said Chet, still bent over Hope, "and rotate them in for the carry."

"Get 'em!" said Bama, who jumped over to try and rally Hope, already slurring her words. Chet grabbed Hope's wrist and checked her pulse.

"We're getting her down," said Bama, stepping close and looking right at me, spit flying off his lips. "You hear me?"

We had a debt to pay, known only to ourselves, and the fear and panic of adding to it thrust us right into each other's face.

"We gotta get going," I said, only half-aware I was gripping Bama's arm.

Everything inside me felt like ice. Reggie's legs were gone, but he somehow backtracked up the trail to try and enlist anyone big and fit enough to help.

We grabbed the litter and wobbled off with five carrying: Bama,

Chet, and I, and the two Juniors. We fought like crazy, hell-bent to hang on and keep busting down the trail; but our hands opened after 100 feet, and we half-dropped Hope to the ground. She forced a smile, but couldn't hold it for long. Bama jutted between trying to reassure Hope and swearing at creation. We had a hard mile to go.

Reggie returned with a half a dozen guys, all strangers to each other. Two grabbed the litter from each side as a big Newfie took the front, and another guy took the back, and the train charged down the switchbacks. Bama shot ahead, calling out obstacles and guiding the carry.

I kept swapping out up front with the Newfie. I could only manage three or four minutes at a go but, without something to do, only jogging alongside, my mind kept attaching to events from the past which brought on that weird freeze and made my bones chatter. I could only warm out of it by grabbing the litter again.

Others joined as we descended: an Italian in soccer shoes, a burly Kenyan diplomat, a pilot from the Indian Air Force, and more random strangers we shagged off the trail, and who spontaneously found a teamwork that thawed me out as Hope and the litter jounced down at speed. Ankles twisted. Shins barked off rocks. Grunting sounded in multiple accents—but quietly—so as not to disturb Hope, all as Bama drove the train for greater speed.

Chet kept checking on Hope, who started nodding in and out, and he made us set her down where the stream cut across the trail. Hope's eyes were open but focused on infinity.

Bama grabbed her shoulder and said, "Talk to me, girl."

She moved her lips but didn't say anything, just stared straight up and a thousand miles past us. Bama gently shook her again. Hope cocked her head a little to the side, as if she recognized something in outer space. Bama couldn't stand it, and said, "What you looking at?"

She wasn't looking at anything. She was listening—to whirling mist and water rolling down the slabs below the falls. Sounds only she could hear. She closed her eyes and breathed out the words, "It's . . . okay.

Okay . . ."

I pictured Hope following those sounds down the trail, left across the buttress to the streaming foggy slabs below the falls. Her body might last another few hours. But the Lost World, I figured, if it was ever a place at all, was always the last stop.

Chet told Bama to call for the Med Evac. The little valley clinic couldn't handle this. Hope needed to get to a trauma unit.

"It's gonna be tight," said Chet, who'd interned that summer in a Calgary ER, in Alberta, where his mom came from. Bama called it in, nearly screaming into his radio, the veins jumping off his neck.

Reggie grabbed him by the shoulders and said, "Ain't nobody quitting here, Bama, so don't go sissy on yourself and lose your shit. We got this."

For a second, Bama trembled like an anxious boy and said, "You think?"

"I know, you fucking hillbilly," said Reggie, who'd probably waited years to say those words, and which put the thunder back in Bama. He checked Hope then yelled, "Load her up!"

Eight females emerged from nowhere and strode to the column. Word had trickled up the trail and they'd raced down to help. They were members of USA Volleyball, tall as oaks and fit as antelope. One woman grabbed the front of the litter, another the back, as four setters and spikers took each side and we trundled off, Bama jogging ahead, yelling, "Watch the ledge!" and "Left between the rocks!"

Twenty men trailed, ready to spell the ballers, but grateful for the relief as we flowed down widening switchbacks, pausing at the hairpin turns.

Bama blared into his radio, "Where's the goddam chopper?" The Valley was graying over.

Hope hadn't spoken for a whole bunch of switchbacks, and her silence was deafening. The volleyball team swapped out with the trailing column, and Chet checked Hope's pulse for a tenth time. Thin but steady.

"Where's that fucking chopper?!"

Deep shadows bled over the southern rim of the valley, streaking down the deepening draws, gulches, and rearing North Faces. We charged, the bathroom lights in Camp 4 shining through the gloom as the sound of thumping copter blades ricocheted up the valley.

We passed Hope from person to person over a lopsided staircase of railroad ties, racing her past the last switchback to the trailhead and reaching the dirt parking lot and the idling Mede Vac right as the sun started setting.

Twenty-five exhausted people bent over the litter and watched Hope's green eyes dim. And she faded, in the way a ballad or a movie ends. The medic strapped a blood pressure cuff onto Hope's limp arm and pumped and pumped. But he couldn't pull a reading. The trauma unit in Fresno was ninety-three miles away, he said, and he said no more.

They slid Hope into the cargo hold and Bama and I stumbled out onto the loop road—blocked for the rescue—and watched the chopper, and Hope, fade to black. We walked away in different directions. I never saw Bama again.

≙

The Jumbo Jet jounced off some turbulence. I dropped from a dreamless sleep and found myself on a plane. Took a minute for my eyes to pull focus on the small video monitor mounted on the seatback, the flight tracker showing the little yellow line edging out across the Atlantic.

I spotted Hope shuffling down the aisle, holding something in her hand and squinting in the blacked-out cabin. She'd find me eventually, so I stood and waved an arm. She took a well-practiced fall into the aisle seat, flipped open the tray table on the empty middle seat, and plunked down a plate with a key lime pie. Dessert from first class. She handed me a fork—a polished metal one, not the plastic articles they give you in economy. The wine, evidently, had worn off.

"Sorry about getting all heavy on you," she said. "But I'm in a kinda strange place these days, and I keep pulling people into it without trying. My boyfriend told me so, when he left for Colorado."

I told her to forget it and handed her back the fork. I never took food for granted. Back in my climbing bum days, we rarely had the good stuff and, even years later, a full fridge always amazed me. But I wasn't hungry. I still felt cold inside, even after napping for an hour. I tossed off the triple-shot can of espresso I had in my carry-on, and my head began to clear.

"What takes you to England?" she asked.

"I'm a writer on a show, and we're shooting in Wales next week."

"Good show? Have I seen it?"

"It's fluff," I said. "Bottom-feeder stuff."

Hope shrank back in her chair. "We did a concert last week in Baton Rouge," she said. "I'm a singer, by the way, and before the last set, I race backstage and change into heels and this fuck-me dress. I go back onstage and start belting out . . ." She paused, and jammed the fork into the pie. "Second we hit the bridge I have this sinking feeling that everyone knows I'm a poser. I can do pop, but it's not my jam. I'm not too good for it. Never said that. But there's hell to pay when I fake anything."

"You can afford it, anyhow, being all rich and shit."

"The Devil doesn't take cash," she said.

"Sounds like a song right there," I said.

"Don't do country, neither," she said with a hayseed twang. "Know how I got through that set? I saw myself back in that litter, at the end. All fog and liquid space. I let the rocking push the words outta me."

She was edging me back to the Valley, and we both knew it.

"Let's not do this," I said.

"Sorry," she said, grabbing my arm. She wasn't sorry. But it all went miles beyond Hope. This reckoning caged me like a mob loan I'd refused to pay off, and the vigorish was sucking me dry. I ran my finger over the gossamer tattoo circling her wrist.

"You asked about Bama and me," I said.

She raised a hand and said, "Doesn't make your business mine."

"Does now."

My tongue started swimming from the triple shot. I didn't fight it.

"Couple weeks before your accident," I said, "Bama gets word the sous-chef at the Yosemite Bar and Grill had gone missing. We both know the guy—a trail runner who'd set a bunch of records for out-and-back runs. He'd jogged out to Cloud's Rest. This big granite dome in Tenaya Canyon. When he doesn't show at work that night, Bama grabs me and we go searching next morning."

The plane bounced off some currents again and we nearly lost the pie.

"The trail's pretty good," I said, "but it's seven miles back to Cloud's Rest, and it takes us a couple hours to get there. No sign of the sous-chef, so we follow a watershed up toward the dome. Then some wild animal starts howling. Like it's gutshot or something. But it isn't an animal. It's the sous-chef. He's slumped in a heap at the base of Cloud's Rest. Legs shattered and twisted around. Got open fractures on both arms."

I glossed over how the sous-chef had somehow wriggled into a sitting position, with his back against the rock. He must have climbed the low-angled slab just above him, because the views up there are worth it. But he'd fallen, headfirst, bouncing and sliding straight into the ground. Whatever face he had was still up on the slab. Eyes, nose, lips, and cheeks—gone. All his front teeth were knocked out and his skull had been ground through in spots.

It seemed impossible any creature could still be alive like that. I only told Hope enough to paint the picture—that the sous-chef was unspeakably fucked up.

"His chest kept rising and falling," I said, "but he hadn't moved or made a sound—till his limbs started flailing like he's on fire. And that heinous wailing again.

I ripped open the first aid kit and Bama grabbed the morphine auto injectors, the kind they use for buddy-aid on the battlefield when somebody gets their legs blown off. Lucky a stick graphic showed us how to use them."

I'd compartmentalized the rest of this into a space so small and dense that light couldn't enter or escape. Now it exploded and I could picture it all lit up, like a film on the seatback monitor. I just narrated what I saw:

Bama pulls off the safety plug, rams the injector against the sous-chef's thigh, thumbs the firing plunger and twenty MGs of morphine race into him. His limbs stop flailing and his shrieks die off. Bama stumbles over to some scrub and throws up. Then the chef is wailing again, and his busted limbs start flapping against the rock. Bama grabs another injector, pulls off the plug and holds it over the sous-chef's thigh. His hand shakes so badly he can barely hold the thing. That'll kill him, I say. You know that. And Bama says, It better! Now we're playing God. I don't say anything and Bama yells, What would you want? The sous-chef wails again. I reach and cup my hand over Bama's and we fire home a second dose. He flatlines in less than a minute.

I'd waited so long to put words to this it rushed out of me like a flash flood. It took me a minute to catch back up with myself. The images still played on the monitor, but weren't solid like before and the details kept thinning out, as New York fell behind us on the flight map. I didn't feel so cold anymore. Just hollow.

"We wrapped him in the tarp," I said, "so the animals couldn't get him. Bama radioed in and a team met us on the trail for the carry-out.

We got him back to the road head around nine p.m. The doctor at the clinic, who signed the death certificate—he told us no human being could ever survive those injuries. The chief ranger said we'd done the right thing. But we'd done it for the wrong reasons: not to help the chef, but to kill his awful wailing. To make him dead so we could wrap him in the tarp and not have to look at him anymore. That's why Bama and I couldn't look at each other. We made sure we didn't have to—till you went and pitched off the Falls Trail."

We sat there, hurtling through space, saying nothing.

"If I was that chef," Hope finally said, "all I'd have wanted is for you to make it go away. You start in with your reasons, and do nothing, I blame you both forever."

I told her how the chef's friends hiked his ashes to the north rim and dumped them over Yosemite Falls. I pictured the kitchen crew emptying an urn into the torrent gushing off the lip, a half-remembered force much older yet running straight through the you and me.

"I wanna get back there," said Hope, "but probably not with this knee. Maybe you and Bama can carry me up the trail some summer day. If you know where he's at."

"I heard he's teaching music at some community college in Tuscaloosa," I said. This could have been hearsay, but it made me curious about the music she did like.

"Torch songs," she said. "Me and a piano in a smoky little room."

"You'll never earn a first-class seat from singing 'Cry Me A River.'"

"It's yours if you want it," she said, thrusting her chin toward the front and the six empty rows of first-class seats, where I could compartmentalize myself, solo in the dimness.

Sometimes I heard a wailing. The sound felt monolithic. Now it mingled with wind and mist, as water streamed over the rock. The Lost World was not so much a place as a crossroad for ghosts and living ghosts. And I wasn't so sure I wanted to leave just yet. A ghost doesn't feel, doesn't bleed. You just float in the mist, neither here nor there.

Hope kept talking, taken by the way things mattered. The wonder in her words, her daring as she leaned in, fetching the whole catastrophe— all these things were beacons of a world beyond the sous-chef.

Hope lowered her seat back all the way and said, "Maybe it's gonna be okay." Then she handed me the fork and gazed at the pie. "You gonna eat that, or what?"

ICE

I started pulling the rappel ropes, doubled through the anchor up above, when the free end got stuck in the crack.

"Shit!" Ed yelled. "We're toast . . ."

Warming days (which melted the high-country snowpack) and freezing nights had rimmed El Capitan with ice. Small beer when gazing from the Loop Road, a mile away and three thousand feet below the rim. But scope it through binos and you'll see an ice crown forty feet tall and just as thick, with hundred-foot icicles dangling below. Once sunlight hits the crown, chunks calve off and torpedo the lower slabs.

The sun was already wrapping around the East Buttress. We had to get off this thing. Like now.

By the time we freed the rope, the ice crown gleamed like a mirror. Huge drops, impossibly cold, pocked the face left and right. Ed shot down the last rappel at 20 MPH, touching ground as the first icy missiles dashed the face.

"Go! GO!" I yelled, but didn't need to.

Ed shot off and down the moraine field, hopping block to block. Slaloming around bushes and towering pines. Then gone.

Lashed to two bolts, I was a hanging duck. I hurried to thread the rope through my rappel device—then the CRACK, thousands of feet above.

A glimmering mass the size of a school bus slowly rotated in midair, freefalling straight for me. I pill-bugged as the chunk fell half a mile, which must have taken ten seconds. An eternity. And the whole time I'm cursing myself for misplacing my girlfriend's keys the previous night, both of us searching for hours, chastising the other for losing them. And how things heated up early that morning and I got pissed off and bolted up here at 6:30 a.m. with Ed.

The giant chunk of ice detonated on the slabs above. Huge ice bollards shrieked past like meteors, exploding off the rock. Crashing off the talus at the base. Shrapnel caroming 100 feet into the moraine field and blowing limbs off trees. That I wasn't smeared off my belay anchor was the dumbest luck.

I rappelled to the ground in seconds as another barrage carpet-bombed the talus. I dove under a little overhang—a granite awning to deflect direct strikes—but ricocheting shards stung like buckshot, and I bled from a thousand little cuts.

A short lull; and just as I'm set to dash for it, a big thump sounds from the slabs above. Followed by shrill whirring, like the antiaircraft missiles I've seen in war docs.

Not fifty feet away, right at the edge of the trees, a five-story, diamond-hard icicle augered straight into the deck, dematerializing into an exploding cloud of shards and cubes, as the end chased after, consuming the point. Then—nothing but splattering drops.

I hand-checked myself. Nothing mashed or missing. My heart banged away but my mind felt clear, and I saw where I'd put the goddam ring of keys last night. I didn't appreciate that a shockwave had blown me back a day, and I remembered the last thing I'd forgotten—till Ed shouted up from the tree line.

For a moment, I sat as frozen as the ice crown. Then jerked, like I'd grabbed high tension wires, and jumped to my feet.

"Still here!" I yelled back.

"Run for it, dumbass!" Ed yelled.

That's why they call them "partners."

I dashed after Ed, taking cover behind the downhill side of big Jeffery pines as grenades exploded all around. Finally, we cleared the impact zone.

On the loop road at last, I drove straight to Sherri's cabin and pulled the big ring of keys from the trunk lock in her rusty Dodge Dart. She met me at the door.

"My bad," I said, holding up the ring. "I left them stuck in your trunk."

She grabbed the ring and held it to her chest. She ran the night desk at Yosemite Lodge, and the ring had her work keys on it.

"Whatever happened to you," she said, frowning at the cuts on my hands and face, "you deserve it."

She'd searched all morning for those keys, while I went climbing. A selfish move, and I said so. She finally cracked a little smirk—meaning I was forgiven, again—and said, "You look dehydrated."

She grabbed a plastic bottle of Gatorade from the fridge, then opened the freezer. I grabbed the bottle and pushed the door shut.

"No ice."

NEVER KNEW HIS NAME

I was eighteen and had lived in Camp 4 less than a week. An hour before found me storming up 300-foot Arch Rock and sweating in a t-shirt. Now, I sat dead-still with my arms wrapped around my torso, as shadows stole over the valley. The towering walls had lost their sunny grandeur and seemed to sneer down at me with hostile intentions.

A mile straight across from me, Sentinel soared off terraced approach slabs like a prodigious black tombstone. A shudder rattled through me. Would I ever get up these walls? Did I really want to? For months, I'd thought about little more than finally getting right here, in the presence of the giants. But in all the books and magazines I'd read about Yosemite, no one had ever mentioned how this paradise could scare the living shit out of you.

I'd bolted for Yosemite the second school let out, and naturally, I'd run my mouth about my big plans. Now I could actually see where those plans would take me. For a long while, I sat on top of Columbia Boulder in an edgy daze, wondering which option I might survive: slinking out of the Valley some lonely night and living with a wimp's laments, or packing the haul bag, jumping onto the vertical unknown, and fighting the beast of my own doubts.

I could have gone either way, when a "Hey, John," startled me back to the present. It was Roger Rudolph, the then head backcountry ranger, and allied with the budding Search and Rescue Team.

I scrambled down and Roger gushed out a mouthful: an accident on the East Buttress of Middle Cathedral, two pitches below the summit; a leader fall and a head injury. A helicopter was en route to ferry the valley czars Jim Bridwell and Mark Klemens to the top of Middle to conduct a rescue. In case that plan failed, the Park Service needed another team to trudge to the top of Middle, schlepping a huge green backpack containing first aid and camping gear. If the Bridwell/ Klemens team hadn't set down by the time we gained the top, I'd rap to the victim and . . . well, we'd flesh out the plan from there.

"You handle that?" Roger asked.

Roger was about fifteen years older than me and a mentor who had skied 100 miles across Tioga Pass in winter, carted injured hikers out of the backcountry on his back, and ran a government department with forty people. A solid outdoors athlete, but out of his depths on a 1,600-foot face. By coincidence, he was also my first cousin. I was mostly clueless, but if Roger thought I was worthy, I'd go with it.

"Meet me back here in five," Roger said.

I dashed for Camp 4's rescue site, ranging table to table, desperate to find someone experienced who could help with the job. Luckily, I found Englishman Ben Campbell-Kelly lounging around camp, recovering from an early ascent of the North American Wall (then one of the hardest big rock climbs on earth) with his countryman Bryan Wyvill. I explained the situation, that I didn't know what I was doing and needed him along. Ben got to his feet and said, "Let's go, man."

Roger, Ben, and I manhandled the pack into Roger's cruiser and a few minutes later, he dropped us at the turnout below Middle Cathedral.

"Only got about three hours of daylight, so you'll have to bust ass," said Roger.

"You know where you're going?"

"Roughly," I said.

I'd climbed the East Buttress the summer before, but it took all day and we hacked down the descent gulley at night. I didn't remember a thing about the gulley.

I shouldered the pack and we trudged up through the pines toward the bushy slot left of Middle. I couldn't have had a better man alongside me than Ben Campbell-Kelly, a proven veteran of these walls, solid as Solomon.

Shortly, we entered a steep labyrinth of dead-end trails, teetering minarets, and low-angled choss corridors. We hadn't a clue about a proper path and never found one.

For two hours, we flailed and cursed our way up that gully, sometimes hand-carrying the pack and shoving it through a pinch when we couldn't wiggle through with it on our backs. We could more easily have dragged a waterbed up that gulley than that pack. About halfway up, we heard a copter circling above, and Ben and I wondered if we were killing ourselves for nothing.

When we finally broke out onto the shoulder beneath Middle's shapeless summit, Ben said he'd burned more gas and lost more hide grappling up that gully than he had climbing El Capitan. I shouldered the pig, and with Ben shoving from behind, we angled up grainy slabs toward the top. Only the crown of El Capitan glowed in light. We had maybe an hour before night fell like an iron gate.

A few minutes later, we met a team who'd just topped out on the East Buttress. Both were in their late twenties, wore colorful, long-sleeved rugby shirts, and thin, white navy pants, formal livery of the '70s Yosemite climber. I wondered about these guys' lives, and their jobs that allowed them to have fixed—for the convenience of rescuers who they knew would be along shortly—two costly new ropes above the injured climber, before dashing back to San Francisco for work and family. They'd fetch their ropes later, or never.

The two men said gusting winds kept the copter from landing on the summit, scrubbing the Bridwell/Klemens rescue effort. I confirmed as much with Roger over the walkie-talkie. We thanked the two San Fran climbers and moved over to the fixed lines. I clipped in and started down, battling not to get pulled over backward by the pack.

Ben shouldered the pig for the last rap and we touched down on a terraced recess by a big pine tree festooning the rock. The injured climb-er—I never learned his name—lay curled on a sloping ledge scarcely bigger than his body. His partner, Peter Barton, sitting dejectedly on a shelf ten feet below, had tied the victim taut to a cluster of anchors.

Ben and I rigged a line off the victim's anchor and moved to a ta-pering ledge ten feet lower. According to Peter, the victim had taken a tumbling fall and banged the back of his head. Though partially respon-sive at first, he hadn't moved in two or three hours.

I asked Ben what he knew about first aid and he said, "Nothing." Since I was the son of a doctor, Ben reckoned I'd absorbed essential medical knowhow by osmosis, and suggested I climb up the rope to the victim and play medic.

The victim's breathing seemed smooth, though hurried. He mum-bled incoherently. A patch of hair was raked off his scalp on the back of his head. No blood or troubling dent, but this guy was in trouble. Whenever a life hangs in the balance, the stakes suck you into a hy-per-real space where you see and remember the gurgling sounds, the acrid smell of fear, the pinched timbre of our voices—alien details that stood out in sharp relief. And yet how the victim looked, or even his age, I cannot say. Had he glanced at me, or said something instead of burbling and lying inert, I might remember his eyes, or his face. But now it's all a blank.

I reported the victim's condition to Roger and he said to pack the guy into a sleeping bag—there was one inside the giant pack—and to keep his airway clear. It took all three of us to wheedle the victim into the sleeping bag. I felt useless, knowing this guy needed assistance we couldn't hope to provide. Roger said there wasn't much more to do. Settle in for the night and hope for the best. Back at park headquarters, Bridwell and two rescue rangers were devising a strategy for tomorrow. Pray the victim somehow holds on. Over and out.

Ben and I returned to the lower ledge and sat back. The slab dropped below for twenty or so feet, then the wall steepened and plunged out of sight. Peering off that perch, I hunkered down for my first bivouac on a rock wall. We dug into the pack and found a headlamp, several gallons of water, a 12-pack of lemonade mix, a wall rack, a lead rope, a great mass of pulleys and bewildering rescue tackle, a frightening twelve-inch knife, two balaclavas, a second radio, several packs of batteries, a first-aid kit that folded out like an accordion, a shovel, a compass, two Ensolite pads, and a bunch of other stuff I can't remember—but not so much as a breadstick to eat.

"We're fucked," said Ben.

Thankfully we had a couple packs of smokes between us and we lit up, gazing into the gloom. Far below, the earth seemed to open up, then night crawled out and swallowed the wall and the world.

Ben, 30, had a rowdy head of red hair and an elegant sideburn-goatee constellation befitting the British academic he was in public life. His calm, rational manner was a balm to my willies, which after an hour in pitch darkness, reared up like wild horses. To divert myself, I pried Ben about his many adventures on big walls in Norway, the Alps, and of course, most recently, the great El Capitan. His comments were so understated I came to believe that sitting there on that tiny ledge in my flimsy white navy pants and a t-shirt was no big deal after all. I admired myself for throwing in with the Yosemite hardmen and, around midnight, figured I was nearly one myself. Then it got very cold, and the victim started wailing. Peter asked what the hell we were going to do, and things went south from there.

Ben and I took turns hold the man down as the other made sure he didn't swallow his tongue or do something worse. The guy bit our fingers horribly, and sometimes his arms flailed and his legs churned inside the bag. We couldn't have been less helpful.

Around dawn, the victim quieted, and might have died for all we knew. The notion frightened me, so I hand-walked the rope up the slab and found him still alive, but apparently in a coma. We couldn't do a thing. I returned to the ledge, emptied the pack and pulled it over my legs. I never knew a person could feel so wasted. Then Roger cut in over the radio. A copter was blading in from Livermore Air Force base to attempt an "extraction." This was long before cliff-rescue techniques had been standardized and neither Ben nor I knew what they were talking about. Roger explained.

Bridwell had reckoned that at our present location, the wall was sufficiently low-angled to allow a copter to hover some hundreds of feet above and lower a litter down on a cable winch.

"That should be good theater," said Ben.

And we'd be seeing it momentarily, as the percussive thumping of copter blades echoed up the Valley.

"Will you look at that bugger!" Ben yelled.

Whatever copter I had envisioned, it wasn't the monstrosity heaving to several hundred feet above, big as a Greyhound bus. Two enormous blades spat pulsing thunder that rattled our bones and shot down a shaft of prop wash that swirled every pine needle and bit of turf into a choking tornado. I thrust my head into the big pack and when I pulled it back out, the surroundings looked as if they'd been scrubbed with a wire brush. The contents of the giant bag were blown into oblivion.

A soldier stepped from the open cargo bay door of the copter and lowered down on a cable, like a dummy on a string. He sat on a "Chaparral Leveler," a bullet-shaped cylinder the size of a fire hydrant with two fold-down metal flaps on the bottom. (A Vietnam vet later told me they used to swoop the Leveler through "hot zones" and pluck out of the fire anyone who had the minerals to mount the Leveler at speed.) The giant Sikorsky "Hercules" stayed glued in the sky and the soldier slowly descended perhaps 150 feet until finally touching down on the slab a short ways below our ledge. Whoever piloted the ship was a deadeye who couldn't have been more accurate had he delivered the guy on a spoon. With his huge helmet and smoky visor, plus the dashing Air Force jumpsuit, the soldier looked like Flash Gordon.

The moment Flash stepped off the Chaparral Leveler, he was unroped, 1,200 feet off the deck. His mountaineering boots skedaddled on the slab as his hands pawed for a hold, and we knew right off Flash Gordon was no climber.

Ben quickly anchored off a loop of rope, hand-walked down, and clipped in Flash, who pulled up his smoky visor and barked out his orders. The plan sounded basic and, surprisingly, went off without a hitch.

The copter lowered down a litter and we loaded up and lashed down the victim, who was winched straight into the hovering ship.

"Okay," said Flash, staring at the ship still hanging directly overhead. "Who's going with me?"

"How's that?" Ben asked.

We'd figured Flash would ascend the fixed lines with Ben, Peter, and me. But he wanted no part of any rock climbing.

"I'm going out on the Leveler," said Flash, "and it gets squirrelly with one man. I need another guy to balance the load."

"I'll go," I said without thinking.

"Atta boy," Ben replied.

He'd climb El Cap in a snowstorm, but he wasn't daft enough to volunteer to get winched off a Yosemite wall on a kite string. I wasn't courageous—I'd just opened up my mouth and blurted.

Just before sitting on the Leveler, Flash said not to worry and to simply hold on tight. We sat face to face on two metal flaps barely larger than my hand. This set us up like two guys bearhugging with a flagpole between them. There were no straps or tie-ins at all.

The cable twanged taut and my stomach fell into my boots as we were pulled off the wall and into mid-air. After ten feet, we started yawing side to side and the copter motored out away from the wall, initiating a harrowing pendulum a couple thousand feet off the treetops. The pilot swept even farther out into open space, away from the wall, which set us swinging in wild horizontal arcs.

Only vaguely could I feel the winch pulling us up as we sliced through the air like trapeze artists hitched to the moon. I remember flashing on the saucy French tourist girl I'd met in the cafeteria, and how she'd probably have to spend the rest of her life without me now. The shit that goes through our heads in the thick of it . . . I enjoyed the view as best I could.

About fifteen feet from the cargo door, right when we stopped swinging, we began spinning, faster and faster. In thirty seconds, I felt so dizzy I could barely hang on. Then they shut off the winch and we dropped a few horrible inches and wrenched to a stop. I glanced up and saw a flurry of airmen fiddling around the winch, which started back up with a lurch and then stopped again, with Flash and me dangling about waist-level with the open cargo bay door. Flash was nearest the ship, and one of the airmen reached down and yanked him on board. This instantly rocked the Leveler out of balance and I nearly fell off. For a moment, the airmen, with blank looks on their faces, stared down at me dangling in space.

Then Bridwell appeared from somewhere, grabbed a strut on the door, and reached down his hand. We locked arms; Bridwell yanked and I shot off the flap and bellyflopped into the bay. The Bird (Bridwell's nickname), who'd been spotting for the pilot, gave a thumbs-up and the big ship banked and headed for El Cap Meadow.

Several medics huddled over the victim. His vital signs checked out and they figured his chances were good, which amazed and relieved me. (I later learned he did survive, following operations to relieve pressure on his brainpan.) Several minutes later, the big ship touched down. In a fifty-yard radius, the tall grass in Yosemite Meadow was pummeled flush as the pitch on a putting green. Bridwell and I jumped out and the ship thumped off for the trauma unit in Fresno.

Roger rushed up and smacked my arm. Ben had just checked in over the walkie talky. He and Peter were just starting down the descent gully. So in practical terms, the rescue was over. I'd expected an official reception, or at any rate a swelling tourist mob. But it was barely seven in the morning and the three of us found ourselves alone in the middle of the meadow. In a few short minutes, as the giant copter bladed out of the valley, everything went still and quiet, as if nothing had ever happened.

The summer after the rescue, Peter Barton (partner of the victim on the rescue) and I teamed up for several big climbs, including the first ascent of Stoner's Highway, also on Middle, a Yosemite Valley classic. A year later, while ferrying loads up to the West Face of El Capitan, Peter lost his footing on a steep bit and perished in a tumbling fall. A helicopter flew in from Livermore to recover Peter's body. Over the steep moraine below the West Face, the copter experienced mechanical problems and ditched in the boulders. The crew barely escaped when the ship burst into flames.

Peter's relatives had his remains cremated, hired a private plane, and from a height of 500 feet above the southern rim of Yosemite Valley (anything lower is illegal), released Peter's ashes over Middle Cathedral Rock.

DR. BROWN

An intern found the scratchy, 16-inch 33 1/3 rpm Vitaphone soundtrack disc in the bottom of a steamer trunk. For seventy years, it had gathered dust in the basement of the Malibu City Library, which has one of the finest collections of mountaineering texts in the US. The narrator on the Malibu disk (Damon Runyon) recounts the life of a doctor and amateur mountain climber named Nathan Brown, whose ancestors purportedly arrived on the Mayflower. By 1850, the Browns grew more Virginian tobacco than anyone and had four family members in congress.

During the Great Depression, while Nathan's stepfather served in the U.S. embassy in Mexico, the family relocated to Mexico City. Here, young Nathan learned Spanish and, on weekends, joined several young embassy staffers for *aventuras de escalada* on Popocatépetl and Iztaccihuatl, the towering volcanoes north of the capital. Nathan also favored bullfighting, mescal, and girlfriends lured from the untouchable peon class. All of this reflected poorly on the Ambassador, so at eighteen, Nathan was shipped back to Virginia for college.

Nathan excelled in school, but there were incidents. Nevertheless, Nathan finished his medical studies and was immediately found *in flagrante* with the daughter of the pathology professor, a fierce man who launched a crusade against Nathan and his family.

Nathan's stepfather, recently returned from Mexico City, gave him $300 and showed him the door. If Nathan was at all honorable, he would leave—forever.

Nathan went into the study and threw a dart at a map of the United States. The first toss stuck in Pennsylvania. He removed the dart and threw it again. This time it stuck in Arizona. Nathan scanned the map, saw 12,600-foot Humphrey's Peak, and was on the next train heading west. Nine days later, standing on top of the peak, he gazed out over the plains. These mountains, and this broad and empty land, would have to do.

Nathan made his way to Flagstaff, then just a wide spot in the road, where he let a room above a dry-goods store and opened up shop. One of his first patients, a woodworker who'd lost a finger in a lathe, made him a little wooden sign that he tacked to the bottom of the staircase: "Doctor Brown - Office Upstairs."

Town managers thought he should work out of the local clinic, but Dr. Brown continued seeing patients in his little room above the dry-goods store. The many Mexican immigrants living in the dusty barrios just outside of town had no problem with Dr. Brown or his office. Here was a doctor who spoke their language and didn't require cash money. Frijoles, *sopa de albondigas*, chickens—anything would do and no one was turned away.

Rumors persisted. Dr. Brown liked playing cards and drinking tequila with undesirables. Dr. Brown and his Mexican house cleaner were known to share the same bed. Dr. Brown stole medicines from the clinic and sold them to the poor—which was only half true. He gave the medicine away. And every week, Dr. Brown risked his life in the mountains. The park ranger himself told how the doctor had climbed every surrounding mountain a hundred different ways, usually alone, never using any safety equipment. Dr. Brown, said the ranger, was a rash and reckless man. Without fail, Dr. Brown would trudge back from his mountains to find the infirm sitting on the stairs of his "office."

Then the daughter of a local merchant went and fell in love with Dr. Brown, and the two were to be married. An engagement banquet was arranged, and important people invited from as far away as Phoenix and Prescott. Here was the chance to draw the doctor back into society, where his talents could be appreciated and rewarded.

But on the morning of the banquet, Dr. Brown was called away by a Navajo man who said his daughter was ill. Since Dr. Brown had no car, they rode on the Indian's horse. It was a long ride. The girl had dysentery, and over the next few days, the doctor nearly lost her several times. When he returned to town, his fiancée's father met him on the stairs with a Colt .45. He would not have the reckless doctor as a son in law, who was forced, at gunpoint, to beg for his life. For the first time in memory, the doctor went to a saloon in the barrio north of town and was thrown out for *borrachera y pelea*—drunkenness and fighting. He left for the mountains that night.

Two days later, a storm hit Humphrey's Peak just as the doctor reached the summit—or so the rangers figured. On his way down, he apparently ran into a three-man party in bad shape. They were stranded, and were unprepared for the storm.

Evidence suggested that the doctor tried to get the three down the mountain in the snowstorm, which lasted two days and two nights. The youngest victim, a boy of fourteen, was wearing the doctor's hat and parka when they found the four bodies, frozen into the slope. Doctor Nathan Brown was thirty-one years old.

The sheriff discovered that the doctor barely had enough money in the bank to buy a pine coffin, with nothing left over for the burial. They needed to get this business quickly over, so the town manager alerted a few of the doctor's acquaintances to dig a hole on the flanks of the cemetery, which they managed the first day. An old Navajo man and two Mexicans lowered Dr. Brown's coffin into the ground with a rope. The woodworker shoveled rubbly earth onto the coffin and planted a wooden cross. Then the small group wandered off for home.

All but the woodworker, who sat down and stared at the grave. For a man like Dr. Brown, a fancy marble headstone was not quite right. And who could afford one, anyhow? But two scraps of two-by-four nailed into a cross wouldn't do either. Then the woodworker remembered.

For many years afterwards, when someone wandered out to the rocky edge of the cemetery to have a smoke or relieve themselves, they'd come across a grave marked by a simple cross, upon which hung a little wooden sign: "Dr. Brown - Office Upstairs."

RIPCORD

YOSEMITE VALLEY. Dawn. Mike Lechlinski and I are just stirring in our hammocks, lashed high on the granite face of El Capitan, when a whooshing sound shatters the silence. Louder, closer, building to a roar. Rockfall. Heading right for us: we're dead. I instinctively brace for impact as two BASE jumpers streak over our heads, only a dozen feet away and traveling at 120 miles per hour.

It seems impossible that two falling bodies can make such terrifying, ear-splitting racket, like God is ripping the sky in half with his bare hands.

We scream, craning our heads from our hammocks, our eyes following the jumpers plunging into the void. Their arms dovetail back as they track away from the cliff. The pop of their chutes fires up the wall like shotgun blasts. They swoop over treetops and land fifty feet into the meadow as a beater station wagon screeches to a stop on the loop road. The jumpers bundle their canopies, jog over, and dive into the jalopy, which speeds off. If the rangers catch them in the act, they're going to jail. We howl because we're still there, still alive.

"I think I pissed myself," says Mike.

In 1984, the adventure world caught fire and every serious player tried to blaze like hell. From our first sorties free climbing big walls to jungleering across Oceania, the mantra never changed: capture the burning flag. Our cousins in big wave surfing, kayaking, cave diving, and mountain biking were also charging hard, and the most visually dramatic show of them all was BASE jumping, the acronym for parachuting from a *B*uilding, *A*ntenna, *S*pan (bridge), and the *E*arth (cliffs).

A couple years after my close encounter on El Cap, I needed something bold to gain traction in the TV business, where I hoped to quickly score the trophy girls and crazy money. I was two months out of school, with a fistful of so-what degrees and a junker Volkswagen Beetle, determined to leave Yosemite behind.

British talk show maven and future Richard Nixon interviewer, David Frost, had a boutique production house with Sunset Boulevard offices. I hired on as a writer and associate producer, knowing zero about the television racket. The salary didn't dazzle but my future glowed. We had several hour-long *Guinness Book of World Records* specials that we needed to style out with electrifying content. Previous episodes featured a dull parade of magicians, carnivorous spiders, and an English mastiff named Claudius, the world's largest dog. I promised to hose out the dog shit, clean up the show, and boost the numbers.

I knew going in that staging world-class adventures for television was sketchy, but so what. I was handy with danger and eager to debut BASE jumping on primetime national television. The plan felt like money. That left the tricky bit: collaring someone to do the jumping.

My immediate boss, Ian, urbane, sardonic, and classically educated at Eton, favored exciting acts. BASE jumping was one of several adventure pursuits, each riskier than the last, that I'd scribbled onto our dance card, and which the network, indemnified of responsibility, could promote to the moon. Ratings were everything, but in Jack Daniels moments Ian sometimes asked, "We're not going to get anyone killed doing this, are we?"

"Not if I can help it," I'd say.

The stars aligned and, in late June, I flew to London and joined Carl Boenish and his wife, Jean. Carl, 43, later dubbed "the father of BASE jumping," was a free-fall cinematographer who, in the 1970s, had filmed the inaugural jumps from El Capitan, plus many other "first exits" off high-rise buildings, antennas, and bridges.

For sheer burn and ebullience, Carl had few peers. Jean, nineteen years Carl's junior, brainy, wholesome, and distant as polar ice, lived her life in a language I didn't understand.

From London, Carl, Jean, and I flew to Oslo. The Norwegian airlines had gone on strike, so we packed six duffel bags into a rental station wagon and headed for the Troll Peaks in the Romsdalen valley, eight hours north. The narrow road meandered through evergreen valleys, dark as tourmaline, laced with alpine streams and glinting under the midnight sun. We stopped for beers at an inn (ginger ale for the Boenishes, who took no liquor), and I marveled at the year, 1509, chiseled on the stone hearth.

Finally, we crept into the sleepy town of Åndalsnes, surrounded by misty cliffs, including the Trollveggen, Europe's tallest vertical rock face, a brooding gneiss hulk featuring several notorious rock climbs and the proposed site for our world-record BASE jump. "Built when the mountain was built," folklore says of Åndalsnes.

Carl and I breakfasted on pickled cod, peanut butter, and black coffee, and zigzagged up a steep road to the highest path and set out on a leg-busting trudge for Trollveggen's summit. We were joined by Fred Husoy, a young local, among the finest adventure climbers in Europe, who knew the Troll massif by heart—critical in locating our jump site.

The first few miles climbed a glacial plateau, broken occasionally by lichen-flecked boulders and gray snow drifts that never melted, carved by wind into gargoyles and labyrinths. The lunar emptiness hadn't changed in a billion years, and held the silence of the dead when the wind died down. It was so big and so blinding that it seemed even the birds felt lost in it, crying out to break the stillness.

From the moment we'd hit the trail, Carl hiked so slowly that I finally took his pack; but halfway over the huge white plane, he'd once more fallen well behind. Fred pulled on his raincoat against the drizzle, warning we had to hike faster or get blown off the mountain by afternoon storms. We slogged ankle-deep through a snowfield. When Carl caught up, wet clouds draped everything. No coaxing could make him hike faster. A little stone hut twenty minutes shy of the summit ridge offered a welcome roof from the shower.

Carl limped in, collapsed, and pulled up a pant leg. Fred and I stared. Right above the ankle, Carl's femur took a shocking jag, as if he'd snapped it in half and the bone had healed inches off plumb. I felt small and mean to have pushed him. How did a person hike at all with a leg like that?

"Jesus. When did that happen?" I asked.

He'd shattered his leg in a hang-gliding accident several years back, said Carl, who clenched his way through a wonky exposition on natural healing.

"I don't know, Carl," I said. "A bone doc could surely fix that. It's hideous."

Carl swished the air with his hand. Who needed doctors when God Almighty would set things right? His fingers trembled as he pulled up his sock. It felt staggering and recklessly bold to stake my future on a man living off stardust and voodoo.

≜

A week before, we'd organized the venture at Carl's house in Hawthorne, a small L.A. suburb. From the moment I stepped through the door, Jean eyed me with steely reckoning, as though if she glanced away, I might pilfer the china. Her clothes were Mennonite-plain, the house immaculate, all cups and chairs and handcuffs in their place. Nothing admitted she and Carl dove off cliffs for a living.

As Carl raked through his garage, overflowing with gear, he'd bloviate about St. Peter, Coco Joe, or whoever. Without warning, Carl would dash to his piano and butcher some Brahms or Brubeck, then jump back into conversation, randomly ranging from electrical engineering to terracotta sculpture to trampolines and particle physics, galvanized by a screwy amalgam of new age doctrine and personal revelations. Often, he would heave all this out in the same sprawling rant. Ian thought he'd dropped acid. But Carl laughed so loud and burned so hot I found myself giddy by the inspired way he met the world. We lived in different keys, but we both craved the intimacy of risk. And in the fellowship of adventurers, folks like Carl Boenish drove the bus.

Outside our little stone hut in the Troll Peaks, the rain slacked off and we continued over snowy slabs toward the mile-long summit ridge, all dark clefts, precarious boxcar blocks, and pinnacles digging into the sky, as twisted and multidimensional as an M.C. Escher landscape. The wall dropped 6,000 feet directly off the ridge and into the Trondheim valley. The rubbly slabs angled down behind us to the high glacial plateau, where perpetual snow framed a tiny lake glowing aquamarine. Black-and-white clouds gathered, masking the ridge, cutting visibility to several hundred feet and making it difficult to navigate. Without Fred's knowledge of the labyrinthine summit backbone, we would have wandered blind.

The clouds parted and we lay belly-down on the brink, sticking our heads out over the immediate, sucking drop. Carl rubbed his leg, laughed, grimaced, and laid out his requirements.

The wall directly beneath his launch must overhang for hundreds of feet, he said, long enough for a plunging BASE jumper to reach near-terminal velocity. Only at top speed, when the air became thick as water, could his layout positioning create enough horizontal draft to track and fly out and away from the wall (the now-ubiquitous wingsuit wouldn't be invented for another dozen years) to pop the chute, as Mike and I had witnessed on El Capitan. The new parachutes didn't simply drop vertically, but sported a three-to-one glide ratio—three feet forward for one foot down. But twisted lines could sometimes deploy a chute backwards, wrenching the jumper around and into the cliff.

"Here, that would be fatal," said Carl with buggy eyes, peering back over the lip.

The most prominent spires along the ridgeline were named after chess pieces. Out left loomed The Castle, a striking, 200-foot spire canting off the brink like the Tower of Pisa. An exit from the summit, hanging out over oblivion like that, had to be safer than leaping straight off the summit ridge, making it an obvious feature to scout.

Carl hung back as Fred and I tied on a rope and scrambled up the water-logged Castle to the top—a flat and shattered parapet, perfect to start our rock tests. We wobbled a chair-sized boulder over to the lip and shoved it off. Five, six . . . *Bam*—a sound like mortar fire. Debris rattled down for ages.

"No good," said Carl, yelling from the ridgeline. "Way too soon to impact."

We tried again. This time, I leaned over the lip and watched a second rock whiz downward, swallowed in fog 300 feet below. Three, four . . . *Bam!* My head snapped up. There had to be jutting ledges mere feet below the fog line. We shoved off more rocks and kept hearing the immediate violent impact of stone on stone.

"Forget it," Carl yelled. "The Castle will never do. It'd be crazy." The flinty smell of shattered rock wafted up as Fred and I rappelled off the pinnacle and joined Carl.

For another hour we continued the rock tests at successive points along the rubbly brink. Trundling rocks off most any other cliff could kill people. Not there. Any climbers on the wall and we'd have known about them. And below the towering upper wall spilled a massive, low-angled slab, terminating in a sprawling moraine field where nobody but climbers had reason to go.

All around us loomed forces and forms so elemental they had never organized into life. Nothing native to this place could even die. But we could. That's what made the testing so heady. Each rock we shouldered off dashed the wall within seconds. When lightning cracked off the lower ridge we ran for the valley. Carl hobbled behind.

≜

Norwegians are a handsome race, normally demure, until you pull the cork on Friday afternoon and the dritt hits the vifte. That night, all the young locals in town crammed into the pub in the hotel's basement, where we drank Frydenlund like mad, chased it with beer, and danced to The Who. Several gallons in, a tall brunette with a stylish bob grabbed a handful of my shirt. She acted more curious than courageous, and couldn't find the words. So I trotted out the one Norwegian phrase I had memorized from a handbook in my room: "Hvorkanjegkjøpe en vikinghjelm?" (Where can I purchase a Viking helmet?)

"Are you a Viking?" she asked in flawless English. I said I'd try to be one for her, and she said, "You will marry me." That night I saw eternity and it looked like this: a girl and a boy dancing in a crowd on an unswept floor in a bar on a thousand-year-old street.

Aud came from the next town over, and worked some dreary retail job in Åndalsnes during summer break from nursing school. We spent our free time together, and I learned there are moments where nothing is so grim as being alone. I usually went it alone, a shark who survived by staying in motion. Until Aud drew the restlessness from me like a thorn, and a little light leaked in.

≜

The next day, as Carl recovered in his hotel room, Fred and I slogged back to the summit ridge for our first of many recons, trying to locate a viable launch site. The existing world's longest BASE jump, first established three years before, exited the ridge well east and some 400 feet lower than the Castle. That left us to scour the chaotic, quarter-mile-long ridge between The Castle and the old site—a confusing task for sure. Over the following weeks, when we weren't kicking around the Troll-veggen's cloudy ramparts, Fred and I would snag Aud and go bouldering on huge, mossy erratics, or hike up spectacular peaks or along jagged ridges snaking through the sky. I was twenty-six; Fred and Aud were in their early twenties, all of us novice adults, searching for our niche in the world.

Twice more, Fred and I explored the summit ridge, ever dashed by hailstorms.

The rain, meanwhile, kept washing our budget into the talus, and my inability to locate a jump site was wearing us out. Norway completed our production schedule, and the crew looked toward holidays in Paris, the Greek Islands, or home. We had to get this done. On the ninth scout, after a nasty piece of scrambling and several tension traverses on crappy rock, we located the highest possible exit from the ridge: The Bishop, to use the old chess name. But again, we got weathered off before we made our rock tests.

We returned early the next day and, lucky for us, the sky shone all blue distance, the entire ridge fantastically visible and spilling down on both sides for miles. After weeks spent wandering about in the fog, it felt like a vision from the Bible, the entire rambling cordillera unmasked before us. We definitely were on the apex, walking unroped on an anvil-flat, 10-by-50-foot ledge that terminated in an abyss as sudden and arresting as the lip of the Grand Canyon. If the rock tests checked out, we were halfway home. The easy half.

I lashed myself taut to two separate lines, bent over the drop, and lobbed off a bowling-ball-sized rock while Fred timed the free fall. The rock accelerated ferociously and dropped clean from sight. Twelve, thirteen . . . I glanced over at Fred and smiled. This could be it. Seventeen, eighteen . . . *BANG!* A faint puff of white smoke appeared thousands of feet below. That rock had just free-fallen three quarters of a mile. No question, The Bishop was our record site. Fred pointed out the original launch spot (or exit site), still far left and 300-something feet below. I chucked another rock and we watched it shrink to a pea and burst like a sneeze near the base, the echo volleying up from the amphitheater. I tried to imagine strapping on a chute and plunging off, but couldn't.

And I couldn't yet imagine ever climbing this towering heap. From a distance, Trollveggen looked classic, a 2,000-foot-high talus slope topped by a 3,600-foot rock wall. At its steepest, the summit ridge over-hung the base by 160 feet. Up close, however, the greatest rock wall in Europe was all fractured statuary, a vertical rubble pile top to bottom. And so utterly, unspeakably *other,* existing in that in-between space where the living feel like phantoms and the inanimate expanse is the geological expression of a mood, sinister for its indifference, yet touched by forever. However one might describe this gray place, it spooked me more by the day and the week.

We ascended our fixed rope, reversed the traverse and, as the first raindrops fell, Fred and I hoofed it to the valley with the good news.

For the next five days, Aud, Fred, and I stayed glued to the Oslo news channel, frequently stepping outside and glancing through thundershow-ers for some providential patch of blue. Mostly we milled around the production HQ in the hotel basement, living off chocolate scones and espresso. Helicopters stood on standby, film cameras were loaded, every angle reckoned, logistics planned to the minute. Meanwhile, journalists throughout Scandinavia streamed into Åndalsnes. The local paper ran full-page spreads in a town where the breaking news trended toward a farmer hooking a record lunker in a secret stream. When approached and pried at, Carl would laugh and let fly his exotic babbling as journalists nodded and smiled but took no notes. Finally, Jean—normally laconic as the Venus de Milo—would answer with several cold facts and figures.

A celebrated Oslo stringer, newly arrived, cited previous BASE jump-ing accidents and questioned something that had every official chewing their nails. As starry-eyed admirers gathered to touch Carl's jumpsuit, she all but screamed that the emperor had no clothes. The glossy hype and big money spent was nothing but a made-for-TV flim-flam in the service of a maniac who, by the sound of him, had flunked kindergarten and had little regard for his own safety. The worry on her face and edge in her words betrayed her annoyance that The Jump had a gravity even she couldn't escape. None of this was simple.

We slunk around. Rain fell in sheets. Tension mounted. With all the media hoopla, all the delays, each emerging detail raised the story's sails sky-high. Norwegian television ran nightly updates. The big Oslo station sent a video truck. With a week's momentum, the production took on the pomp and blather of Hollywood—precisely what I'd hoped to avoid.

Several journalists took to quoting Carl directly. The translation to Norwegian vexed but the waiting game was somewhat relieved by trying to guess what the hell Carl had said.

The sky growled at us. Scandinavia stood by. Each day in limbo meant thousands of dollars lost to feed, liquor, and house the crew. This quickly morphed into an impatience for what required steadfast deliberation. Throughout, the Boenishes were ready to jump and at 8:00 p.m., July 5, 1984, the weather broke.

Everyone scrambled, desperate to shoot something, even in bad light. In two hours, cameramen choppered into position. The helicopter dumped Carl, Jean, Fred, and me into a small notch 40 feet from the launch site on The Bishop. This avoided having to wheedle the Boenishes across the traverses, fitted with fixed ropes, that had given Fred and me fits owing to loose rock.

Carl pulled on his flaming red jumpsuit and paced around like someone waiting for the electric chair. Jean began assiduously studying the launch site. I pitched off a rock that whistled into the night. Other rocks followed to verify my estimates, but disclosed another hazard.

"Sure, they drop forever," laughed Carl, "and that's a good thing. But they're never more than ten feet from the wall."

That left no margin for error. If they couldn't stick the perfect, horizontal free-fall position, if they carved the air even slightly back-tilted—head higher than feet—they could possibly track backwards. Carl demonstrated with his hands, one hand as the wall, the other for the jumper. When his hands smacked together, Fred and I jumped. Jean, cool as the Romsdal Fjord, rolled more stones toward the lip. The light faded to a gray pall. Far below, the great stone amphitheater swallowed the night.

The radio coughed out: *"Come on, mate, let's get on with it!"* The crew was freezing and the director of photography feared it would quickly get too dark to film.

"Hey," said Carl, lucid as water, "I can't be rushed to jump off this cliff."

I quoted this word-for-word into the radio, and the crew backed off. They'd planned to jump in tandem—Jean first, followed closely by Carl—but for this run-through, Carl chose to huck a solo jump while the cameramen previewed and assessed the angles. The sun, at the wee hours, was too dim for full glory, but a practice jump could help the cameramen dial in the details. The sky, though darkening, remained clear and flawless so, with some luck, the good weather might hold. After Carl's trial jump, we'd resume in a few hours, when full light returned.

Carl strapped on his parachute and I tried to capture his kinetic energy on film. But I couldn't pull a focus in the gloom. I packed away the Ariflex, grabbed a still camera, and turned to the drama before the jump.

"Ten minutes," said Carl, bug-eyed, jaw working, hands fidgety. Jean helped Carl with the last straps. Cued by days of front-page spreads, the road below swarmed with cars and people, headlights winking in 1:00 a.m. murk.

"Five minutes," said Carl.

Carl pulled some streamers from his pack. Leaning off the ropes, I lobbed them off. No wind. They fell straight toward the base, shrinking to a blur. Everything looked *go.*

"One minute," said Carl, his voice high and tight. He cinched his helmet and slid twitching fingers into white gloves. I pitched off a final rock and Carl tracked it, visualizing his line.

"Fifteen seconds."

Carl unclipped the rope and stepped over to the lip. Horns sounded below. I was tied off to several ropes, my feet on the edge, with a panoramic view for the ages.

Carl's shoes tapped like a rhythm machine, eyes unfocused. He started his countdown, which Fred mimicked into the radio: "Four, three, two, one!" And he was off.

Watching someone jump straight off a cliff like this is so counterintuitive to a climber's instincts that Carl might as well have jumped into the next world. The void swallowed him alive, his streaking form more easily imagined than described. The air froze in my chest.

After a few seconds, Carl's arms went out to stabilize, his legs bending and straightening while his jumpsuit whipped like a flag. With roaring speed, Carl passed several ledges with ten feet to spare, body whooshing, ripping the air with a violent report. After 1,000 feet, his arms snapped to his sides as he flew horizontally away from the wall, tracking 50, 100, 150 feet, at 120 miles per hour, a swooping red dot. Thirteen seconds, fourteen, fifteen . . . *Pop!* His yellow chute unfurled big as a circus tent, and he glided down, over the slab and moraine field to the meadow. The picture-perfect jump.

Fred and I crabbed back from the lip, gaped at each other, and howled. Some called Carl an idiot for risking his life over something that didn't matter; but we'd just watched him rogue fear with imagination, and dive into the unknown. And if that doesn't matter, nothing much does.

Back at the hotel at 3:30 a.m., the chaotic crews, gnashing producers, frantic journalists, film loaders, battery chargers, pilots, and hangers-on, all guzzled espresso and ducked out to check for clouds, everyone anxious to film the jump and clear out. A chartered jet sat gassed and awaiting the crew once we finished filming, hopefully by noon. At 4:00 a.m., I laid down with Aud for a short nap, but couldn't settle for all the caffeine and apprehension.

At 6:00 a.m., two helicopters ground up through Persian blue skies and deposited us on The Bishop. Half an hour later, after some rock tests, and rechecking their rigs, the laces on their shoes, the film and batteries in their helmet-mounted cameras, Jean tiptoed to the lip, with Carl inches behind her. I stood five feet away, lashed to a rope, toes curled over the brink, shouldering a 16 mm film camera. 100 feet straight out in space, the helicopter yawed and hovered like a dragonfly. Fred gave the order to roll cameras. The Boenishes stepped off the lip and dropped into the void. Jean later wrote:

Eyes fixed on the horizon, I raise my arms into a good exit position. Then from behind, 'Three! Two! One!' For an instant my eyes dart down to reaffirm one solid step before the open air. Go! One lunging step forward and I'm off, Carl right on my heels. Freedom! Silence accelerates into the rushing sound as my body rolls forward. I quickly realize that the last downward glance has been an indulgence now taking its toll, for I roll past the prone into a head-down dive, which takes me too close to the wall. The first ledge is rushing towards me as I strain to keep from flipping over onto my back.

Through the viewfinder, I watched Jean dive-bomb and slowly cant over onto her back. I panicked and ripped away the camera as she plummeted, her toes nearly brushing the first ledge.

"Holy shit!" Fred yelled.

Jean somehow arched back to prone, her hands came back, and the duo swooped away from the wall, shrinking to colorful specks, still flying, 200 feet out, still free-falling. Their training, from thousands of skydives and hundreds of BASE jumps, steered them down the face. But watching the pair, as they streaked toward hungry boulders, stopped my heart.

"Pull the chute!" I screamed. Sixteen seconds, seventeen: *POP! POP!* A world record, no injuries. Cameramen raved over the radios. Newsmen and bystanders swarmed the Boenishes after their pinpoint landing. The world toppled off our shoulders.

Fred and I were done, and drained. Nothing but smiles, chocolate strawberries, and champagne back at the hotel (ginger ale for the Boenishes). Ian and I both thought we had a shot at an Emmy with this one, and my career in television glowed. Aside from the delays, the jump had gone exactly as planned, but the crew scrambled to pack and leave on the charter. Ian was so worried about an accident that he rushed to clear out lest something happen retroactively. That afternoon, the charter jetted for London, and those left behind, including half the kids in Åndalsnes, moved to the bar in the hotel basement, where several storylines began to converge. I could never have guessed where this junket was about to take us.

$$\triangleq$$

A Norwegian named Stein Gabrielsen and his fellow countryman Eric (last name unknown) had arrived in Åndalsnes only hours before. I met them in the bar, thinking they were another two Euro BASE jumpers drawn there by the big news, now splashed across Europe. In fact, while Fred, Carl, and I had begun scouting Trollveggen's summit ridge, Stein and Eric (both working in America, and unaware of our plans) had purchased one-way tickets to Norway to attempt the world-record jump off the Troll Wall, something they'd planned for three years. They would have gotten the record, too, except they'd gone on a ten-day bender the moment they met with friends in Oslo. When a girl showed Stein the newspaper story about how Carl and Jean were already in Åndalsnes, waiting for the clouds to lift, he and Eric bolted directly, arriving in town late that evening.

They walked to the base of the Troll Wall, still glowing under the midnight sun, both men eager to scope out their record site. That's where they met "a drunk old Norwegian dude" who pointed at the dark cliffs and said, "That is the Devil's mountain." They walked back to town and spent their last krone on beer at the pub, where several dozen of us were finishing our wrap party, a Hollywood tradition.

I remained the final holdover from the American production crew, there to settle accounts and hang with Aud. Stein and Eric, both flat broke, joined the bash only to learn the Boenishes had scooped them by a few hours. At best, they might repeat the record—the adventure-sports version of an asphalt cigar. Their consolation was the $500 of production money I had left to blow on booze.

"Eric and I found Carl," said Stein, "congratulated him, and asked about his launch site."

Carl said he jumped from The Bishop. Stein had surveyed the ridge and believed The Castle stood higher.

"Check a chess set," said Carl. "The Bishop is always taller than The Castle."

"Either way," said Stein, "Eric and I are jumping The Castle tomorrow."

"Carl became visibly nervous," Stein later wrote, "and suggested we meet at their hotel for breakfast next morning, around 10:00 a.m. Then we could go jump together."

A free meal sounded good, so Stein and Eric agreed. We closed the bar and half-mashed on Aquavit, Aud and I staggered to her apartment and I passed out for twelve hours.

The following morning, Stein and Eric met Jean at the hotel. Jean said Carl was in town, arranging their travel back to the States, and she invited the pair to breakfast. An hour passed and still no Carl. Jean kept glancing at her watch, out at the driveway, back at the map of Trollveggen hanging on the wall. Something felt fishy.

Jean said she was sorry. She'd deceived them. Carl had been afraid they would usurp his record (as The Castle is higher on the ridgeline than Carl and Jean's launch site on The Bishop), so he'd left at sunrise to go jump The Castle. Jean figured he had already jumped and was at the landing field, waiting for a ride. She suggested Stein and Eric take the rental Volvo, snag Carl, and head back up to The Castle for round two. Jean needed to pack. Stein and Eric had gotten snookered and sent to fetch the culprit. One can imagine their conversation as they drove to the landing zone in the big meadow, to talk things through with Carl Boenish.

Back at Aud's apartment, I sorted gear for a one-day, racehorse ascent of the Troll Wall. I'd changed my mind a hundred times, but couldn't blow off Europe's biggest cliff when it was right down the road. A quick rap on Aud's door. It flew open and Fred rushed in.

"Carl's been in an accident," he said, "and it looks bad."

A car accident? No, said Fred. Early that morning, Carl had hiked back up to Trollveggen and jumped off The Castle. Say what? That couldn't be right. After the last two days tromping around, Carl would be resting his bum leg for sure. Our production had caused such a stir that, for going on a week, jumpers like Stein and Eric continued streaming in from Sweden, Iceland, Denmark, and beyond. Any accident was theirs, I said, not Carl's.

Fred shook his head. Carl had enlisted two teenage brothers, both local climbers, to hike him up. One, Arnstein Myskja, had witnessed Carl's accident and stood there next to Fred, trembling in his boots.

Ten minutes later, I was dashing across peat bogs, seeking a vantage point with the lower Troll Wall in clear view. I frantically glassed the lower face, nearly a mile away, finally spotting Carl's big yellow parachute, unfurled and breeze-blown on a shaded terrace near the base.

"Goddamn it, Carl. Get up . . . signal . . ." The canopy billowed gently from the updraft. "Carl!"

Fred arrived and put a hand on my shoulder. Carl hadn't moved. I followed Fred to a grassy field surrounding the grand manor of an expatriate British lord. A pall tumbled from gray clouds as the media streamed in, occasionally stealing glances our way. My center could not hold much longer.

The police chief arrived and I couldn't meet his eyes when I told him I'd spotted Carl on a ledge near the base. The part about no movement ended our conversation. I didn't have the courage to call Jean, but the chief did. Barely. Tears flowed from his eyes though his voice remained calm and stoic. I will never forget his face as he talked with Jean.

"I . . . regret to inform you that your husband has been in an accident, and it doesn't look good." This last detail took enormous bravery to admit.

Jean's voice sounded eerily detached over the speaker phone, soberly seeking details as every soul in Åndalsnes stomached the fear and chaos on her behalf. I stormed outside and pulled on my harness. Nobody knew if Carl was dead, or even seriously injured, and I yelled as much, confronting some with the news. They nodded slowly and shrank away, huddling under trees, waiting.

The *whop, whop* of the giant military rescue chopper thundered up the valley. It landed in a clearing, arching trees, buckling photographers, scaring all with its powerful thumping. Fred went and I stayed behind, shivering in my t-shirt and glaring up into the rain. Aud came over but I couldn't talk or look at her. I thought about nothing, vaguely hearing the chopper's hammering pitch in the distance. It set down and the crew filed out, staring at the ground. Fred walked over, his face hard as stone. Six photographers clicked shots as we fled back to the lord's house.

As a free citizen, Carl could do as he pleased, but The Castle? Carl himself had called the place crazy as a jump site. The doctor, little more than thirty years old, requested that I go aboard to identify the body.

"For what?" I begged.

The doctor stared up at the ceiling and had no words. The ordeal was far from over, and spared nobody. I felt like the Ugly American who had barged into a quiet little town with a small army and a wad of television money and broke every rule and every heart in the place.

We walked through wet, knee-high grass toward the helicopter. Amber light glinted off new puddles. How dare beauty show itself when Carl was dead? We moved through the chopper's huge rear hold and back to Carl's body, looking as though he'd laid down to get a load off that leg. No sign of regret on his face. The young doctor and I stood there, mourning a life cut in half, gazing from death as if unhurt. But he'd screamed a music too high to scale, and the cold mountain got him. The distance Carl had tracked away from us brought back the birds and their keening, high on the glacial plateau.

I joined the crowd gathering on the grassy field, everyone gazing confusedly at each other. Someone had to know why and how come. We watched the coroner and two policemen heft Carl's black-bagged body into a white van and roll off into the mist. It felt criminal to leave it at that; but Carl could not die again. That was all. The end.

Fred and I silently drove to Aud's place and I wandered in a traceless land. Even Aud couldn't help me now. Why had Carl jumped from The Castle? I'd never felt such helpless confusion.

That evening I went and found Arnstein who, along with his younger brother, had guided Carl that morning. It had taken them nearly five hours to short-rope (drag by a tethered line) Carl over the glacial plateau and up to the top of The Castle. Carl conducted rock tests and, in seconds, as before, they smashed off outcroppings jutting directly into the flight path. But Carl was determined to go. Arnstein grabbed his camera. As he described to me and others, Carl was dead the moment he launched off the lip, or tried to. On his last exit step, he stumbled and, unable to push off and get some little separation from the wall, he frantically tossed out his pilot chute. With so little airspeed, it lazily fluttered up, slowly pulling his main chute from the pack. One side of the chute's chambers filled with air and flew forward. With one side deflated, the inflated side wrenched the canopy sharply, whipping Carl around and into the cliff.

He continued tumbling, said Arnstein, his lines and the canopy spooling around him like a cocoon. Five thousand feet later, Carl's tightly wound body impacted the lower slab "and bounced thirty feet in the air like a basketball." Arnstein was so sickened by what he'd just shot on his Nikon that he yanked the film from the roll and tossed it into the void, so the images of Carl's last moments were lost forever.

A few days later, Jean hired several local climbers to hike her up to The Castle, where she checked the site firsthand and did what a wife does where her husband has died. Then she traversed the ridge to the original 1981 launch site, jumped off, and touched down for a perfect meadow landing.

I couldn't sit and kept pacing around Aud's tiny apartment. For several weeks, I'd agonized over leaving Norway without her—a puzzling concern for a nomad like me. But life kept shifting. TV work had stretched off like a cargo cult runway, inviting a rich future to appear. Then Carl crash-landed and it felt likely I was one and done with production work. Staring at the white stucco walls in Aud's matchbox, I couldn't see any future at all. I don't recall saying goodbye to Aud and Fred, but I must have. I only remember driving through the dark dawn shadow of Troll Wall, heading for the airport in Molde, the giant cliff felt but unseen for all the clouds and rain.

Over the following decades, Carl and Jean's Norway jump became a seminal event in BASE jumping's short history. Several magazines ran feature articles on the couple, but they'd taken a novelist's wand to Carl's accident, and I couldn't read them through. I wasn't surprised when a producer called about a feature-length documentary on Carl, now in production, and asked if I might fly over to Åndalsnes and do an interview. Time had worked the sharpest edges off Carl's death, and a trip to Europe sounded excellent. I found myself back in Norway a few months later.

The Trondheim Valley, and that towering junker, Trollveggen, were far more daunting than I remembered—which wasn't much. Åndalsnes had modernized but still resembled a suburb of Camelot. My feel for the place had gone. Thirty years can blunt the sharpest memories. Mix in drink, work, a failed marriage, and it's a miracle I remember anything. Fred and I reunited and immediately went bouldering at the old haunts— the mushy fields and cow pies, the scabby orange lichen on the rock, gaping up at the monstrous Troll Wall, "doing the joking" as we floundered on short climbs we'd once hiked with ease. The memories stirred. I talked to Aud on the phone and her voice pulled me back. But I still felt lost as the birds on the glacial plateau.

The next day, I met the film crew at a grassy campground directly beneath Trollveggen, rearing a mile beyond us. The director was a jocular young woman from Los Angeles, with heaps of passionate intensity. The director of photography, a pondering Swede, would tuck an entire tin of snuff behind his lower lip and pace, mulling the next shot and spewing vile brown pools like the spoor of a wounded elk. The two went back and forth about the lighting, arguing like they meant it, so I didn't sit for the interview till around noon. It started raining.

They'd paid handsomely to fly me there, so I felt obliged to drop into deep thoughts and important feelings. But I couldn't peel off my armor. The director bore in. As I recounted the details, and Carl's eccentric stoke and fearlessness, the sludge from far below came bubbling up. I spoke without color, owing to the gray way the past came back to me. The questions moved to The Castle, and the rescue chopper. Standing in a drizzle and glaring up, I slammed through the looking glass.

For several minutes I said nothing, sinking lower in my chair. The rain beat down and we stopped filming. I didn't move. The director pulled a blanket over my shoulders. For an instant, I could see my life with jarring clarity as it ran from that July day in Åndalsnes, three decades before, and how my native love for cinematic narratives never made it off that rescue chopper. The part of me that can actually write was wedged like an iron strut between then and now as I continued to muddle along in productions I didn't believe in, without passion or inspiration, an also-ran in an industry made for me—a selfish take on "The Jump," as they called it, but Carl's death was the ogre who prowled my unconscious, setting me on my screwy course in life.

Over the next half hour, I'm uncertain what I said, but I meant every word—and it was mostly news to me. Then the director asked why I thought Carl had risked a jump that he'd previously called "crazy." For years, this question had lingered over The Jump, adding texture and intrigue to the strangeness of Carl's last words.

As Arnstein had later told Stein Erik Gabrielsen, as Carl stepped toward the edge of The Castle, he abruptly paused and asked, "Do you boys know the Bible?"

Wide-eyed and anxious, they said, "Yes, of course."

"Remember when the Devil takes Jesus high up onto the temple roof," asked Carl, "and tempts him to cast himself off, for surely the angels will rescue him?"

"Yes," Arnstein had said. He knew the story.

Carl reached one hand over the other shoulder, patted his parachute, and said, "I don't need angels."

The man who would walk on water and fly through the air—is he closer to God, or possessed, gaslighted by glory, adrenaline, and a lifetime of narrow escapes? Carl turned, took two steps toward the edge, and, on the third step, he stumbled.

That night I sat alone in my room, muddling through an old issue of *Granta* I'd nicked from the hotel lobby. For years, I'd stepped on the gas and whoosh—the far side of life was fast approaching. Scrolling back, I could finally sense the penumbra of Aud, like perfume on an old pillow. We'd spoken several times and thought it best not to meet in person. When I called and asked her to reconsider, she arrived in the lobby ten minutes later.

We stared at each other, dazed to realize that once we'd been young together. I could have ridden that feeling into the ground. Instead, I powered up my laptop and showed Aud photos of my two daughters: Marjohny, with all the freckles, and Marianne, a recently minted MD, both stunners because they take after their mother. When Aud's daughter arrived, I was staring at Aud herself—a young woman exuding life the way a lamp gives off light. She looked at me curiously. A man from her mother's past, standing before her and looking at the future. It's all magic.

Stein Gabrielsen and his friend, Eric, had barely arrived in the Romsdalen valley when a local drunkard pointed to Trollveggen and said, "That is the Devil's mountain." Eight hours later, Carl died quoting the Devil tempting Jesus to fly.

Eric, a wizard in the air, jumped the Troll Wall three times over the days following Carl's death. On his last jump, Eric logged a thirty-second free-fall with a two-second canopy ride before landing in the rocks, miraculously unhurt. He declined to document the record free-fall because the only way for someone to top it was to bounce.

"Get me out of here before I die," he told Stein.

Stein quit drinking on the spot and hasn't jumped since.

Eric is currently a healer in Berlin and skydives regularly. Stein runs a small church (Saint Galileo) and teaches kite-surfing in Miami. He still gets occasional flashes of Eric nearly going in during his thirty-second free fall. "For now," he later wrote, "I am content with the knowledge that I am a fool. Every day I thank my angels and pray for wisdom."

In winter, 1989, Arnstein Myskja, the teenage guide who witnessed Carl's last jump, was swept to his death by an avalanche while climbing the Mjelva Gully, rising above the Mjelva Boulder, the moss-covered stone where Fred and I practiced climbing, waiting for the clouds to part on Trollveggen.

Aud is a nurse's supervisor, has two teenaged daughters, and is married to a fellow Norwegian who manages oil platforms in the North Sea.

Fred Husoy went on to climb many new routes in the Trondheim Valley, the Alps, and the Himalayas. He led the local rescue team for many years and, through innovative, often perilous efforts, saved dozens of climbers injured on the Troll Wall. He is married to a doctor and has two sons.

Half a dozen years after The Jump, while parachuting onto a limestone Tepui in the Venezuelan rainforest, Jean Boenish open-fractured her leg, greatly curtailing her BASE jumping career.

The film about Carl Boenish, called *Sunshine Superman*, earned critical acclaim. Producers felt robbed that it didn't earn the Academy Award for live-action documentary. The director invited me to a private screening shortly after the premiere, thick with industry people, but I left early. It took me three times to finally watch the film through.

A few months after returning from Norway, I came tumbling down in a climbing gym, of all places. The first thing I saw when I rolled onto my ass was my tibia jutting from a fist-sized hole in my shin. I spent the next forty-five days in the hospital. One time in the wee hours when I couldn't sleep and the morphine carried me off to the ethers, I gazed down and saw a girl and a boy dancing to The Who in a bar on a thousand-year-old street.

SHIVA

For a decade, maybe two, whenever David swooped into mind, I shoved him back to the blue yonder because all I could hear was dirt raining off his coffin. Then the piano plinking in his mother's house, once the *shiva* began. The black ribbon, ripped in two, lay on the dining room table. Candles burned. All the mirrors were covered.

The Rabbi kept glancing at Nate and me, but what could he say? His nephew, David, the nuclear wunderboy who went rogue on the big rocks in Yosemite and the wildest rivers on Earth, had gone where the light never shines.

Caterers ghosted through the house, carrying trays of blintzes. We couldn't stomach food so we drank coffee from a big chafer urn, the eyes of the gathering crowd playing over us—graciously, when met. But who were we?

Finally the Rabbi led us up some stairs to a room full of books and paintings, a couch, and a big roll-top desk. The former study, I imagined, of David's father, a history professor at UC Fresno, now dead. David never said when or how because once he hit that first big rapid, his life ran ahead of him—till a moving van t-boned his Ford Pinto, and all we had of David was the past.

David's mother sat behind the desk and smiled, but couldn't hold it. David's kid sister, teetering close by her mother, drew halting, jagged breaths. It might have helped us all had she screamed.

"Truth is," said the Rabbi, "we haven't seen much of David these last five or six years." The room seemed to swallow his words. "There's a lot to be proud of. Or so we've heard."

"We're not sure who David became," the mother finally said, looking at Nate, squirming in the ravenous space David left behind. It was now Nate's job to try and fill it. Nate hadn't said a word on the two-hour drive down from Yosemite.

"Whatever you might tell us—" said the Rabbi.

Nate gazed at the desktop, arrayed with magazines and catalogues, each showing David on the cover. Mostly kayaking shots.

"Couple years ago," said Nate, his voice flat and parched, "I got the wise idea to solo the North Face of Sentinel. No rope. Night before, I tell David to keep an eye on me, and he hands me a little walkie talkie he borrowed from the rescue cache. Can't be lugging needless stuff up that wall, but David says, 'You're taking it.' So I did. I set off at five the next morning, with a bullet pack, a quart of water, a couple energy bars, and that stupid walkie talkie."

Nate pressed on. Hating it. Not so much talking as blurting, to get it over.

"There's a good ledge a thousand feet up," said Nate, skipping ahead, "but I'm going so good I don't stop, and never see the sky greying over. Hour later, I'm 1,500 feet up the wall, charging for the summit, when the first big drops bomb down. Then the rock's pouring water. I burrow back into the chimney. To wait it out. The rain turns to sleet, then snow. It's dark and butt-cold. I've only got sweatpants and a fleece sweatshirt. I'm shivering like crazy. No way I'll last till morning. By midnight I just want it over. Then David calls on the walkie talkie."

"Because he'd been watching you up there," the sister cut in. "Just like you asked him to."

Nate looked at us all in turn, like he needed our regard to pull him through it.

"Of course he was," said Nate. "And soon as it starts snowing, he bolts up the trail and scrambles up Sentinel Gulley, just left of the cliff. Takes him hours to reach the ridge, which is all glazed over. And his headlamp's no good in the storm. Somehow he traverses over to the top of Sentinel and hunkers under a boulder, maybe two-hundred feet above me. When his voice cracks over the walkie talkie, I think I'm hearing stuff. So I don't respond till David starts yelling at me to wake up."

Nate moved over by the desk and stared down at one of the magazines.

"I'm hypothermic. Shivering like crazy. We both know if I drift off, I'm done for. But the batteries are half-dead on the walkie talkies, so David only talks a few seconds at a go. Every twenty minutes. Screaming at me not to quit. I wanna give up but he won't stop calling. I tell him to leave me alone. He yells it. 'Wake up, you fuck!' And it goes like that till dawn, and David can get down to me on a rope."

David's mom looked up at Nate and said, "David always told me: 'If ever I go missing, find Nate.' I'm grateful to you, Nate."

The Rabbi had driven up to Yosemite the previous evening to tell Nate about the accident, and was much obliged that we'd driven down for the service. He walked us down to the street and Nate and I piled into his beater van, the Rabbi pausing beside the open driver's side window.

"You know," said the Rabbi, "I heard that story before. But the way David told it, he got stuck up on that big rock, and you went up and got him." He handed Nate a plastic bag and said, "Something for the drive."

Nate passed me the bag and we rolled off. Not till we cleared Fresno and were driving up the 41 for Yosemite did I check the bag. It was full of blintzes and a little bag of weed, probably found on David's person, when they cut him from his Pinto with the Jaws of Life.

We still didn't feel like food, but we smoked the weed.

ACKNOWLEDGEMENTS

I bought a hat just to take it off for my editors, Cody Wooton, Jeff Jackson, and Willy Rowberry.

AUTHOR BIO

JOHN LONG was an original member of the legendary "Stonemasters," a core group of California climbers who lit the fuse on the modern adventure sports revolution. His incredible feats include the first one-day ascent of El Capitan in Yosemite Valley. Long describes himself as "a writer who just happens to get caught up in climbing and adventuring."

John Long has written over 40 books, with nearly three million copies in print. His literary short stories have been translated into many languages. He is the recipient of a National Book Award, the H. Adams Carter Literary Award from the American Alpine Club, and has won the Grand Prize at the Ban Film and Book Festival.

John Long has two beautiful daughters and two grandchildren. He currently resides in Venice Beach, California.

ABOUT THE PUBLISHER

Di Angelo Publications was founded in 2008 by Sequoia Schmidt—at the age of seventeen. The modernized publishing firm's creative headquarters is in Los Angeles, California, with its distribution center located in Twin Falls, Idaho. In 2020, Di Angelo Publications made a conscious decision to move all printing and production for domestic distribution of its books to the United States. The firm is comprised of eleven imprints, and the featured imprint, Catharsis, was inspired by Schmidt's love of extreme sports, travel, and adventure stories.